It's Not the Size of the Tiger in the Fight But the Size of the Fight in the Tiger

by

Mark Hudson

**Grosvenor House
Publishing Limited**

This book is published by
Grosvenor House Publishing Ltd
28-30 High Street, Guildford, Surrey, GU1 3HY.
www.grosvenorhousepublishing.co.uk

A CIP record for this book
is available from the British Library

ISBN 1-905529-78-3

Printed and bound in Great Britain by Biddles Ltd., King's Lynn, Norfolk

Contents

**It's not the size of the tiger in the fight
but
the size of the fight in the tiger**

Acknowledgements

This book is dedicated to:

Amanda, Jess and Sophie. Thank you for all of your support and patience.

To my mam and dad for always being there.

To the Castleford Tigers supporters: loyal, loud, Cas and proud

Some of lives events do put everything into perspective and however much we are all wrapped up with our team and the sport we love, it is only a game and nothing is more important than life itself.

In June 2004, my good friend Steve Mardy's 5-year-old son, Callum, lost both of his legs after a complication post chicken pox. Callum was on life support for weeks. This happened during the Castleford Tigers relegation season of 2004.

It put everything into perspective.

Callum is now well down the long road to recovery. He is back in full time education and his family are looking forward to him living as normal a life as possible.

My mum died in April 2005. I took a call from my sister Bev, whilst we were at a Tigers game at Boundary Park, Oldham. My mum had been poorly for a while and her condition had deteriorated.

She died in St Gemma's Hospice, Leeds the following day.

Her funeral was on the day after our victory at Barrow. We all went to Barrow because that is what she would have wanted.

Somehow that win wasn't what life was all about.

Mark Hudson
December 2005

The banner that got us back into Super League

It was Saturday 8th October 2005. This was no ordinary Saturday. It was the day before the Grand Final. The day before the biggest game in Castleford Tigers long history.

With another 5 minutes to go against Halifax the previous Sunday in the qualifying game, our season and our future would probably have been in tatters.

Halifax came out all guns blazing with nothing at all to lose. The Tigers just about hung on for victory and were now heading for the Grand Final at Widnes to take on Whitehaven for the ultimate prize, a place in Super League.

One game, winner takes all and hopefully a return to the promised land that is Super League.

The defeat in the qualifying final at Whitehaven before the Halifax game was hard to swallow. I had an interesting conversation, before that game in the Gents with a man claiming to be a Director of Whitehaven. He claimed that "whoever went up would struggle and what incentive was there for the players to get promoted, knowing that some would not be offered contracts in Super League?"

Good points I thought, but something I bet he wasn't thinking about as the final hooter went. His team were now red-hot favourites for promotion.

Whitehaven were right to enjoy that day. They had just collected their first ever trophy and they displayed a 'champi-

1

ons' banner for all to see as we entered their ground. That was a stroke of genius, and I am sure they enjoyed goading us as we left the Recreation Ground for the tortuous 150-mile journey home. 18–0 up and we fell apart.

Isn't Cumbria a nice place to go on a day trip?

The Lake District looked fantastic and we promised ourselves that we would go back there one day for a proper look. We also said that on the way to Barrow and on the way to Whitehaven earlier in the season. It's a bit like when you go to the cinema, have a great night out and say, "we should do this more often".

I wonder whether a Cumbrian side ever grace the big stage?

Back to the Saturday before the Grand Final. Our kitchen was out of bounds for most of the day. It was time to make the Grand Final banner.

There were 11 of us going to Widnes and the banner had to be big enough for us all to hold up.

'It's not the size of the tiger in the fight but the size of the fight in the tiger'.

I took the inspiration for its title in June 2005, whilst in Disney's MGM studios in Orlando, Florida. It was on the back of a large Americans T-shirt and instead of 'Tiger' it had the word 'Dawg'. I am guessing that those 'Dawgs' were a sports team somewhere in the USA and that the chap would never have heard of the Tigers from Castleford.

I scribbled it down on the back of a credit card receipt, something you seem to collect a lot of in Florida, tucked it away in my wallet and thought one day that will come in handy.

It did come in handy and only my eldest daughter, Jessica knew where it had originated. The rest of the family thought I was some kind of prophet capable of coming up with magical one liners. Alas not.

The banner took ages to do. We all had our turn with brush in hand. My nearest and dearest Amanda put her own touches to it in the shape of tiger paws. She thought that those touches made all the difference, and who was I to argue? My youngest, Sophie was worried about actually been seen by any of her friends anywhere near the banner.

Wherever we are, the T.V cameras seem to take a shine to us, so her concerns were genuine.

The banner was made from materials, a large roll of sugar paper and paints, 'acquired' from an unnamed local school, by our friend and fellow supporter Janet Simpson. That school will never know what role they played in our Grand Final success.

We have always been into banners and flags, and have tended to give the proper ones away at the end of the season to players we are not likely to see in Castleford colours again. Proper ones are the Union Jack/St George's flag/ Tigers flags, sewn together.

I wonder what old boys Mark Lennon and Paul Mellor did with the flags that we had given them over the last couple of seasons. Perhaps they had them framed and have them hanging on the walls in their luxury apartments somewhere near a beach in Australia. Isn't that how all Australians live?

My mother in law, Janet Kirk had made a flag for us to take to the Northern Rail Cup final against Hull K.R in July 2005 at Bloomfield Road, Blackpool. It was 4 flags sewn together to make 1. Two St George's crosses, a Union Jack and a white rose of Yorkshire, with a couple of Castleford flags also attached for good measure.

Anyone who takes time and effort to fly their clubs colours

in public deserves a medal. The really massive flags that you see at football grounds across Europe are interesting. You know the ones that the crowd passes over their heads. They often get passed right around the stadium. They are catching on over here now. I have a few questions. Who pays for them to be made? Who makes them? How big are they before they are unravelled? And most importantly, how does the flag get back to the person that brought it in, in the first place?

I remember setting off to Blackpool thinking we must get some good photos with our giant flag on the promenade. We got some great photographs, but lost that game 16–18.

In August 2005, it came with us to Craven Park (or is it Robin Park?) Hull one of the most interesting environments known to man. We also lost that game.

We took it to Whitehaven for the qualifying final and we lost that game.

Our dip in form wasn't down to having a small squad, poor coaching or a lightweight pack; it was down to that bloody flag. 3 appearances and 3 defeats.

That flag was retired and never saw the light of day again. In fact we never followed the tradition of giving it away at the end of the season. It would have been like the kiss of death to the poor recipient.

Going to Widnes for any occasion is always an adventure. To go there for the Grand Final in October 2005, was special. Our last trip to the Halton Stadium in the relegation season of 2004, ended in a rare away victory.

Widnes is one of those grounds that you never go to the same way. People who go for a meal to the Ryther Arms in Ryther near Selby will have the same feeling.

We managed to park up for free near to the ground. I am

always suspicious of parking near to any ground for free and for some reason am always suspicious of parking up in Lancashire, or is Widnes in Cheshire?

I think this comes from a story my dad tells about the time he was 'taxed' many years ago at Maine Road, Manchester by some scruffy youngsters who were prepared to mind his car for 50p. That has always stuck with me every time we cross the Pennines and interestingly enough, my dad who is now in his seventies, and a Jungle regular, always likes to tell the story every time we venture to that part of the world.

The streets and pubs around the ground were full of White-haven fans. It was bordering on slightly hostile and this was hours before the kick-off. One comment I heard was "I hope they are going to give us a game this time".

Where were you at the end, my friend?

I am one of those people that likes to get into the ground the minute the gates open. I love the pre match build up, if not always the pre match entertainment.

We had reason to get to Widnes early that day. We wanted to see Bramley and Batley play in their respective finals. I have a colleague in the Prison Service who has championed Bramley R.L.F.C since they were reformed and it was great to see him at Widnes in his capacity of official club photographer. Well done Mick Wormald, the game needs characters like you.

Mick and his son Andrew are the types who, for the right reasons, stalk touring teams at their hotels. Credit to them. I am sure they were on first name terms with half of last years Australian touring party. Their collection of rugby league memorabilia is also growing. Bramley lost on the day, but I bet the Wormalds took home some great photographs as well as some more memorabilia.

Another Prison Service colleague, Craig Lingard, plays for Batley. I had been in regular touch with Craig all season by e-mail. It was great to see the Bulldogs survive in National League One on the very last day by defeating neighbours Dewsbury. I had been having Craig on all season about bringing him a flask and some sandwiches for when Batley played at the Jungle, in anticipation that he might be spending a considerable period of time behind the sticks.

There was a lot of support for Dewsbury on the day from the Cas end, and in particular for ex Tigers Darren Rogers and Franny Maloney.

It seemed a lifetime ago since Franny sunk that drop goal for us to snatch a 7–6 victory at Widnes in the relegation season.

A funny incident happened a couple of years ago at Widnes. We were walking to the ground and Janet Simpson's husband, David was, as usual, putting his fleece on. Unfortunately for Janet, a pair of her 'Bridget Jones' style knickers were attached to the velcro on the said garment. With an opportunity to cause maximum embarrassment, David duly began waving the knickers around his head. No doubt he would have been in bother that night.

Throughout the world of rugby league, David is known as 'Fleeceman' for his love of fleeces even in these days of summer rugby. It could be 80 degrees in the shade, and David will still have his fleece with him, "just in case".

We always travel in convoy to away games and we travelled to Widnes in a convoy of three cars, two in front and the third about an hour behind, due to the youngest in our clan, 10 year old Josh Morley (Gibbo) playing football.

Josh is the nephew of David and Janet and cousin to their daughter Cal.

Look out for Josh in a few years time. He is on Huddersfield Towns books and apparently has the left foot England are crying out for. World Cup 2018?

I call Josh, 'Gibbo', because he had Gibson (Damian) on the back of his shirt one season. For some reason, I also thought that his surname was Gibson, so Gibbo stuck.

With banner in hand we entered the ground. There were already pockets of Cas fans all over the place.

The banner got its first unfurling at half time during the Batley game. The Tigers team had a walk onto the pitch and I will always remember the Watene boys, Adam and Frank, pointing up to it and commenting to each other. They probably said, "They need to get out a bit more!" or "I bet Amanda painted those paws!"

The hostility we felt outside the ground was never duplicated inside. The majority of Whitehaven supporters must have decided not to bother on the day.

It was their clubs biggest ever game and we outnumbered them about 5:1. Introducing a team into Super League from Cumbria will never happen if people will not go to something like this.

'He who laughs last, laughs loudest' came to mind as the Haven supporters were leaving in droves, long before the final whistle. Sweet revenge for the torment we had received there a couple of weeks before?

Their 'Champions' banner wasn't up for long.

The game and the occasion were unbelievable. Despite being 26–0 up at half time, it wasn't over. We had been there a couple of weeks before and blown a big lead. At 36–0 the game was in the bag and we could now begin to celebrate. I remember looking at my lot when we conceded a try to make it 36–4.

They looked worried to death. By the time Whitehaven had crossed again on the hooter, we were all celebrating, the team included. 36–8 victors.

It was like when Blackburn Rovers conceded a goal against Liverpool at Anfield several years ago. The Blackburn players celebrated because word had come that although they had been defeated, they were still the new Premiership champions.

We were now the champions and no one could argue that it was thoroughly deserved on the day

The season had been a long one.

Our mercurial half back Brad Davis had come in for a lot of criticism after the defeat at Blackpool in the Northern Rail final. He saved his best game until last. Watching the game when we got home (and several times afterwards), you notice just how good his kicking game was on the day and how our tactics were faultless.

'Form is temporary, class is permanent' was never more apt for that performance by Brad.

Brad announced his retirement after the final. Would this really be his last game in a Tigers shirt?

The banner got one last unfurling, but we were missing too much of the celebrations, so it was rolled up. It is still in the boot of my car, too precious to dispose of. I wondered then if it would ever come out again.

The wording on it sums up the 2005 season for me. We were a young team, with a sprinkling of experience, put together to do a job. The National Leagues are full of big uncompromising forwards who can do you damage, if you are intimidated. We had been criticised in some quarters for the fact that our pack was too small, too inexperienced, not tough enough etc, etc

On the day it wasn't about our size, it was about the size of our fight. The scoreboard never lies and we were most definitely back.

We had made a couple more banners. 'Back where we belong' which had its day in the spotlight. It got passed to the front of the stand and made an appearance in several publications post final.

Another one, 'R U watching Hull K.R?' got one airing, but we thought better of it. This was our day and not a day for goading our rivals like Whitehaven had to done to us. Again, sweet revenge nevertheless for the defeat in Blackpool and the hiding we had got at Hull K.R in the league fixture.

On the way back to the car, we were still singing. Amanda asked "Isn't that Lingard over there?" Sure enough it was. Craig and his Batley teammates were waiting to be picked up from outside the ground. I asked Craig if he had watched our match. "Yes" he said, "from the bar". He was well on his way to being worse for wear by this time. Good on you mate I thought. This is a lad who gives 110% every week, putting his body on the line for the cause and is then back at work at Wakefield Prison the next day. Castleford fans throughout the season had taunted the opposition with "back to work on Monday", since the Tigers had a full time playing squad.

I bet Craig never went back to work that Monday or Tuesday!

The traffic back to the motorway was horrendous, and not surprisingly with it being Widnes we went home a different way from the way we had come.

At a roundabout, I flashed a car to let it out and lo and behold it was our friends the Simpsons, who had parked miles away from the ground. We journeyed back home in the usual convoy of 3 cars and headed straight back to the Jungle just in time to see the team bus arrive home.

Janet even snatched a peck on the cheek from a bemused looking skipper Andy Henderson.

Great day, great night. That team will always have legendary status.

Was it only a year ago that we stood in the same car park commiserating after the defeat against Wakefield had seen us relegated for the first time ever?

The night we were relegated we did come home with some souvenirs. My girls acquired Brad Davis's and Waine Pryce's shorts and my niece Naomi, claimed Waines tracksuit top.

Little did we know on that night, the role these two would play in the 2005 campaign. Castleford legends? Without a doubt.

Conversation at the Jungle on the night of our return to the top flight soon turned to "who would you keep? Who would you get rid of?" This is a cut-throat business. We should have been enjoying the moment and thinking about that later.

Attention also focussed on when we would be going to France to play that new team. At that point we couldn't even remember what their name was.

Chancing her arm again, Naomi asked Prycey for his track-suit jacket. Would she be lucky two years running? No chance, Waine politely refused with a "No".

Our board had obviously been planning for the future with a plan 'A' and a plan 'B'. The clubs future was and to some extent had always been in their hands.

Plan 'A' would now kick in.

We are back on the up and this is the story of what was to come. Super League X1 here we come.

This is the story of Castleford Tigers season back in Super League in 2006.

It was to be a season like no other. A real rollercoaster ride of emotions.

What would the emotions be like when we all returned to the car park at the end of the 2006 season?

There is no point looking back, but out of the relegated team, not many have gone on to achieve great success. Paul Jackson has established himself at Huddersfield Giants and played in the 2006 Challenge Cup final. Tom Saxton and Motu Tony collected a Challenge Cup winners medal with Hull in 2005. As did Jamie Thackray, who also earnt a Great Britain call-up.

Is that because Jamie is a good Hunslet lad?

Growing up.....Clapgate days

My roots are in South Leeds. Ask anyone from that area and they will talk about how proud they are to come from Leeds 10 or Leeds 11, an area taking in the communities of Hunslet, Belle Isle, Middleton, Beeston and Holbeck.

In rugby league terms, folklore going back generations said that if you were from the south of the river, you would not be raised with any inkling of admiration for our friends from the Headingley district.

That was that. The River Aire was the great divide.

You were Hunslet and not Leeds. That tradition is no longer there and driving around Belle Isle, Middleton and indeed Hunslet today, you will often see people wearing the latest Leeds Rhinos jersey.

Their fore fathers will be turning in their graves. Some of the population of Hunslet will not even realise that they have a professional rugby league team.

It would have great to have been around Hunslet a couple of generations ago. If you were born in the 1930's, you were really part of it. In some people's lifetimes, Hunslet have appeared in two Challenge Cup finals in 1934 and 1965. The streets you lived in were a stones throw away from their home ground, Parkside.

The Hudson family lived at 8, Playfair Avenue. It was a district of back to backs, with washing lines attached to the houses on the other side of the cobbled street. I still wonder how people actually put the washing on the line, since the lines were about 20 feet above your head. There was the outside, communal toilet down the street and the key to get into it, used to hang on a hook in the kitchen. You didn't flush the toilet, you 'pulled the string'. People still say that now. "Have you pulled the string?" "Who was the last one in here? And why haven't you pulled the string?"

There are loads of books about 'old' Hunslet and Hunslet R.L.F.C. My dad loves them and takes delight in pointing out everything, and recalling memories about what he used to do and who he used to do it with. "Shaw, Gunney and Poole. The best back 3 ever", my dad proclaimed recently.

I do not think that future generations will be interested that much in their heritage, which is a real shame because at some point in time, all we will have left is photographs and books. People who were there and that actually remember will be gone. It is like watching Remembrance Day parades. Is there anyone left that fought in the first world war?

The Hunslet team throughout the years was always made up of people you had gone to school with or worked with. Despite all of the poverty around, those were the days when neighbours looked out for each other. Children could play out safely and front doors were seldom locked. I suppose people never actually knew that they were living in poverty. That was just how it was.

There was a community spirit with a shop on every corner and the area awash with pubs and picture houses.

Hunslet was also the industrial backbone of the City of Leeds. The industry and factories are long gone. The trendy city centre dwellings are now drifting out towards the borders of an area that must have once employed thousands of people.

My dad still talks fondly about how he played in the same Hunslet Juniors team as the legendary Brain Gabbitas, who won the Lance Todd trophy at Wembley in 1965, when Hunslet lost a classic match against Wigan. He also claims to have kept Billy Langton out of that junior team. Langton went on to be one of a hand full of professional players who played and scored in every game in a season.

I would love to meet Brian one day to see if my dads' claims are true.

My dad completed a period of National Service. He served in the R.A.F and although he claims to have flown many a daring mission over Korea, we all know he was a potato peeler that never ventured far from his camp in North Yorkshire. He is at an age now where he likes to read the obituaries in the local newspaper to see how many people he knows have died and is always saying, "There is nothing to get old for".

One of the first rugby league games I ever played in was for Clapgate School in a local cup final at Parkside Stadium.

I think I was 8 or 9 at the time. I still remember how long the grass was, the coal fire in the changing room and the big bath.

Clapgate has produced 2 world famous pupils, former Hull, Leeds and Great Britain rugby league captain, Garry Schofield and more recently model Nell McAndrew. Is Nell world famous or just famous according to Belle Islers?

Garry played in the school team a couple of years below me. The same team as another future Leeds player, David Creasser and my own brother in law, Mark Bramley (Bram). That school team went years without losing and without conceding a point.

Our Deputy Head at Clapgate was affectionately known as 'Jeppo'. He had the ability to launch chalk at you from every angle. I am sure he could even send it flying around corners. Bram claims to have been the victim of a disciplinary measure known as the 'shaker maker'.

Jeppo is still around the rugby league scene today. Mr. Harry Jepson is now the President of Leeds Rhinos. Good on you Sir, you have devoted the majority of your life to our sport.

Until recently, Garry Schofield was still living in Belle Isle and running the 'Omnibus' pub, which is less than a mile from Clapgate. It is not a pub I have frequented very much over the years, despite it being what you would call my local. The first time I ever went in was with my long time friend and later best man, Russ Hanwell, a staunch Bradford Northern (Bulls) supporter.

We walked into the Omnibus one Saturday evening and everyone stopped and stared. It was a surreal moment when we might as well have been from another planet rather than from just down the road. My local was full and nobody knew me. There was a DJ on that night and when Meatloafs 'Paradise by the dashboard light' came on, everyone in the pub sang along. This was long before karaoke. The boys sang the boys bits and the girls sang the girls bits.

"I remember every little thing as if it happened only yesterday, parking by the lake and there was not another car in sight, and I never had a girl looking any better than you did, and all the kids at school they were wishing they were me that night".

Not exactly Lennon and McCartney, but nevertheless a classic track from the best selling 'Bat out of hell' album. I still think about that moment everytime I hear this song. It didn't take me long to learn all of the words and I can still do a fair rendition of it today from start to finish.

I am not sure that Clapgate even play rugby league these

days. We were banned from playing football at school, even in the playground. In saying that all the lads would return on an evening and play regular football matches between the Belle Islers and the Miggy lads. Miggy is short for Middleton, which was the next place up Belle Isle Road. There are no noticeable markers to show where Hunslet finishes and Belle Isle starts or where Belle Isle finishes and Miggy starts. You just knew whether you were a Belle Isler or not. Unlike nowadays, the lads were never interested in playing with the girls. We weren't interested in them or what they were up to.

If there were enough of us, our football game would be played on a pitch that had hockey goals. I cannot remember a time when anyone at the school ever played hockey, but for some reason we had a hockey pitch.

If there weren't enough players for a full game, it would be 'jumpers for goalposts' and a game of 'shots in', or 'cuppie'.

'Shots in' was when somebody went in goal and the others played against each other. The rule was if you scored 3 times, you were then goalie. The tactics for 'shots in' were to goal hang (which meant you loitered near the goal and let the others do the running) and make sure you only ever scored twice so that you never went in goal

The rules for 'cuppie' were different in that if you scored one goal you were through to the next round. The last one to score then had to go in goals.

Team selection for the full games was done by the nominated captains, with first choice going to the lad who won 'fish and chips'. This was when the captains stood about 10 yards from each other for starters and then took it in turns, putting one foot in front of the other, until one touched the foot of the other one. The one to touch first got first choice for his team.

As the feet were in motion, one would say "fish" and the

other "chips". If it sounds complicated, it wasn't, but wouldn't tossing a coin have done the same job?

You could have named the teams without 'fish and chips' because it generally ended up with mate picking mate so that Belle Isle v Miggy rivalries continued.

Once the teams were selected, you would hear the cries "laggy goalie" and "seggy laggy goalie". These were the calls you made to avoid being in goals.

If there wasn't enough players for a full game, but too many for 'shots in' or 'cuppie', 'goalie when needed' came into play. This meant that anybody could be goalie. The expressions and rules were not common to our group. I later found out that they were used in other areas of Leeds. There were variations on the theme. In some parts of Leeds 'goalie when ned' was used and cuppie was known also as 'Wembley'

In all cases it seemed that you had to avoid being in goals at all costs. With the ball handling skills the Clapgate lads had acquired from rugby league, surely one of us could have been a half-decent goalkeeper.

We played football all year round, and also played cricket during the summer. What you played was seasonal. It's a bit like the Council tennis courts which only seem to be used when the Wimbledon tournament is in full swing.

We had the essentials, some stumps, a bat and a ball for an adequate game of cricket. That was all you needed. There was no need for gloves, pads or a protective box, despite the bowlers tearing in at you with a 'corky' in their hand. A corky ball is a proper cricket ball and if it hit you, you knew about it. I think there was some rule about how fast you could bowl, so most bowlers mastered spinners or what would be described as gentle medium pacers. Any movement off the seam was down to luck.

We didn't know anything about how to in-swing or out-swing and we were completely clueless about the 'l.b.w' rule.

We never had the need for a wicket keeper, because we set the wicket up near to a fence. The fence also acted as the slip fielders and if you edged one into the fence, you were out, caught.

There were also impromptu games of cricket on our drive. The shot that got you most runs was a little dink or chip of an 'on drive' that sent the ball about 6 feet over a privet hedge and into next doors garden.

You could run at least 4 whilst the fielder had to negotiate all sorts of obstacles in an attempt to retrieve the ball. I mastered this shot, but it also got me out at least 3 times when we started playing proper cricket matches against other schools. Our school team were once all out for 12.

Cricket played a big part in our lives over the big school holidays in summer. We would often catch the no.74 bus from Belle Isle, which took you straight to Headingley cricket ground at the other side of the City. It was a real adventure. Being a Yorkshireman meant that you were proud of the counties ruling that you had to be born in Yorkshire to play for the team. Geoffrey Boycott was the epitome of what a son of the county is all about. Gritty and determined. We used to hang around the changing rooms collecting autographs throughout the day, to break up the boredom of watching the cricket.

All of our after school activities took place on the school playing field. Unlike today, it wasn't frowned upon.

We tried golf when somebody got some golf clubs and even javelin throwing when one lad produced a home made javelin. It was a long piece of wood with tape for the handgrip and a nail in the end. It was effective though and could be launched for miles.

Every school year had a 'cock', which is nothing to do with what you might imagine.

The cocks of the school were the hardest boys and the hardest girls. There was never a contest or fight to decide who the cocks were. Everyone just knew who they were. It was always a good tactic to get the cocks on your side regardless of the game you were playing.

Most of the cinemas around Leeds have long gone as cinemas, but we did have one in South Leeds. The 'Rex' was a bus ride away. The person collecting your money as you went in also doubled up as the person selling the ice creams during the interval. Ice cream at the pictures came in tubs and tasted differently to any other ice cream.

We had to collect our rugby kits on the Friday, before the match on a Saturday morning. We always seemed to play on a Saturday morning, without ever realising that the teachers were giving up their own time. We were all responsible for getting our own kits washed and back to school for the following Monday. Mine was the right centres No. 3 shirt.

My dad taught me how to clean my boots. I used to clean them straight away after training and after every game. I used to put dubbing on them to protect them from water. Nowadays, children very rarely clean their boots or indeed their shoes. Modern science is great and the liquid polish we use today does save you time, but the art of polishing should not be lost.

Transport was at a premium, so anyone who had a parent with a vehicle, came in very handy. My dad used to take groups of us all over Leeds.

He still remembers all of the lads names that played in the Clapgate team and that was over 30 years ago.

When Clapgate got its own mini bus, the teachers then

doubled up as drivers, leaving the parents redundant as taxi drivers.

I am not sure who brought them, or who cut them up into quarters, but we always had oranges at half-time. Thinking about it, I am not even sure that oranges were the best things to eat half way through playing a game of rugby league.

In those days a pass was still a pass and not an offload. When you were going forward, you were attacking, not on the offence. Set plays and power plays were not even in the dictionary.

Our captain at Clapgate was a lad called Andrew Clark whose dad was Mick Clark.

Mick captained Leeds in the water splash Challenge Cup final of 1968, the match when Don Fox, poor lad, infamously missed the kick in front of the posts to win the game for Wakefield Trinity in the last seconds.

There was no greater feeling than pulling on the blue and white striped Clapgate shirt and playing for Mr Dougall, and later Mr Ahm. Mr Ahm now manages the Leeds Rhinos and Tykes training facility in Kirkstall, Leeds. He used to come to School in a revolutionary yellow 'kit car' which he apparently built himself.

I was never the greatest player at school, but I have still got the shield for player of the season in 1973/74. Mr Ahm, was also the woodwork teacher and he made that shield.

I won the shield not because of my exceptional talent, but because I never missed training. You got a point every time you trained and two points if you were man of the match. I got the man of the match in a game against our arch rivals Royal Park School, by scoring the only try in a 3–0 win. That game was played at the Archie Gordon ground which is situated right behind the afore mentioned Rhinos training ground. I wonder if Mr Ahm ever thinks about the school teams he has taken there over the years?

Mr Ahm was once refereeing a home game against Royal Park and had to stop play to twist my ear and give me a right dressing down after I had decided to kick an opponent whilst he was on the ground. It was the most malicious thing I have ever done in my life.

It taught me a lesson, and wouldn't it be good to see referees chastising their charges in the same way today?

Training sessions used to start with us kicking the ball in the air as high as we could for someone else to catch. This stopped once the teacher came out. Young footballers do a similar thing by just shooting at the goalie has hard as they can. They count that as their warm up.

Another regular sight at rugby training was lads taking kicks at goal. There was no science then and you literally had to plant the ball. There were no kicking tees and you either dug a big hole with your heel, or created a tee by making a mud mound to stand the ball on. No matter what technique I adopted, I couldn't kick goals. It is a much harder skill than it looks and the really great goal kickers are gifted.

We only ever had two rugby balls for the whole school. They were brown leather balls and both had Clapgate written on them in white. It makes me smile that even in todays ultra modern game, professional teams still have a need to write the clubs names on the balls. Is this to ensure rival teams do not steal them?

I did represent Hunslet schools and played in the shirt of legends. Wearing the myrtle, white and flame shirt and running out of the pavilion of the Arthur Thornton ground was like running out at Wembley when you are only 12 or 13 years old. It was at training with Hunslet Schools that I was first introduced to the delights of circuit training. I never had a problem with bench pressing the old wooden benches or the medicine balls, but I could never climb the rope that was attached to the apparatus. Not many lads could, and what was the point of rope climbing anyway?

These were the days before weight training was ever thought about. The 'bullworker' was about though and regardless of the "I got a bullworker, but wasn't strong enough to get it out of the box" line, it was a revolutionary device for building strength and stamina. Everyone had a bullworker at one time or another, but the only things we ever wanted was big biceps.

Are clubs missing a trick these days by not recognising quality players in schools at an early age? Garry Schofield was always going to play for his country. You could tell that he was special even in his early teens.

Is there a generation of future superstars being produced in our schools today, and how good are the scouting systems? Playing rugby league is like playing no other team sport and the discipline and respect you get from playing at an early age would generally stay with you forever.

I still have many fond memories of Clapgate. I remember the excitement when the school got a home economics classroom. The first thing we did in cooking was to make a coffee out of milk, and in a saucepan. We later ventured onto fruit salad and then onto rock cakes, which were real jaw busters. I can still make a mean coffee and a more than average fruit salad. I cannot say that rock cakes have been my forte over the years.

The only thing I ever disliked at Clapgate was when we had to go swimming to St Josephs baths in Hunslet. The baths are now long gone, but had stood there for years.

There were individual changing compartments where girls changed down one side of the pool and boys down the other.

The doors on the compartments didn't go to the floor, and it gave all of the lads a great deal of amusement looking under our doors as the girls got changed.

That was about as funny as it got. Once you were in the water you were for in for it. The instructors were not our teachers and they didn't know you from Adam. If you couldn't swim, they tested your courage by ducking you. They also had long sticks with big metal buckets on the end. I was never sure what this contraption was supposed to be for, but they used it to pour water over head as you were struggling to do ten yards 'doggy paddling'.

You were always encouraged to get your swimming certificates at school. The good swimmers could swim for miles. There wasn't any coaching, they just got in the water and swam for miles. I was chuffed to bits when I claimed my beginners certificate, which was for swimming a 10-metre breadth of the pool. The big test was the next step up when you had to venture to the deep end to do your 25 metres, and gain the 'first' certificate.

I must have warmed to the swimming at some point, because a group of us used to go back voluntarily on an evening, probably in the safe knowledge that the instructors who dished out the torture would not be on duty.

Our treat before going home was a wagon wheel from the vending machine. Those were the days when wagon wheels were massive, not like the ones you get today. We were also introduced to Chinese takeaways, but we only ever dared have a bag of chips. Those chips tasted differently to normal chips, but after all, they were oriental and our taste buds were being educated. You never got pizza or spaghetti bolognese for your tea. I had to get married to sample the delights of a takeaway pizza from a box for the first time.

A Vesta beef curry was as extravagant as it got. Just add water and stir. The rice that came with the powdered curry was obviously sided off and replaced by proper chips, but having curry and chips was really living life on the edge.

I always liked to get the cream from the top of the milk. The milkman, delivering glass bottles to your doorstep, is now a forgotten occupation. Everyone used to get full cream milk. I didn't even know that there was any other type of milk. Birds used to peck open the milk bottle top and pinch the cream from the bottle. I wouldn't even think of drinking full cream milk now. It tastes lousy. If you were really posh, you also had bottles of fresh orange delivered by the milkman.

Getting the cream was as satisfying as getting the crust from the loaf.

I wasn't brought up with tomato or brown sauce either and as a result I cannot stand either, although I can honestly say that I have never even tasted them.

Talking about dying trades what about the mobile shop? There used to be a big green van that came down our way called 'Ruddock'. My mam used to say, "Ruddock is here". I used to think that 'Ruddock' was a style of shop, but I guess Ruddock was the name of the man that drove the van who then doubled up as the shopkeeper. He sold everything from bread to sweets to 56lb sacks of potatoes. He always used to sound his horn as he pulled up and people used to queue to get in the van. It was a community thing that was probably replicated across the city.

Bonfire nights were great.

There seemed to be an agreed time when you started to 'chump' and build your bonfire. Chumping was going around and doing the leg work of knocking on peoples doors and asking them if they had any old wood. I was never interested in fireworks. I couldn't see how lighting them and throwing them at other people would give anyone a sense of gratification.

Our level of devilment was 'raiding'. Raiding was as it sounds nicking the wood from other bonfires. As we were raiding one, our own was usually getting raided so you generally ended up with what you started with. You could always leave a 'guard' on your own bonfire, but everyone wanted the adventure of raiding and no one wanted to stay back to guard. It never crossed our minds to set light to someone else's bonfire. That was an unwritten rule.

Christmases were also great.

As a family I remember us going into Leeds on Christmas Eve to see a pantomime. I cannot remember if this was an annual event, but I do remember getting home and having jacket potatoes for supper. This was the first time I had sampled the delight of a jacket tatie. A lump of butter and a sprinkling of salt. Magnificent. You were even allowed to eat the potato skin. Adding tuna mayo, cheese and coleslaw came several years later.

I always used to get a replica football shirt for Christmas. They were not the same ones as you get today and replica rugby league kits weren't even on the market. The football shirts never had any badges or logos. If you wanted a badge putting on you had to buy it separately and get your mam to sew it on for you. In some ways it helped not having a badge and because of the colours, your West Ham kit doubled up as a Burnley kit.

You had to take it back to the shop to get a number ironed on the back. After a couple of washes the number always came off anyway.

One of the best Christmas presents I ever got was a Binatone game that plugged into your television set and allowed you to play tennis or squash either by yourself or against an opponent. This was the forerunner to all of the play station games that are for most adults, too difficult to understand. The Binatone model let you adjust the angle you wanted the 'ball' to go at. You could also have different size bats. We used to spend hours playing, until I mastered all of the angles and became unbeatable. The trouble was everyone was unbeatable, so games went on for hours. You needed your mam or sister to play, to show them that you were still the champion. Where are all of the Binatones today?

Another great Christmas present was a spirograph set. This allowed you to draw circles and other shapes. If you didn't have a compass, the art of drawing a circle for your homework was always a challenge. You had to rely on circular things around the house, like coins, egg cups or saucers.

We also used to trace using the tracing paper that was also the toilet roll in School. You know the sort, one side shiny, one side not.

Modern technology improves household items by the day. L.P's were replaced by tapes, which were replaced by compact discs which have now been replaced by I pods. I am still at the c.d. stage and have trouble understanding how all of that music can be downloaded from your computer and stored on a little plastic gadget. Modern technology brought us infra red grills and pressure cookers. These were revolutionary ways of cooking your food. Our toastie maker came out on a Sunday teatime. You couldn't eat your toastie for hours because the red-hot cheese would burn the top of your mouth. All of the contraptions produced lovely food, but they were also really difficult to clean.

Pop machines or sodastreams came and went. You could make your own pop from tap water. Fill up a bottle, stick it in the machine, a couple of squirts of gas to give it its fizz and then add the concentrate to give it its taste. An easy and cheap way of producing your own drinks? You would think so except the gas cylinders were really expensive and home produced pop never tasted the same as the real thing.

Growing up.....Belle Isle Olympics

When I left Clapgate in 1976 aged 13, I had a choice of a couple of schools. As far as my rugby playing career went, I chose wrongly. Parkside School was the place to go, and I still regret to this day that I never went there, choosing instead to follow my peers to the City of Leeds School. High school wasn't bad for me. The City was a mixed school that brought together a diverse range of children from the 4 corners of Leeds. It had a strict uniform policy of school ties and blazers. Parkside was however the rugby league school.

It was where Garry Schofield's Clapgate team went en bloc a couple of years later. If you played rugby at Parkside, you also played rugby for Hunslet Parkside, one of the finest junior clubs in the country.

This was the club that produced Great Britain rugby league star and England rugby union captain, Jason Robinson as well as future professionals Sonny Nickle and Karl Pratt.

At the City of Leeds the sports field was a bus ride away in the Lawnswood area of Leeds, and there was no rugby league. It was very much a football school. Tottenham and England football starlet Aaron Lennon went there.

Now when we are looking to expand the game away from the traditional M62 corridor, there is still a lot of work to do in traditional areas. Some of the lads at my secondary school from other parts of Leeds had never heard of rugby league never mind played it. I wonder if that is still the case today?

Swimming was still on the agenda. We had to go once a week to the 'Olympics' in Leeds. This was the name given to the International pool. It was known as the Olympics because the big pool was in fact an Olympic size pool. I finally achieved the bronze certificate at the Olympics. For this you had to jump in wearing your pyjamas, tread water for what seemed like hours, take your pyjamas off, retrieve a brick by doing a surface dive to the bottom and than swim for what seemed liked miles.

I fully support youngsters learning to swim at an early age. It is a life skill that may or may not come in handy one day but, how many people do you see on the river bank or sea front dressed in their pyjamas, just waiting to jump in and rescue a brick?

I couldn't surface dive and had to wait for the examiner to look away before retrieving the brick from the bottom with my feet. If there are any bricks out there that needed rescuing, I would still be able to do it, but not by the conventional method.

It took me weeks to get my $1/2$ mile certificate. For this you had to swim about 15 lengths of the 50-metre pool. Going as slowly as you could was sound tactically, but it also meant that you got out of doing English in the next lesson.

Around this time, fashions were changing. It was the time of 'star jumpers' and 'high waisters'. Anybody who was anybody had a star jumper. Mine was red, with three big black stars on the front, black cuffs, with green stripes. A classic style.

What ever happened to the thousands of star jumpers around the country?

Just like the Binatone games, will they ever make a come-back? Most things go full circle, so you never know.

I have got a school photograph of me in my star jumper,

with my long hair. Lads had to have their own hair dryer to look the business.

Our musical inspirations were changing and the once popular 'Top of the pops' L.P's were now out of favour and replaced by 'Tonic for the troops' by the Boomtown Rats and 'Parallel lines' by Blondie. Seeing Debbie Harry for the first time on Top of the pops was fantastic. She was a vision of loveliness.

'Top of the pops' albums always had a scantily clad female on the cover and the songs were all chart songs that were sung by cover artists. It would be a bit similar today to having a compilation album featuring the entire Pop idol or 'X' Factor winners. They were actually rubbish.

Everyone remembers the first single they bought. Mine was 'Children of the revolution' by T Rex. Marc Bolan is still an icon. I would have loved to have changed my name to Marc. I once read that Bolan never washed or combed his hair for years. I had a T-Rex poster in my bedroom alongside one of Olivia Newton John who still looks a knockout today.

Everyone used to buy a comic or magazine and you usually went for the one with the free gift attached to the front. The best free gifts were whoopee cushions and the plastic '45' records that had a message on from David Cassidy or Donny Osmond.

My sister Bev went to see the Bay City Rollers in Sheffield. I wouldn't like to comment on what she looked like in her $^3/_4$ length tartan trousers.

There wasn't much to look forward to on television. The highlight was always on a Saturday when my mam and our Bev would go into Leeds shopping. That meant me and my dad could watch Grandstand from start to finish. We watched it religiously regardless of what might be on. World of sport on ITV was never in the frame until about 4 o' clock when the wrestling came on. That took you up to the teleprinter and the full time football scores. I used to love writing the final scores in on the copy coupon of the pools. Not many people do the pool nowadays.

The wrestling on TV was great entertainment and very believable. The 'tell all the secret' shows on TV take the gloss off things now. You never realised that most of it was put on. It takes the shine off it when you know it's all fake. It's a bit like those magicians who give all of the trade secrets away. I once saw Paul Daniels get a £5 note out of a grapefruit at the Futurist theatre in Scarborough. That was magic!

My dad used to take me to the wrestling at Leeds Town Hall. We saw all the big names, like Giant Haystacks, Big Daddy and Kendo Nagasaki. My personal favourites were Mark 'Rollerball' Rocco and Jim 'Baby face' Breaks, who used to cry when he got hurt. However, that was only a ruse to lull his opponent into a false sense of security.

Seeing wrestling in real life was vastly different from T.V wrestling. The fights always produced blood and often continued outside the ring. What ever happened to wrestling on television?

Grange Hill had started on BBC1 with 'Tucker' Jenkins and 'Gripper' Stebson. Tucker went on to great things in the East end and Sun Hill, but I have never seen Gripper in anything else, which probably serves him right for all of the bullying he did at Grange Hill.

"It's Friday, it's 5 o' clock and it's Crackerjack' and the world stopped still. The slapstick humour was great then, but no one would watch Crackerjack if it were on today. Or would they?

Most children also longed to be the proud possessor of a Blue Peter badge, although no one actually knew how to get their hands on one. Blue Peter inspired you to do things like 'back' your school exercise books with sticky backed plastic. I preferred to use old wallpaper, because you couldn't buy sticky backed plastic from anywhere. Magpie was on ITV and was a poor mans Blue Peter. The only time we ever watched Magpie was when they had an appeal going on. They used to have a strip of red tape going around the walls of their building. The more money that came in, the longer the strip was. Blue Peter never collected cash on their appeals. You would have to donate old toys or tin cans.

'We are the champions' was like a kids equivalent to 'It's a knockout'. Teams of school children competed in various events, but the best bit was at the end when they all jumped into the swimming pool, after the commentator said, "well done kids, away you go!" Great television. I am also convinced that the school grounds where we park up at St Helens was a school that competed in 'We are the champions'.

The worst day of the year was when the budget came around. All childrens television got switched to BBC2 and we didn't have BBC2. Good job it was only once a year.

When you were allowed to stay up late, you could watch programmes like 'The Professionals' and 'The Sweeney'. Bodie and Doyle were really hard men under the stewardship of George Cowley. I always liked Cowley, because in a previous life he was Hudson in 'Upstairs, Downstairs' and I thought he could have been a long lost relative. When you watch the Professionals or the Sweeney on T.V now, they are really corny. Political correctness hadn't been invented and some of the things Bodie, Doyle, Regan and Carter said and did make you cringe.

Not much to look forward to on television? Television was actually great.

At times our house was like a mini 'indoor league'. Indoor league was a show on ITV hosted by legendary cricketer Fred

Trueman, who sadly passed away in 2006. It featured obscure indoor sports like bar billiards and arm wrestling.

In our house we had a dartboard, where games of 501 went on for ages because no one could ever hit the winning double. We often decided games by nearest the bull or highest score with 3 darts wins. Who says dart players are not athletes? Darts is one of the most difficult games in the world to play and in my opinion it should be in the Olympics.

The number of bizarre sports in both the summer and winter Olympics amazes me. How many people have actually tried curling? It looks straight forward enough and I am sure there must be thousands of people out there who could actually represent the country if they had the opportunity to have a go in the first place.

Another one is ten-pin bowling. How easy is that? With a bit of coaching anybody could play that for a living. The hardest part is fathoming out the scoring system. It's a bit like the offside rule in football in that nobody can actually give you a definitive explanation has to how it works.

Trying to operate and understand the computerised scoreboards is impossible for the average adult.

We also played table tennis on the kitchen table. The rules had to be adapted because of the size of the table and the shape of the kitchen. Rebounds off the fridge or off the wall were allowed.

You bought your table tennis kits from the newsagents. The kits consisted of a net, a ball and 2 bats. The bats were just pieces of wood with a pimply rubber cover. If you accidentally trod on the ball, you would try and reshape it, because table tennis would have to be cancelled until somebody went to Leeds to buy a new one.

Matchbox rugby is, apart from blow football, probably the

cheapest game in the world to play, because in most houses a dining table is a given, so you only need an empty matchbox. The rules are simple. You draw a chalk line about 6 inches in from the end of both ends of the table, thus creating a try line. The player kicking off then has to flick (with the forefinger only) the matchbox over the try line. On the line is no good, it has to cross it in its entirety. The second player responds with a flick back and so on. If you do score a try you take a conversion for the extra two points. Goal kicking was always my forte and I could land 'kicks' from the touchline.

The goalposts were made by your opponent placing 2 pointed thumbs together with two fore fingers being placed on the pitch. The arms naturally become the posts with ricochets off the post being allowed. Anyone with a round or oval dining room table was clearly disadvantaged.

When you played matchbox rugby you adopted a team to represent. There were even internationals, when Great Britain played Australia

One of the most exciting times of the year was when the feast came to town. It was like magic. One day there was an empty field, the next there would be a fayre complete with the rides and attractions to keep you mesmerised for hours. The feast only had one big ride, which was the speedway. You had to be really hard to go on that because it went at about 250 m.p.h. I never went on it, but liked to watch others turning green and not been able to walk straight when they got off. The hard lads who worked on the feast stood up throughout the ride.

One night you were at the feast and the next morning, whoosh it had gone, leaving behind just a few tyre marks where the wagons had pulled off.

"We've swept the seas before boys"

My loyalties as a lad growing up in Belle Isle were of course with Hunslet, who in 1973 became New Hunslet and then a few years later, Hunslet again.

We followed them everywhere. I don't think yourealise how grateful you should be to your parents for ferrying you around the grounds of northern England, when the roads and transport systems were not as good as they are today. Clubs like Huyton and Blackpool were still in the existence.

My fondest memories of following Hunslet came throughout their time at the 'dog track'. This was the greyhound racing stadium opposite Leeds United football ground on Elland Road, Leeds. It was the one with the revolutionary American football style 'tuning fork' goal posts. The posts and the ground have long gone.

I once got Roger Millward's autograph has he left the pitch after we had played Hull K.R. Cigarette in hand, Roger was happy to oblige. The autograph was actually on the back of my dads fag packet. Roger was one of the best players I have ever seen. He now lives about half a mile away from us.

Another time when Hull K.R visited there were some disturbances in the crowd and outside afterwards. It made the national news that night. Violence at rugby league games was and is thankfully still a rarity.

You could listen to coach Paul Daley's team talks through the dressing room wall at half time. The dressing rooms were situated at one end of the ground and were best described as something like a large pre-fabricated garage. You could hear every word he said. I even heard words that I had never heard before.

Paul is still involved in the game today with the Leeds Rhinos.

The dog track was the ground where Gary Kemble, one of the greatest New Zealanders ever to play the game, cut his teeth in this country, before carving out a very successful club career at the Boulevard with Hull F.C.

One of my first visits to Wheldon Road was around 1977. It was a Friday night match when Hunslet actually beat Castleford. I remember that game because my cousin Steve Hudson was playing for Hunslet. Some years later, his career ended in tragic circumstances after a road traffic accident.

We stood in the Wheldon Road end that night close by to where we watch the Tigers from today.

Hunslet eventually moved across the road to the football ground at a time when Leeds United were grateful for a lodger and the rent that Hunslet brought in. How times have changed.

By this time my girlfriend Amanda was on the scene and we both got involved with the supporters club. Amanda ran the souvenir shop on match days with a lovely lady named Pam Jones. I wrote the supporters club piece in the match day programme and I also worked as a steward on the players entrance.

That was a great way of sneaking my dad in for free. I felt that he deserved it after a lifetime of supporting Hunslet.

I never played rugby league again until the mid eighties when I turned out for the Station, a local open aged team, playing the Leeds and District Sunday league. Those leagues were and are still tough and rivalries were and are still fierce. Local pride and territories count for a lot. It's like tribal warfare.

I was never fit enough, committed enough or hard enough to make any worthy contribution, although I did pick up a few medals along the way.

Due to being a half-decent team we trained two or three evenings a week.

Based in a pub, it wasn't unusual to turn up on a Sunday morning to find half of the team asleep, recovering from the Saturday night drinking session.

The warm up for the match often started by one or two of the lads being sick at the side of the pitch. It never affected their performance though and I had every admiration for their fitness, commitment and hardness.

I never drank in the pub enough to guarantee a regular place in the team.

Touching wood, I have never been in hospital or had an operation. I did however have to have stitches in a leg wound caused when I was tackled into the corner post. The post snapped in half and pierced through my right leg. The flag post was a length of 4 by 2 timber hammered into the ground.

They say our game is different now. Some say for the better others say not. The only thing I know is that anyone who plays at the highest level of rugby league is a credit to the sport. Players generally remain close to the supporters and still belong in the main to the communities, which is what the game has been built upon throughout the generations. The media frenzy that hit footballs elite competition has not reached our game yet, and hopefully to protect its future, it never will.

The game still belongs to the grass roots and regardless of the level you play at, rugby league is without a doubt the toughest game in the world to play and that includes darts and curling.

In 1986, when the Australian tourists played Great Britain at Elland Road, the Hunslet stewards were invited to work alongside their counterparts from the football club. I was stationed in the Kop end of the ground. It served a purpose. I got in for free, had a good spot to watch the game from and got paid for my troubles. This was before stewarding became more professional. There wasn't much stewarding done by me that day.

That Aussie touring team in 86, similar to the one in 1982 were in a different class. They played a style of rugby based on strength and speed. The backs were the size of forwards and the forwards had the pace of the backs.

On the 86 tour, the Australians were staying for the duration at the Dragonara Hotel in the centre of Leeds. Amanda and I went down to the hotel one evening to get some rugby balls signed for the Hunslet supporters club Christmas raffle. The Aussies were playing at Warrington that night. We got there in time to be in the lift with the giant forward Steve Roach and one of the greatest ever scrum halfs, Peter Sterling. Roach who later went on to play at Warrington ate about 6 mars bars in the time it took us to travel half a dozen floors.

We ended up in conversation with none other than the great Mal Meninga, who agreed to take the balls and get them all signed. He asked us to give him a couple of days to get them done and said we should ring him before coming back to the hotel. A couple of days later I was on the phone to Mal Meninga and then I was knocking on his hotel bedroom to collect the balls. Not only was Mal a great player, but he seemed a really nice bloke.

One of the signed balls 'accidentally' ended up in our loft. Its value trebled overnight the day I got the Hunslet squad of 1986/87 to sign it!

Castleford came to Elland Road in 1986, for a Challenge Cup quarter-final. There were 14,000 in that day and the rest. That season, 1986/87 was a classic. Coached by former Leeds great, David Ward, Hunslet won promotion to the top flight. It was a team that introduced players like Sonny Nickle and Jamie Lowes to the professional ranks. Jamie later became James and James Lowes went on to have a distinguished career with Leeds and Bradford. Lowes, who is now part of the coaching set up at Salford is a true character of the modern game and a South Leeds lad to boot.

I met a gentleman called Bill Tate through supporting Hunslet. Bill's son Phil was a regular in the side. Little did I know at that time that I would soon come into contact with Bill in a professional capacity.

Hunslet have been in decline in recent times. They are now settled back where they belong at the South Leeds stadium close to their spiritual Parkside home.

Without clubs like Hunslet, there would be no Super League. Who knows what would have happened if the club had been allowed into Super League after winning the right to be promoted a few seasons ago. Their ground was deemed to be not suitable for top flight rugby. An unbelievable decision that cost the club many supporters.

We went to that Grand Final against Dewsbury at Headingley in 1999, but by then we were distant from the club. We applauded their every move and cheered at the end, but we no longer had any real affinity with the club.

Hunslet Hawks now survive on a shoestring, with a band of

truly loyal supporters and a Board very much keeping the club going I would suggest by 'dipping into their own pockets'.

We went to the South Leeds stadium a couple of years ago to see the Hawks play the Leeds Rhinos in a pre season friendly. The South Leeds stadium is one of the most picturesque grounds in the country, with views that take in Middleton light railway, the oldest railway in the world. Despite growing up about 3 miles away, I have never been on that railway. I wonder if I ever will?

It is without exception one of the coldest grounds due to a constant whistling wind that blows through the stand. 'Fleece-man' was in his element.

My cousin's son, Danny Wood was playing for Hunslet that day. Danny is what some would call a 'journeyman'. He had played a few years earlier in the same Rochdale Hornets side as Danny Sculthorpe. Before signing for Hunslet, Danny was being courted by a couple of clubs. He is a Middleton lad and I am sure there was a pull for him to sign for the Hawks and to follow what his Uncle Stephen had done in the 70's and 80's. Proud Great-great grandparents will have been looking down on him.

Danny re-signed for Rochdale for 2006, after a period in the widerness playing rugby union. His comeback was however a short one, and due to work commitments, he has now hung up his boots, but at least he did pull on the famous myrtle, white and flame jersey.

It made me smile when Hunslet beat Leeds Rhinos to win the Lazenby Cup pre the 2005 season. The Lazenby cup is the unofficial City of Leeds championship. It has been played for, for many years. This victory went largely unreported in the local press, but I bet it meant a lot to everyone involved with the Hunslet club.

Good on you Hunslet Rugby League Football Club. You will always be the first result I look for after the Tigers.

The question still remains "how does anyone change allegiance?"

You are brought up to follow one club for life, unless you are a glory supporter. How did the South Leeds lad end up at the Jungle?

From Wembley to marriage to prison

The journey from Elland Road and Hunslet Rugby League Club to Castleford Rugby League Club at the Jungle was an interesting one.

I had left school in 1979, without a bag full of qualifications. This was a time however when there seemed to be plenty of jobs around.

Nationally in 1979, the country had a winter of discontent. There were strikes and there was snow. Both brought the country to a standstill. In the May, Margaret Thatcher came to power.

People say, "It doesn't snow like it used to", and they are right, it doesn't snow like it used to. I remember having to dig our way out of the house and clear the drive and footpaths. Today, you only seem to get the odd day of snow, which can be got rid of with a sweeping brush.

We used to make 'slides'. This was an area of the playground that was worked on for days to produce an area of sheet ice. You could slide for what seemed like hundreds of yards. You were warned about making slides in the street.

The days when workers went on strike are distant memories. Power cuts were a real adventure for children. It meant the candles you had somewhere in the house had to be sought and put to use. Everyone used to sit around their half a dozen candles with their melted bottoms, attached to small plates. You had one candle on it's own to take to the toilet.

Unfortunately power cuts also meant no television and that's when the fun ended.

Compared to now, there didn't seem to be a great deal of careers guidance or any push to get children to think about university or higher education. I started my first job in July 1979. That was the day I also met Amanda who started at the North Eastern Gas Board at the same time. It's funny how fate sometimes deals you a good hand.

Being half decent at Maths at school, I had aspirations about a career in accounting. That never transpired.

I got my maths right however when I spent some of my first monthly pay packet of £135.23 on a 6 × 3 snooker table. The final piece for our indoor league. It was stored behind the sofa in the living room and when it came out, it was out for days and nights on end. There had to be allowances for some shots because of the proximity to the furniture or walls. We had to purchase a two piece cue and that alleviated these problems. However, controlling the cue ball is difficult when your cue is about 18 inches long.

One of my managers at the Gas Board was Eric Gardner who was on the board of Featherstone Rovers. Knowing Eric came in handy when the 1982 Challenge Cup final at Wembley between Widnes and Hull ended up being a draw. Tickets were hard to come by for the replay at Elland Road, but with the right connections anything is possible.

Eric also brought the Challenge Cup into the office after Rovers had beaten Hull FC against all the odds at Wembley in 1983.

I went to the 1983 final with a mate called John Gilmartin. We drove down to Wembley on the night before in my Fiat 127, and slept just off Wembley way in the back of the car. John ended up working in the computer department at the Gas Board. These were the days before I pods, laptops, and palm tops. Everything was still hand written and the computers that were there were big enough to fill a house. Despite doing computer studies at 'O' level, I still never understood what magnetic tape or paper tape were all about.

One of John's colleagues in that department was the referee John Kendrew.

The annual excursions to Wembley for the cup final were always eventful. I went to several with 3 Bradford Northern fans, my future best man Russ Hanwell, his brother Mark and his best mate Michael Hudson.

I had met Russ at Park Lane College in 1979. Being a junior clerk meant that you were allowed day release to go to college. I never really liked it, but I came out with a couple of qualifications and it was like having a day off work for free. The class we were in at college was made up of people of similar age, so none of us were long since out of school. In that respect the social side was good. We found a pub near to the college called the 'Highland'. It was a traditional hand pulled Tetleys, spit and sawdust type of pub, and we loved it. A few pints on a dinnertime accompanied by either pork pie and mushy peas or a roast beef and onion sandwich always hit the spot. Sometimes we just stayed in the pub and never went back for the afternoon lessons. That beat school.

On one of our early trips to Wembley, Bradford Northern played Fulham at Craven Cottage on the Friday night before the 1981 final. The Hanwell brothers are really good with the dry wit and have the ability to wind people up. Stood just in front of us that night was none other than John Kendrew. The evening ended with referee John challenging Russ to a sprint race the length of the field, after some jibe had been made about the referees level of fitness. Unfortunately the race never took place.

On those trips, we never saw much of London, but we did sample what was the uniqueness of the weekend when everyone came together regardless of which club colours you wore. The pubs were full of northerners sharing stories, singing and generally having a good time. I tended to stick to the singing and having a good time, because I didn't have many stories to tell.

At the cup final, supporters are always encouraged to sing the 'traditional' song 'Abide with me'. Traditional it may be, but hardly anybody knows the words and I still cringe with embarrassment when the television cameras pan the crowd to see if they can find someone who is actually singing. My mam always said that rugby supporters were a class above their football counterparts because they always sung the national anthem with gusto. She always felt that football audiences were ignorant in comparison.

In 1981, we were staying in the St Ermins hotel, somewhere in London. Its grandness blew us away when we arrived. In the bar, we got talking to an American chap who had the biggest biceps any of us had ever seen. He didn't need to tense them either to impress us. He told us that he worked in 'aluminum', which we took to mean aluminium. Thinking about it, Aluminum could also have been the city or town where he worked back home!

I fell for Amanda within days of first meeting her, but the pursuit lasted a couple of years. We were soon friends, but apart from maybe going for a drink on a Friday lunchtime, our friendship grew only as work colleagues.

The first time we went out together as friends was to see Superman at the pictures. I still watch it every time it comes on television and was saddened when Superman, Christopher

Reeve had his riding accident that ultimately led to his premature death.

In the summer of 1981, I had my first trip abroad, to Magaluf in Majorca with Russ Hanwell. We were in a bar one night when ex Castleford player Steve 'Knocker' Norton and ex Leeds centre Les Dyl walked in. They were two real characters.

Amanda was away in Spain the fortnight before us, so we went nearly a month without seeing each other. Within a couple of weeks of getting back, it was her 18th birthday and she was having a party at 'Cinderella Rockafellas' in Leeds. My 18th birthday a couple of months earlier was memorable in that it was the day the Yorkshire Ripper, Peter Sutcliffe was sentenced.

It was at Cinderellas that the pursuit came to an end. I still have the invite to the party in my wallet. 'Cinders' was a popular nightspot in Leeds. It wasn't a club or a pub and it wasn't a disco, it was what was called a 'nitespot'. The other Leeds nitespots were La Phonagrapique and Tiffanys.

The world was getting used to new romantics in 1981. Spandau Ballet were in the charts and I still think their debut album 'Journeys to glory' was a classic. It cost me £3.89 from HMV and is now in the loft somewhere. I haven't listened to it in over 20 years, but it is still a classic. I never bought into lads wearing make up and I could never master the 'flick head' haircut modelled by the Human League's Phil Oakey, but the music was different. One of our songs at the time was Vienna by Ultravox. Lead singer Midge Ure, more famous for Live Aid, had sideboards that we all tried to copy, but no one could.

It was around this time that George O' Dowd came onto the music scene. Boy George and Culture Club appeared on Top of the pops and people were fascinated, asking the day after at work "was that was a boy or a girl?"

I was also fascinated by Soft Cell and in particular by singer Marc Almond. I think it was how he had the name spelt differently ala Bolan and that Leeds tried to claim him as a 'home boy'. When it all turned out he actually did spend time in the Leeds as a student, but never claimed to being born in the city.

12″ singles were the rage then too. I have a copy of Soft Cell's 'Tainted love / where did our love go?' which is by all accounts a collectable.

A couple of years ago we went to see Duran Duran at the Sheffield Arena and we were sat near the girls from the Human League. That was the highlight of the evening because Duran Duran weren't that good. One of the last decent venues in Leeds was the Queens Hall in the City Centre. We saw Elton John there in 1984 and later T'Pau. I always fancied lead singer Carol Decker from T'Pau. Just like Debbie Harry and Olivia Newton John from years before, there was just something about her.

I gladly missed out on the punk era by a couple of years. Why would anyone want to dress like that and spend their life swearing and spitting anyway?

Roundhay Park in Leeds put itself on the music map in 1981. We went to see the Rolling Stones on their farewell tour. Not really sure if they ever played together again after that!

It is a great venue and a couple of years later we went to see Genesis, although Joe Jackson stole that show for me with his acapella version of 'Different for girls'. In 1987, we got tickets for Madanna's gig at Roundhay, but I was on nights and I couldn't get anyone to cover my shift. Bram and Sister in law Helen went instead and they still owe us for those tickets! They must have enjoyed that Madonna gig so much that they returned 19 years later to see Robbie Williams play in front of 90,000 adoring fans at Roundhay.

Amanda and I courted for a couple of years. We were very much creatures of habit, going to the same pubs in Leeds on the same nights of the week. Although we worked together and saw each other every day, I still got butterflies everytime I met her off the bus. I was a bit of a traditionalist and didn't believe in going dutch. We only had a few drinks anyway with the real treat being a visit to Pizzaland, where a couple of pizzas used to cost around a fiver.

We got engaged in 1983, in Venice. The moment was meant to be really romantic, as I placed the ring on Amanda's finger. This was all going to be set on a gondola. The planning went to pot really, because our romantic gondola ride for two turned out to be a gondola ride for about 20, with me at one end and Amanda at the other. If you ever go to Venice, look out for the tourist sized gondolas, built for getting as many people on as possible.

The back canals in Venice weren't the most romantic of places. People opened their house windows and just threw litter into the water.

I had bought the engagement ring in Leeds but decided not to take it with us in case it got lost. I bought a cheap ring in Italy, but by the end of the holiday it was going mouldy. Venice, like Cumbria is a place we have always promised to go back to one day, but we haven't made it yet.

We got married on Saturday 8th June 1985 at St Mary's Church in Kippax.

The reception was held at Jane Tumeltys dance school in Castleford, about a mile from the Jungle. The building is now long gone.

That day was memorable for other reasons. As well as it been my new father in laws, Robins birthday, it was also Amanda's grandparents Golden wedding day. Eddie and Doris Lee were also like Grandparents to me and although they are no longer with us, we felt privileged to share that day with them.

It was also the day that Barry McGuigan fought Eusebio Pedroza for the world title at Loftus Road in London. I am still accused to this day of sneaking out of our evening reception to go watch the fight in the Prince of Wales feathers.

I will say once again that I didn't, but I know no one will ever believe me. I also have no knowledge on how Robin lost one of his false teeth that night. The suspicion was that he left it behind in the pub after sneaking out of his own daughters wedding to watch the boxing!

Every time McGuigan appears on our screen, I am still ribbed about my alleged disappearing act.

I always liked boxing. Personal favourites were Charlie Magri, Alan Minter, Dave 'boy' Green and Yorkshires finest Richard Dunn.

When Frank Bruno fought Mike Tyson for the first time in 1989, I went with Bram to the Grand Theatre in Leeds to watch it live by satellite from the U.S.A. It cost a bomb, at £25 a ticket, but was a unique event. The fight was due to start in the early hours, so we get there in good time with a view to having a few beers before the main event. Unfortunately the theatre hadn't been granted a license for serving alcohol, and all that was on offer was alcohol free 'Kaliber'. The bouts leading up to the Bruno fight were really boring and they all went the distance. By the time big Frank climbed into the ring it was nearly morning and the majority of the audience were fast asleep. We just woke up in time to see Tyson pummel Bruno in 5 rounds.

When they fought again in 1996, Sky TV bought the rights to show it live. Robin invited us round and once again it was due to start in the early hours. Bram picked my mate Astley and myself up and we drove the short distance to Robins. When we got there Robin was watching a black and white cowboy film.

We all just sat there thinking that the fight must be delayed or that the satellite wasn't connected. There was no great scientific explanation, Robin simply had the wrong channel on, and by the time he realised the fight was half way through.

One of Robin's workmates was a regular in the Griffin pub which is located on Lock Lane as you enter Castleford. The landlord at that time was Hunslet player John Wolford. John had signed a photograph for us wishing us all the best on our wedding day. He was in a different class and had a fantastic footballers brain. His only shortcoming was his lack of pace. In another generation he would have been one of the greatest.

Looking at our wedding photographs its amazing how many people are no longer with us and how many people you lose touch with over the years. The last time I spoke to John Gilmartin was at Headingley at the Challenge Cup semi-final in 2002, when Cas lost valiantly to a fabulous Wigan outfit. John's son was refereeing the curtain raiser. He couldn't believe that we were now Cas fans after knowing us as long time Hunslet supporters.

We had only been married 5 weeks when 'Live Aid' came around. Like most newly weds we didn't have much furniture. We set our speakers from the music centre up at either side of the TV and had the volume turned up. We watched from start to finish. It must have been fantastic to have actually been there and how much better was it than the second event in 2005?

I have some fond memories of working at the Gas Board, but after about 6 years and a couple of promotions, I decided that working in an office was not for me.

In 1986, I made a career change that was without a doubt a real gamble.

MARK HUDSON

I thought about the Police, Fire Brigade and Ambulance Services, but ended up in mid 1986 sat in the training unit at HMP Wakefield having an entry examination and medical to join Her Majesty's Prison Service.

Hunslet supporter, Bill Tate had worked at HMP Leeds for years and he was full of encouragement when I discussed my possible career move with him at a match.

I had to attend an assessment test and a subsequent interview. A couple of weeks later, I got a letter to say that I had been accepted and that I should report to the Training Unit at HMP Leeds on the 8th December 1986.

Looking back now that was one of the best things I ever did. As a profession I truly believe that the Prison Service is a best kept secret. Joining the service did however lead indirectly to us turning our backs on Hunslet and rugby league.

In those days, when you joined you could be posted to any prison in the country as a NEPO (new entrant Prison Officer). Basically you put in your preferred choice of establishment and then half way through the 8 weeks training course you were handed a brown envelope that contained your destiny.

Sat with 11 colleagues in 'E' section at the national training college in Rugby, we were told we all had to open our envelopes together and say nothing. The tutor then went around the classroom and asked us what our initial thoughts about our postings were.

I was really pleased because my posting was to HMP Full Sutton, located just outside York, but which was still being built at that time. You had to live within a certain distance from your prison, so we eventually moved to Stamford Bridge near York.

Some of my mates were not so lucky. Some were posted to prisons in London, despite living in the North East of England.

There didn't seem much fairness in the system, but I wasn't too bothered. I got what I wanted.

I had to go back to work at HMP Leeds for the best part of a year until Full Sutton was ready to open. Those first few months at Leeds were fascinating and when I left I always knew that I would go back to work there one day.

There were some amazing characters and some even more amazing nicknames. One of the first officers I came into contact with was called 'Wingnuts', because of how his ears stook out. Another officer with a tendency to tell management about what his colleagues were up to was known as 'Pampas', which is a six-foot tall grass.

Then there was 'Jimmy 2 chairs' who took up 2 seats in the staff tea-room.

The tea-room was and is still to this day called the kardomah for whatever reason. There was the 'Duke' whose hobby was painting toy soldiers.

One of my favourite nicknames was given to Officer Carter. 'Minty' Carter was regularly late for duty and often arrived 'after eight!'

Another was nicknamed 'Horace' after being assaulted by a prisoner. Horace was short for Horace-zontal (horizontal).

At 1330 hours everyday there used to be a stick and whistle parade where the tasks for the afternoon were handed out by the Orderly Officer, who was in charge of the prison regime. Whenever Officer Les King got a job, the place was in uproar.

It went something like "unlock the 3's landing, Officer King, L". Then everyone to a man shouted "King, L".

I say to a man, because at that time there were no female staff in male prisons and vice versa.

Another officer at Leeds was Bob Haigh. Bob had a distinguished career with Leeds and Wakefield Trinity and a nicer man you couldn't wish to meet. He once scored a world record 40 tries in a season, not bad for a forward. Bob's forearms are like Popeyes, due mainly to the number of operations and plates he has had inserted over the years.

When we left Leeds for York in late 1987, we also left behind Hunslet RLFC. By this time Amanda was pregnant with Jessica. We used to do 100-mile round trips to attend supporters club meetings on a Tuesday evening. It all got too much really, so with money been tight due to Amanda giving up work and me working alternate weekends, something had to give.

H.M.P Full Sutton is one of the most secure prisons in Europe. That tells you something about the category of prisoners locked up there. That didn't stop one of the most unusual rugby league matches taking place shortly after the prison opened in late 1987. It was a rugby league version of 'The mean machine'. The staff versus prisoners game ended in a nil all draw. It was not short of quality and competitive throughout. The touchlines were full of prisoners not playing and the atmosphere resembled Craven Park (or is it Robin Park?), Hull on a good day. However there wasn't any suggestion of foul play from either side and like most games, players from both teams walked off together in unison. The only difference was that only the staff team went for a drink afterwards before making their way home.

Jessica was born on 27th June 1988.

I went to the tailoring factory where my mam had worked for years to tell her that Jess had arrived. I couldn't actually believe the state of the building and the conditions people worked in. I had to go up a few floors in a wooden lift and then entered a massive room where men and women were set out in lines at sewing machines. I can't imagine that Victorian workhouses would have been any different. How did people work in such conditions?

The delight on my mams face when she saw me was priceless. Becoming a parent for the first time is unbelievably special. To become a Grandparent I imagine is just as good.

We did take Jess to her first Hunslet game at Crown Flatt, Dewsbury in her pushchair. We had missed a lot of the season and by then it didn't seem too difficult to walk away.

At Full Sutton, I worked with an officer called Nigel Howlett, who was known as 'Howlers'. Everyone in the service had a nickname, it wasn't just a Leeds Prison trait. I got 'Rocky' for a while, but there was already another Rocky Hudson (Roger) who had played for several rugby league clubs in a largely unfulfilled career. So 'Hudders' stuck for me, with 'Howlers' anyway.

We are Leeds, we are
Leeds, we are Leeds

A lot of staunch rugby league supporters are also staunch football supporters. Since summer rugby was introduced, if you have an allegiance to the 2 sports, and an understanding partner, you generally win all ends up.

Nigel Howlett has been a life long Leeds United supporter. His rugby league team is Hull K.R.

Nigel tells the story about the European Cup Final in Paris in 1975. United lost that night, 2–0 to the crack German side Bayern Munich. Peter Lorimer had a perfectly good goal disallowed with the score at 0–0 and after the final whistle Leeds fans rioted, wrecking the stadium.

Nigel was arrested and made an alien of France. He could never return to France again.

He said that he was locked up in a cell for the night and when he was initially offered some food, he threw it all over the floor. 24 hours later when he hadn't been offered another morsel, he was on his hands and knees eating the scraps he had previously discarded.

In the late eighties, Howlers asked me if I fancied going to Elland Road one week to watch Leeds United. Leeds had fallen from grace some years before and had been languishing in the old Division Two. I went along and was immediately taken in by the experience.

This was not my first experience of watching Leeds United.

My dad had a season ticket for many years in the west stand at Elland Road, during the Don Revie era. He followed them around the country with his mate Tom.

When United won the centenary F.A Cup Final in 1972 against Arsenal, they then had to travel to Molenuix on the following Monday night to play Wolverhampton Wanderers. If they won that game, Leeds would have done the double. This scenario wouldn't happen today, but rulings like that always seemed to affect Leeds.

My dad and Tom duly drove to the ground, but never got in. They listened to the game on the radio on the drive home. Leeds lost and the Revie team never quite got the accolades that it deserved.

When Leeds eventually went on to win the old First Division title, in 1974/75, their last match was at Loftus Road against Q.P.R. They won 1–0. As a family we travelled to Elland Road late on the Saturday night to see the team bus return and to share in the jubilation. Unfortunately for the many fans that had made the same journey, the players and staff got off their bus and went straight into the ground, without one word for the supporters who had ventured out in the middle of the night. That memory stuck with me. I was 11 or 12 at the time. Why the attitude and lack of regard for the people who paid their wages?

How different to the scenes at the Jungle in October 2005 when we celebrated the Tigers return to the top flight.

In saying that about the attitude, the reverse did happen on many occasions. During the school holidays my sister Bev and I used to look after our younger cousins, Paula, Neil and Andrew Hewitt who lived about 2 miles from Elland Road. We would all go down to watch Leeds United's open training sessions on Fullerton Park, which was right next to the ground.

Fullerton Park is now a car park and you have more chance these days of winning the lottery than walking off the street and watching premiership footballers train.

We used to get all of the autographs and act as ball boys when the balls used to come flying over the fence surrounding the training pitches.

There was a steep banking from the training area to the car park so when you fagged the ball it had to be helluva kick to send it back over the fence. We were little and the footballs were heavy. We once got a roasting from Norman 'bite your legs' Hunter for failing to achieve this. "We haven't got all day, son" were his exact words.

Many families in South Leeds have not ventured far from their roots. The Hewitts are all married now with families of their own and despite living close by, we only seem to come together at big family occasions. Their dad, my Uncle George has recently retired. He is one of those people who can make anything from anything. Andrew reminded me recently about the time George made the lads some cricket pads out of plastic guttering. They were great when the ball hit you, but not too comfortable to run in. They were ground breaking in the fact that they were also black. George once made the lads a snooker table, with an old flannelette sheet for the cloth and onion bags for pockets. The balls used to run all over.

Back then, football wasn't the multi million pound business it is today. Scottish internationals, Joe Jordan and Gordon McQueen used to lodge together in a house near us in Middleton.

I once wrote to Joe at his digs and he sent me a signed photo.

Centre forward, Mick Jones was my hero. My pet rabbit was duly named Mick. My sister Bev called hers Snowy. Both rabbits were white. Calling it Snowy was the equivalent of naming your dog, Rover or your goldfish, Jaws.

We used to race the rabbits down the street holding their back legs. I think that there is a balance between sport and pet cruelty, but neither Mick nor Snowy ever complained.

Having a pen pal was once all the rage. Mine was called Steve Palone and he lived in New York City. Our Bev's was called Marie Christine and she lived in France. After a couple of exchanges of mail, I bailed out on Steve after he sent me a load of stuff about New York. I always thought that there wasn't much about Leeds that would interest a lad from the 'big apple'. Truth be known, I think I was just too tight to consider buying presents back. Bev is still in touch with Marie Christine and has been to France to meet her.

As a club Leeds United were always innovative. My dad always said they were the first team to come to the centre of the pitch, stand in a line and wave to the crowd before the kick off. It seemed to mean something then, whereas today I always think it is very much a token gesture by footballers turning up to perform as actors on a stage every week.

I had a pair of Mick Jones, number 9 stocking tabs. These were worn by Leeds United players on their socks. They were blue in colour with white tassels on the bottom and with the players number on them, also in white.

They measured in at about 8 × 5 inches.

The Leeds and England full back Terry Cooper had a sports shop near Leeds Bridge and it sold 'target 10' footballs. These were blue and white striped plastic balls with a black number 10 at each end. They were endorsed by the midfield genius and United number 10, Johnny Giles.

Just two examples of innovation and a pat on the back to the marketing people at Leeds.

Returning to Elland Road with Howlers in the late 80's, I stood in the Kop end and enjoyed the atmosphere and passion shown by the fans. Leeds had real chance of being promoted back to the top flight and I wanted to be part of it.

I had to go home and persuade Amanda into letting me get a season ticket for the remainder of that season. She said that if I did then that would be the end of going to the rugby. The choice was mine.

I got the season ticket and shared in the jubilation of that promotion season. Towards the end of the campaign, Leeds played Leicester City and if the results went right they would get promoted. The results didn't go our way and the champagne was back on ice. Along with Bram, who had followed Leeds for years, we had arranged to take the wives into Leeds that Saturday evening for a meal and a few beers.

We headed off to an Italian bistro we knew was regularly frequented by the playing staff. Sure enough, in walked one Vinnie Jones who had become very much a cult figure at Leeds.

I never had much time for Vinnie after that night, due to the language he was using at the bar. There is a time and place for such language and that wasn't it. The place was full of families and his performance that night didn't impress, a bit like some of the films he has gone on to make since.

Promotion and the title were sealed at Bournemouth a couple of weeks later. We watched the game at the old Astoria Ballroom on Roundhay Road in Leeds. There was no Sky T.V and the club had acted quickly to ensure that the match was beamed back live to several locations across the city.

It was a great day that ended with a barbecue and a few beers back at our house. I remember putting the hosepipe on

n attempt to revive him. Howlers was of course in
uth.

We lived for a year in Stamford Bridge, just outside the beautiful City of York. It was 35 miles from home. We might as well have been living in London. People came for the day and then went back home. We were homesick and really missing our family and friends. Our neighbours were also strange and we always felt like outsiders in this close knit village. On one side we had a young lad who lived on his own. We called him 'Hermit' because every time you said "hello", he would dive in his house without replying. On the other side we had a nun. Most people have nicknames for their neighbours. Growing up, we had Tarzan living near us. He always walked around with no shirt on. I also recall a Lucy 'no neck' living on the street. She wasn't even called Lucy.

By the time our youngest daughter, Sophie arrived, on Valentines Day in 1991, we had moved back to Leeds after the Prison Service relaxed the rule about living in close proximity to where you worked. We haven't moved since and after over 21 years of marriage, I cannot imagine ever moving again.

It was decision time on whether I should get a season ticket for the new season in the old first division. I did and watched Leeds for a few seasons, including the Howard Wilkinson inspired championship winning year of 1991–92.

If you stood in the Kop, you had your own spot and got to know the people who stood around you. We had a spot near a group of lads from Northampton who travelled all over the country watching their adopted team. This group included a couple of lads we called 'Rixy' and 'Midge', because they looked like the Arsenal player, Graham Rix, with long curly blond hair, and Midge Ure, with the sideboards.

They used to get into some right scrapes with supporters from other teams. For them, that was all part of the package and something they seemed to enjoy more than the football. They once had a ruck with rival supporters in a motorway service station. Managing to steal their rivals car keys, they sped off up the motorway whilst at the same time launching the keys from their own car into a nearby wood. Several miles later they were pulled over by the Police and made to go back and find the keys. The image of Rixy and Midge on their hands and knees in the bushes looking for the keys was priceless.

The Kop at Elland Road sang, "Welsh, spotty virgin, he's just a Welsh spotty virgin", in recognition of a young Manchester United player, aged about 17 or 18 at the time. His name was Ryan Giggs and he had just about forced his way into Alex Ferguson's first team squad. The rest as they say is history.

People still say that the 91–92 season was the one when Leeds didn't win it, but Manchester United gave it away. In all of the football annuals I have seen since, there is a league table and Leeds United are right there at the top of it as champions.

The title was won, one Sunday, when Leeds beat Sheffield United at Bramall Lane and our closest rivals from Manchester lost against Liverpool. That was a great game to be at and a great occasion. On the way back from Sheffield, we pulled into the Post Office pub off the M1, which had been taken over by Leeds fans. Man Uniteds defeat meant that the title was ours. That was a remarkable effort looking at the squad under the stewardship of the very under rated Howard Wilkinson. Towards the end of that season, Eric Cantona arrived and although his departure hurt because of where he went, his contributions were not the reason why Leeds United were now champions of England.

Home matches at Elland Road started for us at around lunch time. A group of us used to frequent the Whistlestop pub in

Beeston, about a 10 minutes walk from the ground. It was a real United pub on a match day. Similar to inside the ground, every one had their own spot, either propping up the bar our sat around in groups. Our group consisted of sister in law Helen, husband Bram, a couple of Brams mates and of course Howlers who by this time had transferred to HMP Birmingham to be a dog handler.

Howlers still made every game, home and away, as part of the Birmingham branch of the supporters club. We got on really well with the staff in the Whistle. You could tell if the game was against a big team by the number of people in the pub. Big teams attracted a bigger drinking crowd. That never stopped us regulars getting served ahead of everyone else. We used to call one of the barmaids Jack, because she had a real gravely voice like Jack Duckworth from Coronation Street.

During this period I also crossed the great divide and played a few games of rugby union. An officer at HMP Full Sutton had played a bit and was keen to take a team to a tournament in Eccles, near Manchester. When he asked what position I wanted to play, I didn't have much of a clue, so decided I could be a hooker. All that I would have to do was throw the ball in at the lineouts, something that seemed simple enough. Our first game was against a team from the Maze prison from Northern Ireland. As the first scrum went down, the opposing hooker decided to give me some old fashion 'chin pie', which didn't go down too well. My dad used to take delight in dishing out the chin pie when I was little. I didn't appreciate it as a grown up. Being able to give somebody chin pie is a power trip. There is nothing that hurts in life more than being pinned down and being on the end of chin pie. The Chinese wrist burn is a close second. I never understood if it originated from China or whether that was added to make it sound more tortuous.

My throwing in at the line-outs was worse than rubbish. The ball went in every direction apart from where I intended it to go. The neck ache I had for several days later didn't go down too well. Rugby union isn't an easy game to play. My career was over before it began. I had a greater regard for anyone who plays the game. If only they didn't have pockets in their shorts and three christian names, they would be okay.

There is a tradition in union that you give three cheers to your opponents as they leave the field. This is done at the same time that your team forms a 'guard of honour'. The opposition reciprocates as you leave the arena. That is a nice touch and despite knocking lumps out of each other for 80 minutes this is true sportsmanship at the end of the day.

I have always enjoyed watching international rugby union and grew up admiring the great Welsh teams containing players like Phil Bennett. England teams always seemed to be class orientated. The Welsh players seemed to be from the mining communities, whilst the England team were all ex public school-boys who were now officers in the forces.

One thing I still look forward to is the singing at the international games in Wales. The Welsh people sing with a real passion and pride for their country. I haven't got a clue what the words to their anthem are, and I have my own version. League fans always seem embarrassed to sing our national anthem at big games.

The codes have learnt from each other over the years.

There was a time when injured players in union games had to be seen by a Doctor before a substitution was allowed. That rule has gone.

Union seemed to frown when the 'big screen' arrived in Super League, but lo and behold it is now used at the big union games.

There should be no rivalry between the codes because the

games are as different as chalk and cheese. There is room for both games, although very few supporters would ever admit to following both codes. Do Leeds Rhinos fans turn up to watch Leeds Tykes play and vice versa?

Winning the first division meant that the football season 1992–93, commenced with the Charity Shield at Wembley. This is the traditional curtain raiser contested between the team winning the F.A Cup and the team winning the title in the previous season.

This was to be the second visit to the twin towers within a few months.

We left getting the tickets for August's Charity Shield in the capable hands of Amanda's Uncle John, who promised us that he had the contacts to get us the best seats at the side of the Royal box, near the Leeds end.

It was a game against Liverpool and we had the most pleasant of surprises when we entered the stadium to find ourselves very much in the Liverpool end. Not the thing you would want when you are donning the all white kit. It's a good job it was the pre season curtain raiser. Leeds won 4–3, with a Cantona hat trick.

Howlers married a fellow officer from HMP Birmingham and we went to the wedding at Walsall Registry Office. The ceremony was on the same day that Leeds were playing Man United at Elland Road in a rearranged evening fixture. I wasn't going to miss that. Howlers was gutted that we had to leave early, but even more gutted that he would miss the game himself.

We left early to ensure Amanda would be able to drop me off in time. Unfortunately with traffic and road works on the way back up North, kick off time was approaching and we were still miles from the ground. There was no other option. I had to run the last couple of miles, still dressed in my best gear that I had worn to the wedding. Stood in the Kop with my suit on caused some amusement that night.

In May 1992, I got pay back for those Madonna tickets from Bram. Live Italian football was now being shown on BSB and Bram became an armchair supporter of Sampdoria. Their team included future Chelsea boss Gianluca Vialli and the future 'divine ponytail' Roberto Baggio. Sampdoria played Barcelona in the European Cup Final and Bram and I were amongst a small band of English people in Wembley stadium that night.

The atmosphere was unique. It was the first time I had seen supporters with those cards that everyone holds up as the teams are coming out. We left Leeds mid morning with the intention of getting to London in the afternoon, get parked up, a few beers etc. In fact the usual match day routine.

We ended up in the pub at the very end of Wembley way, called 'The Torch'. The skills we had perfected in getting to the bar at the Whistlestop came in handy again. The pub was full of Italians and Spaniards who didn't have a clue on how much things cost or on how our currency operated. As they were paying for their beer, they just held out a hand full of notes and coins to the bar staff. I never heard any of the bar staff say "I am sorry Sir, but you have given me far too much, please take this back".

My flirtation with the 'beautiful game' ended a couple of season later.

Half of the attraction was the spirit in the ground and the connection with the players. Winning the title as underdogs was a remarkable and the club can always say that they were the last to win the first division title before the new world of the Premiership kicked in. This new world also meant that all seater stadiums were coming. You could no longer jump about like a mad man with your mates and the admission prices also went up. If you had a seat next to someone you didn't particular like, it was tough because you were stuck with them all season.

Leeds United never kicked on from that period until the David O'Leary era several years later.

I walked away from football when the seats went in and have only been back a couple of times since. I now have trouble understanding why people watch top flight football these days. Normal working people paying extortionate prices to line the pockets of players, some of whom are earning up to and beyond £100,000 a week. How can that be right?

Our next door but one neighbours have a grown up son who left home years ago. As a youngster John Finnigan was always a gifted footballer. He started life as a junior at Nottingham Forest and now captains Cheltenham Town after several seasons playing at Lincoln City.

I once glanced out of our bedroom window to see a line of red and white shirts hung out on his mums washing line. It was obviously John's turn to bring the kits home and get Lincoln City's kit washed.

Football in the lower leagues still belongs to the fans.

Finnagan made a rare TV appearance in January 2006, when his Cheltenham team took on Newcastle United in the 4th round of the FA Cup. It was shown live on BBC1. John had a good game despite his side losing 0–2. I asked John if he had managed to swap shirts with a Newcastle player. He said that he wanted Alan Shearer's number 9 shirt and as captain thought that he had a real chance. Unfortunately he got pulled for an interview as he left the pitch and by the time he got into the changing rooms, the only shirt up for 'grabs' was Charles N'-

Zogbia's. I am sure that will never be a collectable in years to come.

Give me rugby league any day. No cheating, feigning injuries and hurling abuse at the referees. The theatricals of diving to win a free kick must be something footballers practise at training. They have got it off to a tee, because the referees never seem to be able to spot that they are actually doing it. For me, it's cheating the officials, their opponents and the thousands of people who pay good money week in and week out.

There is even a third official who stands and takes abuse from the managers at the side of the pitch.

It has been reported that a number of players who have been transferred from Leeds United in recent years are still having some of their wages paid by the club.

I was just glad I caught Leeds United at the right time, before the media spotlight and finance took the game away from the man on the street.

My family were now growing up and for several years I was fallow as a supporter of live sport.

I took to participation instead and chose one of the better value activities, long distance running.

As for Nigel Howlett? I would have shaken his hand and said, "congratulations" when Hull K.R defeated the Tigers at Blackpool to win the Northern Rail Cup in 2005. I would have shaken his hand and said "congratulations" after Hull K.R defeated us at Robin Park in the league in that August.

I would have stood there and just smiled after our Grand Final victory. It's all about the big games.

The last I heard Nigel had moved to Australia. I bet he still looks out for the football results, the rugby league results and I bet he has never been back to France.

Daughters

The day Sophie was born was my last shift at Full Sutton. It was a typical February day and the prison car park was snow covered when I arrived on duty. Mid morning, Amanda phoned to say that she thought she was going into labour. Even more snow had come down. When I got onto the car park, it took me ages to find where I had abandoned the car a few hours earlier.

Driving the 35 miles home in my wellies and in a state of panic wasn't fun. I got home for Amanda to say that I shouldn't have panicked.

My transfer back to Leeds Prison came through whilst I was on paternity leave.

Getting up for the middle of the night feeds was always a chore and like most dads, I mastered the art of 'throwing a deaf one'. It must be a pleasure nowadays and I bet couples have fewer arguments when it comes to getting up in the small hours. When our 2 were babies, we didn't have central heating or Sky T.V. Whoever got up would come back to bed frozen. Now you can get up and watch a film or sport or the music channels at the same time as administering the night feed.

On my first day back at Leeds in February 1991, someone asked me if I had been on annual leave. I had actually been at another prison for 3 1/2 years. Talk about being missed.

I was considering my first shot at getting promoted to Senior Officer. I had studied hard to pass the promotion exam when I was still at Full Sutton, but I was still a young officer in comparison to the majority of staff at Leeds who all seemed to have at least 30 years service in.

Experience is everything. Prisons are built around goodwill. There is generally a great deal of camaraderie between the staff and good working relationships between the staff and the prisoners.

I worked on 'A' Wing, which was a busy remand wing, where prisoners where locked up 3 to a cell and still going through the archaic ritual of 'slopping out'. There were no telephones or in cell televisions. The events at Strangeways in Manchester in 1990 changed the way the Prison Service operated and led to a massive investment and modernisation of Victorian prisons. HMP Leeds was built in 1847. We were one of the last wings in the country to have slopping out and when the wing closed down for refurbishment in late 1994, Leeds Prison turned a corner.

As a parting gesture, 'A' Wing entered a team in the annual staff 5 a side football tournament held at Armley Sports Centre. We won the event wearing our 50p T-shirts from McDonalds, celebrating the '94 football World Cup in the U.S.A. Bob Haigh played in that tournament (the 5 aside, not the World Cup) and won even more respect by kicking a couple of the prison Governors up in the air.

Having 2 daughters at the same junior school gave us the opportunity to get involved with the parent/teachers association. Every school has a PTA. These are small bands of enthusiastic and hard working parents working alongside a small band of enthusiastic and hard working teachers, to raise funds for the school.

When Amanda was chairperson of the group for several

years, I seemed to get volunteered for all sorts. I ended up being Santa at Christmas and being Fred Flintstone in a 'Seven little girls' sketch. You know the one:

"Seven little girls, sitting in the back seat hugging and a kissin' with Fred".

In this case the seven little girls were all young mums, so it was well worth the embarrassment of wearing a Fred costume.

There was an Easter fun day and I was asked to be the Easter bunny, with a free reign to do whatever I wanted to do around school. To maintain my identity, I hid the bunny suit in some bushes around 200 metres away and kept reappearing as myself in the school corridors. When no-one was looking I would run to the top field don the white bunny gear and hop back inside to terrorise everyone. The suit wasn't a great fit and I couldn't put my trainers on under it, which caused me some anxieties. At one point I kicked my toes against a kerb and let out a, "bastard". Unfortunately the children from Nursery were stood right next to me at the time.

All the time I was hopping around in that white bunny suit, I was thinking, "I wonder what my mates from work would say if they could see me now?"

That experience taught me to hold club mascots in high regard.

From the Leeds/Liverpool canal to New York

A group of us started to run on a lunch time to get fit. The Leeds to Liverpool canal is about a mile away from the Prison and the canal runs gives you a sense of real escapism. The route is popular with all runners based in Leeds City Centre. There were always the same faces and banter as you passed the same group you saw at the very same spot you saw them at on the day before and the day before that.

We decided to put our new found fitness to the test by entering the Leeds half marathon. It was an event I then went on to run for 10 consecutive years between 1994 until 2004. I have a personal best on the course of 1 hour 45 minutes, which is good on a difficult course. As the years went by my enthusiasm and fitness for the faster times waned, and I was happy just to get around in whatever time.

Running became popular across the country and at one time or another we seemed to be taking new training partners on board. One officer, Nigel Baker lasted about 100 metres before declaring in a cockney accent, "I think I am going to have to walk". That was the shortest running career in history.

We once appeared on the hit TV series 'A Touch of Frost'. The make believe Police Station was a building about $^1/_2$ mile from the Prison. There were always camera crews around and we weren't shy in our attempts to get filmed.

Jack Frost, played by David Jason, was in his office in one episode speaking to his boss, when all of a sudden 3 runners went past his window. That was us.

We began to enter half marathons around Yorkshire, including one at a place called Bishop Wilton. It was described as a scenic run through the picturesque Yorkshire Wolds. The course was unbelievably mountainous and the race stewards didn't seem to care as we plodded up another long, steep stretch. One of my mates Placey asked a marshall "where's the next drinks station mate?" to which the marshall replied "I don't know, but when you find it come back and let me know!" After almost 13 miles of torture, that's not what you want to hear. We never went back there again.

I started to play a bit of football for Leeds Prison football club. I was what you would describe as an old fashioned English centre forward.

My striking partner was an officer called Kevin Farley, who is now the physio at Doncaster Lakers.

We were a team of tryers playing mostly in a local astro turf league. We once entered the civil service cup competition and travelled to the North East for a game. Upon arrival there were 3 big, fat lads stood outside the dressing rooms.

Getting changed, somebody commented "no problem against this lot if they are all like that". Unfortunately these big, fat lads were the match officials. We were playing a team of semi professionals and went down 9–1.

It makes me smile when I see cars parked up alongside a football pitch on a Sunday morning. There are still thousands of blokes running around trying to be the next Georgie Best. Someone once said, "The best part of a team is its spirit" and no doubt what these individuals take away from their 90 minutes of toil is the camaraderie with their team mates and the sense of belonging, even if they know their best days are behind them.

Every team seems to have a centre half who is the elder statesman and captain.

He is the stopper assigned to mark the young kid up front. The stopper was once a young kid up front himself, but as the years have rolled by, he has moved from attack, to midfield and now into the defence. Another couple of years and he will be hanging up his boots, going into management and making the odd comeback game when there aren't enough players.

He will then position himself behind the defence almost holding the goalkeepers hand, whilst convincing himself that he could still do a job in the team.

That is until the following morning when he gets out of bed and can hardly walk. Credit to anyone who plays team sport on a weekend and even more credit to the people who give up their time to officiate. My brother in law, Dave refereed for years in the amateur leagues around Yorkshire. The abuse and threats he used to get were way beyond the call of duty. There would be no game without a referee.

Our running exploits eventually took us further afield to the Great North Run, the greatest Half Marathon in the world. There were 5 of us. A colleague Steve Mardy arranged the transport. He borrowed a transit van for the weekend and loaded it for comfort with prison mattresses. We travelled up on the Saturday night with the intention of getting there to see the Super League Grand Final on a big screen in any pub we could find.

Since Mardy was the smallest, he had the job of going into every pub we came across to ask the locals if we could have the rugby on. Persuading Geordies on a Saturday night to put rugby league on their pub telly wasn't easy. After several attempts, Mardy did the business. The serious runners amongst us had a soft drink, namely brother in law Bram, whilst the others Mardy, Astley, Placey and me had a beer.

We watched the match then headed off to South Shields for a bite to eat. South Shields on a Saturday night is bouncing. Well worth a visit in the same way as Cumbria and Venice.

We found an Indian restaurant. The serious runners had an omelette; the not so serious had a curry and a few more beers.

By this time we were ready for bed, and decided to head for a car park on the sea front near to a lighthouse. Imagine 5 blokes in the back of a transit van, 4 of them loaded up with curry and beer.

In fact there were 4 of us in the back, because since Mardy was the smallest, he had to sleep in the front.

We laughed at the situation until our sides ached, but the best was still to come. As we were settling down, we saw the headlights from another vehicle pulling into the car park. Almost immediately another one pulled in. When Mardy got up to investigate (he had to because he was the smallest), we found out that we had parked in the local 'knocking shop'.

Without further ado, the 5 of us had our noses pressed to the windows to watch the action.

We still laugh today about what we would have said to the Police if they had visited the car park that night. "Sir, can you please explain why 5 middle aged Prison Officers are stripped down to their boxer shorts in the back of a transit van in the middle of nowhere, watching strangers doing allsorts to each other?"

We weren't put off though and all ran well on the Sunday. We returned en bloc to retrace our steps the following year, vowing at that time that wherever we were in the world we would come back and do the run every year. After 2 years, we never went back again.

Like most big road races, there are always the official photographers strategically placed en route to capture you at your very worst. If you realise that they are there, you can compose yourself, straighten your hair and hold in your belly. If you don't spot them, you are in for a shock when the photographs land on your doorstep several weeks later. Steve Mardy has a photograph of himself crossing the finishing line, with a clown complete with size 30 feet just in front of him. The atmosphere and organisation at the Great North Run are priceless.

Placey is a great lad. An ex miner from the days of the miners strike, Chris Place is a salt of the earth character and a pleasure to have worked with.

One time at Leeds we had a couple of Eastern European prisoners on the Wing. They had been convicted of importing drugs into the country, on their fishing boat. Trying to speak to Chris in their best pigeon English to resolve a problem didn't work with Placey.

He said "S'nowt t' do wi' me, its tuther S.O tha wants" in his best broad Yorkshire accent. This roughly translates to "Sorry lads, I cannot help you on this occasion, but perhaps you would like to speak to another Senior Officer". They never bothered Placey again.

Nick Astle is my best mate. He was born in Stockport, lived in Shildon, County Durham for most of his life, but has been in Leeds for over 20 years. Having him with us in the north east on the Great North runs was a bonus, for his ability to communicate with the locals. In fact when he was in a conversation with a fellow Geordie, you couldn't understand a word either was saying.

A Newcastle United supporter, Nicks real name is Nigel, but he always gets Nick. Ask him why and he can't tell you. Astley came about after we did a charity run and got a bit of press coverage. Our photo in the local paper named Nick Astle as Nick Astley, so Astley stuck.

He bears an uncanny resemblance to a young Gary Pallister of Manchester United fame.

Besides being a very competent prison officer, Astley also excels in haircuts. He specialises in skinheads. In fact he can't do anything else but skinheads. Amanda didn't speak to me for 3 days the first time I went home with my head shaved to the bone. There used to be a queue of staff at work for a haircut on a meal break. Astley used to use the prisoners' clippers.

One day we couldn't locate the clippers, which almost led to a security alert. Thankfully a colleague called Mick came along saying "Don't worry, I know where they are". "Where are they Mick?" we all asked, to which Mick replied "I took them home last night to trim the dog and forgot to bring them back".

Mick's dog was a St Bernard. After that my appointments for a haircut were switched to Astleys house.

Our greatest running adventure came about by accident. When Leeds prison celebrated its 150th anniversary in 1997, we decided to encourage has many staff to run in the Leeds Half Marathon as possible. It took some organising, but loads did it and we raised a lot of money for a children's charity. Mardy even appeared in a national running magazine explaining how running had changed his life.

In 1999 we ran for another charity and because we raised so much, they donated a prize of a trip for 2 to anywhere in the world for the member of staff raising the most sponsorship. The only catch was when you got there you had to run in a race. It was won by a great lad called Dave McManus, A Manchester United supporter, but a great lad nonetheless.

As time moved on, Dave approached me to say that he was moving house, that his wife had got a new job and that he wanted to give the prize back to Astley and myself. After some emotional wrangling, we decided to go for it and duly entered the New York City Marathon in 2000.

We trained for 6 months solid, going out at 6 o'clock on a weekend for a 15-mile run, deciding that if we were going to do it, we had to give it our best shot. Completing a 26 mile run takes some doing, whether you are a novice or an Olympic champion. It was a new experience for both of us and to this day I don't think we fully appreciated what we achieved.

We had a few beers in New York on the Friday night when we got there. Astley in his Newcastle United shirt and me in a Leeds United shirt. When we got back to the hotel, Astley put his shirt on a hanger saying, "I might as well wear this tomorrow". I thought fair point we had only been out for a couple of hours. Thinking we would save the wifes on the washing when we got home, we donned the shirts every day for the duration of the trip. This included our visit to the designer shops on Fifth Avenue where we were searching for Gucci handbags for the girls back home. We were followed everywhere we went by the security guards who were probably wondering "Gee's what the hells that smell?"

The schedule on the trip meant that we were entered in a 'friendship' run on the Saturday morning taking us from the United Nations building to Central Park.

The event was moving. Everyone was in their national colours and it was a steady jaunt for most, apart from 2 blokes from Leeds who were knackered by the time we got to the park.

It was the day before the marathon and we were shot after

running 6 miles. How would we cope with a 26.2 mile run the day after?

The free food handed out in the park aided our recovery. That night we went to the pasta party in a massive marquee in Central Park. Once again there was free food on offer.

Then it was back to the hotel and early to bed. We had been given some sound advice by another chap in our party. "Get to bed early the night before the marathon, have your breakfast early and take some energy gel on board on the way around the course". He sounded like he knew what he was on about, being the veteran of loads of marathons.

We duly went to bed early and got up early on the Sunday morning. It was race day and the diner ocross the street opened at 0500 hours to cater for the runners needs.

We didn't get much sleep that night. Our hotel window overlooked a precinct house of the NYPD, so we couldn't have the window opened for the continuous sound of sirens going off. The room was that stuffy though we needed some fresh air. During the night I opened one eye to see a naked Astley opening the window. I thought "My God, he's going to jump to avoid doing the run!"

At the diner, one of us had scrambled egg on toast, whilst the other had cheesecake. 0500 hours on the morning of the NYC Marathon and Astley was eating cheesecake. This came about after several attempts to order beans on toast failed miserably. He gave up eventually and asked for a piece of the cake that was lined up behind the counter. Who says New Yorkers can't understand English? It's the thick Geordie accent that they have trouble with.

We even wore the plasters that you stick on your nose for better breathing. They were fashionable amongst footballers at one time. Anything that gave you a psychological edge was worth a try, and they were free.

To be part of the event was unbelievable. The race started on Staten Island and we ran over the Verrazona Bridge to enter Brooklyn. People say that you will always 'hit the wall' at some point during the marathon. I hit the wall on the Bridge and could have jacked it in after less than 2 miles.

One of several unscheduled pit stops for toilet breaks helped me focus my effort.

We ran through all 5 of New Yorks boroughs and experienced 5 different cultures. There was a drink and food station every 2 miles. Too difficult to resist, we decided our tactics had to be sample each of them, so we ran for 2 miles and then dined on pieces of fruit or pieces of bagel, all washed down with water or fruit juice. Just enough to keep you fuelled up for the 26.2 mile journey back to Central Park.

Going through the Bronx was just like you would imagine with graffiti covered buildings everywhere. On one corner a really shady looking character was handing out lollypops. Astley grabbed one, it would have been rude not to, but I dropped mine. Without further ado 'Shady' was running after us to make sure I didn't miss out on the lolly. We considered going back to the Bronx that night to thank Shady, but we thought better of it.

At about 20 miles we saw the gels been handed out, and remembering the advice we had been given, we duly bit off the corner of the sachet and slurped it down. It tasted horrible to the point of making us feel sick. Closer inspection of the packet revealed 'must be diluted before consumption'. Our expert advisor forgot to mention that.

The runners and spectators came from the 4 corners of the world and the support was exceptional. People waving Union Jacks gave you a lift and we really thought that we were in New York that day representing our country.

As we entered Central Park to finish, the crowds were lining the streets 10 deep, each and every one of them cheering you on.

We crossed the line in 4 hours and 26 minutes. It was our first and last marathon. How could you better that experience?

We received our goodie bags and silver foil wrap and headed off to the subway station to get back to the hotel.

As we walked through Central Park, I thought that I recognised a chap sat on the pavement. "That bloke looks like Eric Pollard" I said to Astley. To which the chap replied "Hello lads, enjoy the run?" It was Eric Pollard from Emmerdale, actor Chris Chittel. We had a good chat with Eric then headed back to the hotel, with our silver blankets wrapped around our shoulders.

The first job after showering was to open the bottle of port Amanda had put in my case. Post marathon ideals of rehydrating went out of the window. We finished the port off in no time and headed off into the city that never sleeps.

We went to the official race winners presentation in a swanky Manhattan hotel. By this time the leg ache was kicking in and anyone who has been to New York will know that the kerbs are about 3 feet off the ground. We were struggling to get up and down them and walking in general was painful. At the presentation we felt really sorry for the dozen or so male elite runners who were called onto the stage. Why? Because of their appalling dress sense. They all wore suits that didn't match their shirts or their ties, or indeed their training shoes! It wouldn't have surprised us if somebody had turned up in a 'star jumper!'

Still who were we to crib? We couldn't even get up a kerb.

That night we had been invited to a party at Planet Hollywood. Not wanting to be rude by turning down a free meal, we duly attended. Not long after we arrived in walked Eric Pollard.

Eric made a speech saying, "Whatever happens to you from here, you can all stand up and say you are marathon runners". Nice words Eric.

We decided to numb our aching bodies by having a few drinks and to round off the day grab a bite before heading back to the hotel. The only trouble was the city that never sleeps decided it was going to on this occasion and we couldn't find anywhere open.

We bumped into Eric Pollard again at John F Kennedy airport. He was in the check in queue just in front of us. "Are you coming for a drink?" Eric asked, "Yes" we replied, so we checked in and headed off to the bar determined to spend up. Since we were going back to Leeds and Eric was heading back to Emmerdale, we assumed that he must be on our flight. After a couple of beers and Eric in our sights I had to pay a call, leaving Astley to 'copper up' and get a couple of chasers in. I was stood in the Gents and heard "Last call for passengers Hudson and Astle for the Manchester flight" Can't be I thought. "Final call for passengers Hudson and Astle. Final call". Shit, that was us. I hurried back to the bar. Astley thought I was having him over since Eric Pollard was still in the bar. Taking no chances we ran as fast as we could to get to the check in. We made it just in time, but then had to make our way to the very back of the plane to the last 2 seats. We made sure we caught as many people on the head with our bags as we could.

Eric Pollard wasn't actually on our flight, the bounder.

Going to New York was a trip of a lifetime. We went for 3 nights, stayed in a hotel near to Times Square, and did a few touristy bits, although Astley wasn't taken in by any of it. In fact it took a lot of persuasion to actually get him to go up the Empire State Building on our last morning. He said he couldn't see the point. In the spirit of 'blagging' as much as we could, we even tried to dodge the tourists entry into the Empire State Building, by going into the lifts assigned for the buildings employees. This was pre 9/11 and there we were in our Newcastle and Leeds shirts trying to snake our way to the top of the worlds most famous building.

Astley thought that New York was overcrowded, smelly and noisy. It is all of those things, but isn't that why it is so magical?

All that way and all that effort of running 26.2 miles. The memories will stick with me forever. For all I know, my old pen pal Steve Palone could have been running at the side of me, or cheering me on. If only I had kept in touch.

An officer had arrived at Leeds via HMP Holloway by this time. His name was John Hodkinson. He was known as Butch. I am not sure why apart from his resemblance to another Emmerdale favourite Butch Dingle.

Our Butch had one claim to fame. He went to school in Manchester and was once mates with Liam and Noel Gallagher of Oasis fame. Of course everyone doubted this and asked for evidence. Butch duly produced this evidence from a book charting how Oasis came to be. There he was in all his glory featuring in it several times and on photographs with the Gallaghers in various poses at different music festivals.

Butch is a Wigan 'pie eater' and his partner is a Saint. He is also like most real Mancunians, a staunch blue. This got him into hot water when Manchester City won the first division play off final at Wembley. The following day John called in sick. Unfortunately for him, the rest of the wing had spotted him on Sky T.V jumping about like a mad man at the final whistle.

Mr. Nee, what have you done?

Brigshaw School is in Allerton Bywater on the outskirts of Leeds, close to Castleford, but with a Wakefield postcode. Wigan star and ex Tiger Danny Orr went to Brigshaw as did TV presenter Mark Curry. Who? Exactly.

We have P.E teacher Mr. Nee to thank for reuniting the family with the greatest game of all.

In 1999 there was an offer for any pupil wanting a free ticket to a Tigers game at the Jungle against Salford. The only catch was that a paying adult had to accompany the junior. I am not sure that wasn't a catch, but a really positive attempt to entice more people along.

Why charge people £20 a ticket to watch a match only to have empty grounds, when you could charge 4 people £5 a ticket and fill the place? Is it that simple? I haven't heard any counter argument.

Jess got a free ticket and another one for her best mate Cal who actually went to another school. The same school that produced former Tiger Ryan Hudson.

Will Danny and / or Ryan ever return to the fold in the future?

Jess always said that her motive for wanting to go was to get a Castleford shirt. Little did she know what she was starting.

Having 2 girls wouldn't suit some dads, but I wouldn't

change my 2 for anything. Of course you miss out on the father / son stuff, but that's when nephews come in handy.

My eldest nephew is called George. He is also a pupil at Brigshaw, plays in goal for his local team, Kippax Athletic, supports Leeds United and that rugby team called Leeds something or other. The team that spent millions but never won anything, but then suddenly did win something and called themselves world champions for a while.

Poor Naomi, his sister. Remember Naomi of "Prycey can I have your jacket?" fame? A Tiger and a Rhino in the same house. It's a good job that their dad, Bram is a Hunslet lad. A few Christmases ago, his wife Helen bought Bram a Leeds Rhinos fleece. It never came out of the packet. A Hunslet lad in Leeds colours? Hell will freeze over before that happens.

So Jess and Cal were hooked. Initially myself and Fleeceman alternated between fixtures, but it wasn't long before we were hooked too. I have known David Simpson by association for years. He used to live in Amanda's street when she was growing up. She says that in his younger days, David had a look of John Travolta, but I can't see it myself.

Every season without fail, David goes through the ritual of saying, "look how many different kits Cas fans still wear". He then proceeds to tally them up, adding one every time somebody walks passed with a different style of kit on. I don't think it's a gripe at the club for bringing out new home and away shirts every year. It's more a gripe at the supporters who still walk around in shirts from days gone by.

I have trouble understanding why Castleford fans appear at games in West Tigers colours. If you want to support Wests, move to Australia.

Why wear a shirt from an Australian club when you could wear a Cas shirt?

How many Wests fans stroll around the Leichhardt Oval in our shirts?

It wasn't long before Janet was a Jungle regular with David and because Janet started to go, so did Amanda. David has supported Cas for years and said he once heard a tannoy announcement at Wheldon Road asking "Is there a joiner in the crowd? The door to the bar is stuck fast and there's a pint in it for someone. Mind you I'm not sure if the people inside want to get out"

They don't hand trophies out in December

As soon as the dust began to settle from our Grand Final victory, talk soon turned to who would replace Dave Woods as coach. There were several names banded about and everyone knew someone else who knew someone else who could offer 'insider' information.

"A source at the club said" is the way the press gets around reporting such issues when they probably haven't got a clue what is going on with the club keeping their cards close to their chests

Similar to Leigh in the previous season, we were disadvantaged from the off with regard to recruiting a squad for Super League X1. Throughout the previous Super League season there had been talk of some high profile transfers, such as Leon Pryce to Saints and Jamie Peacock to the Rhinos. These players were committed to another club for the next season, whilst the current season was still ongoing. It happened again when Leeds announced in May 2006, that Chev Walker and Richard Mathers were on their way out of the club. The Rhinos had obviously got replacements lined up from somewhere. How can National League clubs begin to think about recruiting before their promotion is confirmed? This confirmation comes several weeks after the previous Super League season has finished.

After weeks of negotiations, Terry Matterson was appointed first team coach. The news that Brad Davis had been made assistant coach was universally welcomed. The management team to take us forward was in place and all of the speculation was just that, speculation. It wasn't Gary Freeman or Tawera Nikau. Cas had got their men, although Terry Matterson was an unknown to the majority of Tigers supporters.

Pre season friendlies are not always great occasions. A colleague in the Prison Service, Steve Fox, vowed never to go to another Boxing Day game after we had got a hiding against Leeds at Headingley a few years ago. We were actually back in the house when that match finished, because it was such a non event and it was really cold. We never leave before the end of a game, but had no hesitation on that occasion.

I always suspected rather cynically that players hated turning out at Christmas and that games are only arranged to get a few pounds in the clubs coffers.

The Boxing Day fixture for 2005 was against Featherstone Rovers. We had beaten them 5 times in the regular 2005 season. A song was written that said we would never play the Rovers ever again, due mainly to us being promoted and them being relegated to National League 2.

It's a great song, but within a few weeks of the season's end, we were once again facing our neighbours from Post Office Road.

Songs at any sporting event are great and the people who put lyrics to music are in the wrong profession. Who thinks them up? And how do you get everyone singing along? It's not as though song sheets are handed out as you come through the turnstile. A song sheet was actually available for 'Will we play Fev Rovers, no never, no more'

"Super league it waits for me" or was it "Super league awaits for me?" is another example of putting words to music, replacing "Sweet Marie who waits for me" from Peter Kay's, 'Is this the way to Amarillo?'

'Viva Brad Davis' to 'Viva Las Vegas' is another classic.

Some songs get shared between sports. "You're not singing anymore", is a good example. This can be sung by any supporter from any sport providing their team has come from behind. It is always a risky one to sing because if you sing it when you are in front there is no danger that the opposition will bounce it right back when you fall behind.

Supporters generally sing better at away games because they are usually congregated together in one stand. Singing is also better at night matches under floodlights.

Boxing Day games give you an excuse to get out of the house to blow away a few cobwebs after the Christmas festivities. Matches are never classics, with teams full of junior and fringe players. This game was no different. It was easily forgettable. None of our new overseas recruits had arrived, but it was a chance for new coach Terry Matterson to get a feel for a match at the Jungle for the first time. In fact it was the second time.

I had seen Terry at the England Academy v Australian Institute of Sport game before Christmas. He looked frozen to the core that night.

The team Cas put out on Boxing Day would obviously bear no resemblance to the team that played when Super League X1 kicked off at the Jungle on February 10th 2006.

I think a lot of supporters felt that our promotion wasn't celebrated enough. There was no open top bus parade or civic reception. This was the first chance we had of showing our appreciation since Widnes back in October 2005. In between times there had also been several players leaving the club.

The break between the season ending and the new one beginning, regardless of what sport you follow is really frustrating. You don't know what to do with yourself on the usual match day. There is always press speculation on potential signings, but you don't have to wait for the paper to arrive to see who you have signed. Daily visits to the website are essential.

The gap between the seasons is also getting narrower and we now have the delights of the Tri Nations tournament to keep us going as we head towards winter. I am convinced that one day in my lifetime, Great Britain will rule the international stage and that the team will parade around Trafalgar Square and receive honours in the Queens New Years honours list, like their cricket and rugby union counterparts have done in recent years. You just can't see that happening really. Victory, yes but without the national recognition that it would deserve.

Wearing our Tigers colours we ventured to Loftus Road, London in October 2005 to watch Great Britain take a beating from a very underrated New Zealand team. We were proud to be Cas fans in the capital, weeks after our promotion. There were thousands of New Zealanders in the crowd that night. I know London is cosmopolitan, but every Kiwi in London must have been at that game. The only disappointment was that they couldn't be motivated to attend the final a few weeks later in Leeds. London to Leeds is not that far.

At Loftus Road, we paid £5 for a childs ticket, which is great value for international sport. We took our Jess and Rhino George to the game, whilst Sophie and Naomi went to a West

End show with Bram and Helen at a cost of over £50 per ticket, which I consider to be a bit of a right rip off.

Coming away after the match reminded me very much of the atmosphere you used to get on those Wembley weekends. One wag waiting for a train at tube station asked "Is this the queue for the Hogwarts express?" I think he was from Cumbria.

The same wag led a rendition of 'Hey Jude' on the journey back to Central London. This included 'women only' and 'men only' bits on the "na, na, na, na, na, na, na, na, na, na. nar, Hey Jude" chorus. True musical genius.

On the tube, we were stood next to a family who had just flown in that very morning from Auckland, New Zealand. They never joined in with the singing and must have wondered what was going on. They must also have wondered "eh?" when Amanda said to the little girl in the party, "I bet you're jiggered". I don't imagine jiggered is a word they have ever heard before or are likely to hear again.

Amanda is always having a go at me for my accent. She has room to talk.

Once whilst on holiday, we were on a cycle ride on a bike made for 4. We passed an American family and Amanda asked, "are you flagging?"

We still rib her about that. She would have been good company for Astley in New York trying to order beans on toast.

The 2005 Tri Nations final at Elland Road was a real anti-climax, but at least we saw the Australians at last beaten in an international tournament. It's just a pity it wasn't by Great Britain. It had filled a few weekends in until Super League X1 began.

One of the greatest upsets in international sport was in 1992 when Great Britain beat the Aussies 33–10 in Melbourne. Former Cas coach, Graham Steadman had a blinder that day.

Bram and Helen had got BSB by then and although they were away on their holidays, they left their house keys and said I could go round to watch the game live. I missed most of the first half trying to fathom out how to work the 3 remote controls. Life was a lot simpler when you used to actually have to get up to switch channels.

The biggest disappointment about the Boxing Day game against Featherstone was that we some of our team had to wear odd socks. It didn't look particularly professional or impressive. What did look impressive was the way the young team stood as one against a Rovers team that took some really cheap shots.

Another disappointment was that the new replica kits for 2006 were not in the shops for Christmas. When Rhino George was parading around on Christmas morning in his new Leeds shirt, we had nothing. Perhaps this is again because our promotion in October gave the club little time to get sponsors confirmed and kit suppliers lined up to produce the goods. When our new shirts eventually arrived, they were better than the new Leeds one. George said that he didn't like the style and design of his new Leeds shirt. They were the skin tight design and no good at all for anybody with anything less than a 6 pack, which ruled out George straight away.

Singe

I was watching the local news on T.V on New Years Day, 2006 when I heard about Singe. I couldn't believe it. Singe had been stood near us on Boxing Day at the Jungle.

I never knew St John Ellis, but the words spoken and written about him after his death tell you everything about the man. The game lost that day and the minutes silence at the Jungle before our first real pre season game said it all.

Even before the minutes silence was announced, the crowd was singing "There's only one St John Ellis" and applause at the start of the minute soon turned to deafening silence.

Where Singe had been stood 4 weeks earlier was the same mate he had been stood with. My heart went out to that lad.

Let's hope the Doncaster Lakers do the business in 2006, in Singe's memory.

I am sure he will be looking down on their every game.

Who are ya, who are ya?

Wakefield Trinity came to the Jungle in mid January 2006 for the first time since that infamous match in 2004, the game that saw us relegated. I am not sure that their supporters took a lot out of sending us down. They might have enjoyed it on the day, but as a consequence they lost a fixture on their doorstep and there are no greater fixtures than local derbies.

Whatever people say about local rivalries, they are mostly friendly in this game.

There are rivalries, but supporting is about experiencing everything to do with your own team. Not many people have animosity towards other clubs. They may not like the other clubs but there isn't the genuine hatred that exists in other sports. Post match, you can still walk back to the car discussing the game with supporters from the opposition.

Not many have any feelings one way or the other for London, because they are so remote and a lot of people believe that their involvement with rugby league will not be long term. I suppose it depends on what you describe as long term, but it seems a while ago since we were stood at Craven Cottage watching London against Bradford Northern in the 80's.

Throughout the week leading up to the Wakefield game speculation had been rife as to whether new signings Willie Manu and Richard Fa'aoso would even be in the country. They arrived 2 days before the game and the final pieces of the jigsaw were coming together.

The start of every new season brings a great deal of optimism. This would be no different. Some people had seen Willie and Richard before the Sunday and word on the street was they were huge in stature.

In the time we had, the club had recruited well. Danny Sculthorpe is one of the most under rated forwards in the country. He has that rare ability to look to pass out of nearly every tackle. Keith Mason whose dad played for Hunslet (as did Paul Handforths) joined from St Helens on a similar year long loan as Scully.

A core of the side from 2005 had earned the right to play in Super League.

They deserved their day on the big stage. Others left to join clubs in the National Leagues. Anyone who played a part in getting Castleford back to the top flight would almost certainly be guaranteed a heroes welcome if they ever returned to the Jungle.

Throughout 2005 it was pleasing to see Andy Lynch and Wayne Godwin at the Jungle, stood amongst the Tigers fans. Both left at the end of the relegation season to join Bradford Bulls and Wigan respectively. I am guessing that they are still and always will be Cas fans.

Some of the players that bailed out after our relegation were branded as traitors. Lynch and Godwin were not in this bracket and gave their all for a club that they obviously still cared a lot about.

The biggest coup was Danny Nutley, signed from Cronulla Sharks in Australia. Nutley is a top quality prop forward with a wealth of experience in the NRL and over here with Warrington Wolves. 'A non stop workaholic of a prop', not my words but those that described Danny in the match programme when the Tigers entertained the Wolves in July 2000.

With two weeks to go until the Super League season started, the situation with another potential signing was still unresolved. Ryan McGoldrick was apparently on his way from Cronulla Sharks in Australia, when the Wests Tigers stepped in to say that he had signed for them for 2006.

You are never sure who will be coming until you see the whites of their eyes and the photograph in the newspaper, holding up the club scarf or shirt.

If McGoldrick was going to play for Cas, he would have been at the club by this time.

For some of the squad the season would also provide them with the opportunity to take their careers to the next level. Andy Kain (Kainy) although small in stature never shirks his responsibilities with the tackling and he poses a threat in attack when near the line. The question was posed whether the lack of a top quality halfback would cost us in the long run. Again when you are playing catch up with recruiting the top quality is not always there. Australian and British players have usual committed to new clubs long before we were in the market.

Cas fans still remember our last top quality stand off from Australia, Sean Rudder. He had a nightmare stay in 2004 and his contract was terminated half way through the season. Rudder was now in France with the Catalans.

The club came in for criticism from some quarters for looking overseas to fill out the squad for 2006. The inference being that short term fixes never work and the national team would never improve because clubs never give home grown talent a chance. I think it's more a case of there isn't enough home grown talent to go around. On a selfish front, who really cares about the national team anyway? As long as your own team is winning.

Super League brings television exposure and television money. Our first game back was the one chosen to kick-off the season with Hull F.C as the visitors. Whenever the cameras are in town, they have a tendency to follow the family around. We are generally spotted on at least one occasion when Sky broadcasts our matches.

In the summer of 1999, we all went to Headingley to watch the last day of the cricket test match between England and South Africa. It was one of those days when play would only last for a couple of hours, so admittance was free. Since the game was in Yorkshire and entrance was free, the ground was full. Astley, our families and myself still managed to get on the TV celebrating an England victory.

Later on the very same day, Astley, his son Mark and yours truly headed north to St James's Park, Newcastle to watch a pre season football match between their beloved Newcastle United and Juventus. The game was shown live on Channel 5.

As we got near to the ground I was approached by a reporter who started to ask questions about Newcastle's under fire manager Kenny Dalglish. I said that I was probably the only person there that night that had no interest in Newcastle United. I told him to speak to Astley who at that time was in the burger queue.

When the reporter asked Astley, "what do you think of Dalglish as the manager?" Nick replied "give him time, give him time!"

Nick duly appeared on Channel 5 that night, but it was the 'kiss of death'. Newcastle were looking for a new manager a few days later.

Not only were we always on telly, but we had started to get speaking parts as well.

In 1999 I was working in the Training Unit at HMP Leeds with a colleague called Steve Staker who I used to call 'Fenner' after the character in ITV's prison soap, 'Bad girls', a programme we watched for research purposes only. This Fenner is a closet Rhinos supporter.

We were approached by the producer of 'What the Victorians did for us' a series being commissioned by the BBC. They were interested in coming to have a look around a Victorian prison. I showed the producer around the prison and a couple of days later he was back in touch to say that they would like to return with a camera and sound crew to do some filming. They also wanted me to appear in it.

"No problem" I said. The day of filming arrived and with new shirt on and trousers pressed, the filming took the best part of half a day. I had a microphone clipped to my tie and had to answer questions prompted by the producer. When the programme came out months later, my shot at stardom had been whittled down to about 2 minutes and you could tell by my voice that I was trying my very best to cover up a broad Yorkshire accent.

I failed miserably.

The programme is still doing the rounds on the obscure satellite channels and I am still awaiting my big break and my payment for that performance.

Steve Staker and myself were approached by staff from a college of further education, who asked us to come along and do a careers type presentation for their students about the Prison Service. We decided to do something novel. One of us went in full uniform as a Prison Officer and the other went in a full prisoners uniform, as a serving prisoner. We carried off the sting with the audience being taken in until the very end, when we revealed that Steve was in fact a Prison Officer too.

The only thing that never dawned on us was what we would have said to the Police if we had been pulled up on the M62 motorway on our way from Leeds to Huddersfield. There we were motoring along, with the officer in the passengers seat and the prisoner doing the driving.

We won the friendly against Wakefield comfortably in the end, 33–20. Wakefield had had a game at York City Knights over the same weekend, so came with a scratch squad. Still you can only beat what is in front of you and it was good to go into our final warm up game against Huddersfield with 2 wins out of 2 in pre season. It was also good to have our first look at the team that would be carrying the clubs destiny on their shoulders for the next 10 months.

Luke Dyer scored on his debut with just 78 seconds gone according to my watch. I have the habit of setting my stopwatch as the referee blows the whistle to kick off. It is something I cannot stop now, but it does get annoying when matches are tight and people ask, "How long is left?" Nobody ever asks, "how long has gone?"

Like every other year it takes time to get to know whos who in the squad. The crowd spends half of the early matches asking the person next to them "who's that number 10? Who's that number 17?" or shouting "Go on lad", because they don't know a players name.

It wouldn't be long before we all knew who everyone was, because we were heading for Super League, a place with squad numbers and names on the backs of shirts and not an odd sock in sight.

Innovation is great and the person who thought of putting players names on the backs of shirts was a genius. The only problem is of course when somebody leaves the club after you have paid £39.99 for a shirt and then shelled out a few more pounds to have a name and number printed on the back. There are still several Orrs (6) walking around. Vowles (13) and Eagar (4) were reborn for a few games in the promotion season.

The squad numbers for 2006 were announced at the end of January with no number for Ryan McGoldrick.

The half back shirts went to Andy Kain and Paul Hand-forth.

Would these 2 local lads do the business or would Brad Davis be forced out of retirement at some point?

The Jungle experience

The clubs sharing a football ground such as Wigan and Huddersfield have excellent facilities. It was a shock when we went to the Galpharm (or was it McAlpine?) Stadium, Huddersfield pre season in the relegation year to find out that it was £16 for adult admittance. Spectators outside had to beg, steal and borrow to get in. Charge £16 and people won't come. Charge £8 and you will attract twice as many. Simple sums really. This was for a pre season friendly on a Friday evening in a game that ended in a 0–36 defeat for the Tigers. Not a great start to what turned out to be a disastrous season.

The Jungle is an old ground with true character. Throughout the season in the National League I lost count at the number of supporters from Super League clubs who said that they hoped we got promoted because they loved the Jungle experience.

One day there is a real possibility that the Tigers will leave the Jungle and move to a new ground. That will be a sad day when we bid farewell to this special place. There are not many grounds left where you are on top of the pitch and where you can swap ends at half time.

One thing you always get at the Jungle is youngsters who bring their own rugby balls into the ground. There are groups all over passing the ball to each other. Young Josh 'Gibbo', is one of them he never goes anywhere, home or away, without his ball. Pre and post match there are always impromptu games of touch and pass on the training pitch.

For 2006, the scoreboard changed but not much else. The playing surface as always looked like a snooker table. The pre match entertainment is second to none, although the routine of dancers dancing, mascots coming on and dancers dancing with mascots is becoming a bit tired now. Even the smaller children don't bat an eyelid when the presence that is Mr. Purrfect enters the arena. The only time they do seem interested is when Purrfect or his trusty sidekick 'J.T' have something to give away.

Our dance squad, Claws had some new signings for 2006, including our youngest daughter Sophie.

What ever happened to that chap who used to commentate at the Jungle on the pre match junior games? His "Ee's like shit off a shovel" description of a youngsters pace was a classic line.

Regardless of the sport, the media always like to preview and predict what is going to happen at the start of any season. Not surprisingly some pundits predicted that we would finish bottom of the Super League. It always amazes me that predictions are made without seeing the goods first. I suppose that is what a prediction is and I guess predictions sell newspapers.

With 2 weeks to go before the big kick off, the popular opinion seemed to be Saints for the title and a quick return to the National League for the Tigers. What's the point of playing 28 weekly rounds if it's all sorted at the end of January?

We had 9 months to prove the 'experts' wrong. Some bookmakers were even offering odds of 25–1 for Cas to win 6 games or less.

The Huddersfield Giants came to the Jungle for our last warm up game. The Giants are a club full of tradition. My dad says that the Huddersfield team of the 1950's was one of the best teams ever.

Huddersfield supporters still shout "Fartown, Fartown", which is a legacy from days gone by.

A bonus for being back in the big time was that the senior academy games were played prior to the main attraction. Roll on summer rugby. The academy game against Wigan had a 1245 hours kick-off. It was bloody cold. In all we were stood for over 4 hours and despite the tomato soup, I cannot remember a colder day watching rugby league.

New signing Willie Manu played in that game. He scored a hat trick but for most of the match he looked like he would rather be somewhere else. The cold weather must have been a factor, but Willie was also due to fly back home for an ongoing court case in Australia. Who could blame him if his mind was elsewhere? His look and style of play would make him a fans favourite in 2006.

It is a bit of a gripe, but why can't clubs be bothered to produce match day programmes for pre season games? All you get is a team sheet handed out at the turnstile. Not everyone has access to the internet or teletext and they rely on the match programmes to be kept informed of developments within the club. Surely clubs could also do with the extra revenue programmes sales would bring in?

There was a whisper going around the Jungle that the club had won the tug of war with Wests Tigers for Ryan McGoldrick's signature. It wasn't a rumour; McGoldrick was in the country, was on the team sheet and made his debut against Huddersfield. The vibes coming out of the Jungle had been positive through-out the chase for 'Goldie' and it was pleasing to see the deal done. The number 23 shirt now had an owner.

There was a real poignant moment that day. I spotted Wigans ex Tiger Wayne Godwin and Jon Hepworth. Jon was in our promotion team and played in the Grand Final. His career had taken him in another direction and he was now playing rugby union for Leinster in Ireland. There were embraces all round when members of the current squad Waine Pryce and Craig Huby spotted their former colleagues. Hepworth's stay in Ireland was a short one. He is now plying his trade with Leeds Tykes.

The Huddersfield game was a true test. Both teams were almost at full strength. Robbie Paul was now a Giant after 10 years as a Bull.

How good would it have been to have Robbie in a Tigers shirt?

Several supporters were wearing the new away shirt. Fleeceman's annual "Let's count the number of different shirts" competition was just around the corner.

The Huddersfield game wasn't a classic, but it was a good game. We lost by conceding a try in the last second. Defeat didn't hurt and people were going home really positive for the start of the season.

Ryan McGoldrick made his debut less than 48 hours after his arrival in the country. He apparently met his team mates in the dressing room before the game.

The pre season friendlies were out of the way and we were less than 2 weeks away from the season's opener.

The new Gaffer

Terry Matterson is one of those characters that always seems to wear either a bobble hat or baseball cap. In his bobble hat he looks a bit menacing.

I first met Terry at the Jungle a couple of days after the Huddersfield game. Although he was disappointed that we had lost he was taking a lot of positives from the match.

Terry was watching a re-run of the game whilst Brad Davis was sat with Ryan McGoldrick discussing the debutantes' performance.

"A few of them got a reality check" was one of Terry observations.

The 2006 squad was on paper much stronger than in years gone by. The only problem being that every other team had also improved. Since the introduction of the salary cap, the gap between the top and the bottom had narrowed. In Australia, the Grand Final winners in 2004, Canterbury Bulldogs finished outside the top 8 in 2005. The same thing happened again in 2006, when the Wests Tigers failed to make the top 8 less than 10 months after challenging the Bulls for the world club championship.

Super League hasn't got to that point yet, but this year it doesn't look like any of the teams are in the competition to make up the numbers. Last years bottom 2 clubs, Leigh and Widnes, were poles apart from the rest and despite a couple of creditable performances, the writing was on the wall for them long before the seasons end.

The interesting slant for 2006 was the introduction of the Catalans Dragons. If the Dragons finished at the bottom of the league with no points, they wouldn't be relegated. The Catalans had been given a 3 year exemption from relegation in an attempt to establish the game in France. The team finishing second from bottom would be relegated.

Everyone knew the rules at the start of the season, but imagine the outcry if one of the big teams just happened to finish second from bottom and ended up getting relegated whilst the Dragons survived without winning a game?

Terry Matterson arrived at the Jungle from Canberra Raiders as an unknown quantity. He had groomed himself under coaches like Wayne Bennett and Matthew Elliot in Australia. Terry's reputation over here was made as a London Broncos player and he had a level of respect throughout the game. He now had the job of gaining the respect of the Castleford faithful.

Hopefully the head coach would be a magnet for top quality signings for years to come.

The lack of a quality half back led to more rumblings when current Australian scrum half Craig Gower appeared unsettled at Penrith Panthers. If Gower had have landed at the Jungle, it would be one of the greatest signings in the clubs history and a sure sign that the new gaffer had the magnetism to attract the best. He didn't land and the rumblings went away until the next time.

Managers from all professions and with varying degrees of experience shape their teams differently.

When I was the Principal Officer on D Wing at HMP Leeds

in 2003, I managed 5 other managers and a team of 40 staff. The number of staff involved is similar to the numbers that a Head Coach would manage, including his assistants and then the first and second string players. There are hundreds of books and theories about people management and how to develop yourself as a leader. There is a difference between being an effective, capable manager and an effective and capable leader. The trick is to be able to adapt to be both. With my staff, I found that certain individuals got on better with others. Some worked harder than others. Some had a better sense of humour than others. As a Group Manager, I had to recognize the strengths and weaknesses of each person and appreciate that everyone had something to offer. It was all about getting the best out of everyone on a consistent basis. Experienced staff were used as mentors to support and develop new staff. It is all about getting the best out of each other to achieve the end goal, the common goal.

Terry had inherited 15 of the squad who he had never ever seen and I guess will not have heard of before either. Added to that nucleus of a squad, the club brought in players who were released by their current teams, both in England and Australia.

To help their preparations, the Tigers went to Lanzorote for a week on a pre season training camp. Every team seems to go on a training camp. I think they are designed for bonding and generally getting to know and appreciate each other. Outsiders are not welcome as the team spirit, trust and belief begins to develop. Individual and team goals will have been set.

The pre season friendlies were just run outs with the majority of work being done at that time of the year on the training pitch. It would have been a good exercise to have an away friendly to prepare the squad for the away day match experience, but by the time Matterson arrived the fixtures had already been arranged.

The Tigers secured the signatures of several top quality under 17's from the local area. Without Super League and without Terry Matterson, these players would have probably headed off to the Rhinos or the Bulls. It will be interesting to watch their progress in the future.

One day the Tigers will hopefully have a team of players from in and around Castleford. The Leeds Rhinos managed to recapture their successes with a team of mostly locally produced players.

The talk about a new ground continued as we got ready for the new season. At some point we will be saying that this is the last time we will watch the Tigers at the Jungle. As previously mentioned, the Jungle is a great place to watch rugby league. Behind the scenes the story is different.

The Chief Executive doesn't sit in a plush office and I don't think he would ever want to. The players use a small gymnasium to do their weight training and a public gymnasium where anybody can just walk in.

The coaches have a portacabin on the car park. Nobody complains, because that is what life is like at the Jungle. Former Castleford player, Dean Sampson once said that he would motivate his under 18 team by telling them to look at their own surroundings and compare them with the facilities their counterparts at places like Leeds and Bradford had.

A new ground will leave a legacy for generations of Castleford people for years to come. I am sure that all players, officials and supporters from years gone by will wish the Board and

Chief Executive Richard Wright all the very best in their plans for the site at Glasshoughton.

This generation of Castleford supporters would hopefully experience that transition from old to new. Whatever lies ahead, history will record that we were the ones who saw the last game at the Jungle and the first game at the new ground.

"We are Super League, said we are Super League"

Amanda still felt that the Castleford supporters never got the opportunity to celebrate the Grand Final success of October 2005.

The chance to say a public thank you to Brad Davis came around at the traditional shirt presentation which took place at the Jungle 5 days before the big kick off.

This year, there wasn't a great turnout and there seemed to be a feeling of apathy around.

In previous years you could sense the anticipation and spirit amongst the camp.

Perhaps the players were still getting to know each other?

Perhaps this was the level of professionalism we were now operating at?

The players emerged from the tunnel, walked up some steps in the main stand, said a few words, collected their shirt and walked down the steps in the opposite direction. It sounds a simple maneovre but it didn't go like clockwork.

Amanda said she didn't feel a 'buzz' and that we should get used to it as we were now in the serious league. Some players appeared dressed in their new tracksuit tops each individualized with their own initials. Others emerged without any club colours on at all.

Everyone was interviewed with most looking and sounding cringingly uncomfortable. There were some funny stories like the one about Gray Viane who had flown into Manchester airport in the middle of winter, dressed in a T-shirt, shorts and flip-flops.

As Richard Fletcher collected his shirt and was just about to speak, a prankster amongst the group, rang his mobile telephone. Fletch asked, "Who's ringing? Dickhead!"

Amanda felt that none of the interviews really laid down people's individual aspirations for 2006, but dwelt too much on the training camp in Lanzarote. "What was best the Chinese whispers or the egg and spoon race?" must have been asked about 6 times. I am not sure that the majority of people who were braving a bracing February lunchtime wanted to hear about which player was the best at Chinese whispers.

Andy Henderson is popular with everybody and as always he spoke with a real passion for the club. Hendo is a character who was plucked from obscurity and led the team back to Super League. He is a Tigers legend.

Terry Matterson said a few words and then it was over. Brad Davis was missing.

That was the opportunity missed. Brad would have got a standing ovation from the few hundred that were there and I am sure that would have meant a lot to him.

Afterwards in the car park people were getting autographs and taking photographs. Strangely again there was a lack of atmosphere. Some players were even stood on their own waiting for something to happen and probably wishing they were in warmer climes.

Amanda said she was dreading the Hull game. "Would we be made fools of?"

She said that the only thing she was looking forward to was Sophie's debut, dancing with Claws.

On the same day as the shirt presentation, it was the 2006

unofficial championship of Leeds. The Hunslet Hawks retained the Lazenby Cup by once again overcoming the Leeds Rhinos for a second year in succession. One of Hunslets try scorers in that match was Chris Redfearn who lives on our street. So that's the current Cheltenham Town FC captain, a bloke who ran the New York marathon and the Hunslet Hawks loose forward. Our street has some real sporting pedigree.

Hunslet's victory passed again without a great deal of public recognition.

The week leading up to the big kick off was anything but quiet. The Tigers even made an appearance on Sky Sports news, with an interview with our longest serving player, Waine Pryce.

Willie Manu also made the headlines after returning to Australia for his Court appearance. He received a community service order and would not be returning to England until that was completed. It was suggested that he could possibly do his community service over here. That request was rejected by the authorities and he did it back home, making him unavailable for selection as the campaign began.

Danny Ward signed after a well publicised sacking by Leeds Rhinos. Nobody seemed to know the reasons for the sacking, but Ward arrived with a big reputation and was a current Great Britain international forward. He became the third Danny to sign, following Sculthorpe and the new captain Nutley. Danny Ward is the son of David Ward who coached Hunslet to success in the late 80's. It's when things like this happen that you realise you are getting old. On paper our pack was taking shape, but we went into the first game still with a nagging doubt about the lack of a quality playmaker.

It was an early start to the evening to watch our academy side play their counterparts from Hull FC. The interview with

Waine Pryce on Sky proved to be a real dud. 'Prycey' wasn't even in the first team squad. He played for the reserves alongside last season regulars Craig Huby and Tommy Haughey.

Craig and Tommy have got those names that the public announcer at away games never gets right. You regularly hear "Craig Hubby" or "Tommy Hockey". I bet they have had that all of their lives. To complicate things we now have Richard Fa'aoso, Willie Manu and Gray Viane.

The early start at the Jungle interrupted our traditional Friday teatime routine, but life is full of sacrifices. When I first started going out with Amanda, we always went to her Grandma and Granddads for egg and chips on a Friday teatime. Not just us but her whole family. As the years went by, the family was getting bigger and it ended up with about 3 sittings, starting with the youngest and finishing off with the elders who then sat around conversing and putting the world to rights.

Years later, Amanda's mum and dad now play host to the 12 in their family. It's the same menu, but we are now the elders. Who are we to put the world to right?

An hour before the kick off and the Jungle was filling up nicely. Rugby league supporters are notorious for getting into the grounds at the last minute. This goes back generations, because there never used to be pre match entertainment or the ritual of seeing the players warm up on the pitch for 30 minutes before the game. The only time you used to see any sort of pre match entertainment was at the Wembley cup final and that was in the shape of a marching band.

In Turkey, crowds at football matches get into the ground up to 12 hours before the kick off. The atmosphere and hostility must have an affect on the opposition. The Jungle had been a fortress in 2005. If we were to be successful this year we would have to win the majority of our home games. The role our supporters played would be vital. It was us against the world.

With the season ticket renewal information, Chief Executive Richard Wright said, "Thanks in no small part to you, the future looks bright, and I hope that you will want to continue to be part of it".

As well as sporting their club colours, supporters also have the opportunity these days to trim up their cars. Car flags are all the rage.

Towards the end of 2004 to demonstrate our togetherness as we tried to stave off the threat of relegation, the club gave away 'staying up' car flags. The supporters amongst the ranks who were still flying these flags before the start of this season were either really tight or really pessimistic.

I am not sure that 'staying up' was the message we wanted to be showing the rest of the rugby league world, before the first whistle of the new season

There were 10180 people in the Jungle for the big kick off. For some it would have been their first time back since we had been relegated. For others it may even be their first visit ever. Everyone there was paying their money and supporting the Tigers in what would be the biggest season in the clubs long history. With 28 games in front of us, we had to get off to a flyer.

We had to wait 12 games into the relegation season before registering our first victory. That came at London Broncos and we had a lucky charm with us that night. Astley made his one and only appearance of the season.

It was a Friday game and we journeyed south on one of the organised club coaches from the Jungle leaving just after lunchtime to get to the West London ground for the evening kick-off. There was another example of the game belonging to the people, when our coach supervisor Jason got on his mobile to call our CEO to ask him if the kick off could be delayed. The Tigers travelling support was caught up in the snarl up of a typical Friday evening on the M25. Sure enough word came back and there was a 15 minute delay to the start of the game. We got there just in time to see the kick off. Can you imagine the same call going to a CEO from a Premiership football club?

I had promised Astley a few beers when we got there. The Broncos home ground at that time, Griffin Park has a pub on every corner. We never got to sample any of them, but we did see the Tigers victorious. There were no surprises when Astley appeared on television jumping up and down in celebration.

For the opener against Hull, we had only 7 survivors in the squad from 2005, with 10 players making their competitive debuts against the team that won the Challenge Cup in 2005 and who had added a couple of quality players to an already formidable line up. Hull F.C are an established top 6 team, have a great coach and magnificent stadium. They are on their day are a match for anyone.

The game was billed as a local derby and although there is 50 miles between the two, it is Hull's nearest away game. Their away support is a credit to the club. They are isolated on the East Coast and every 2 weeks they have to travel miles to follow their team.

I heard one comment from a Hull supporter on "How it was great to be coming back to a proper ground".

That was a nice thing to say, but it didn't stop a couple of friendly choruses of, "Sing when you're fishing, you only sing when you're fishing".

The game saw the first return to the Jungle of Tigers old boys Motu Tony and Jamie Thackray, which added a bit of spice. Thackray will be in the 'world class' bracket if he continues to make the same progress as he did last season. On attack, he is awesome.

With a Castleford chorus of, "Are you watching White-haven?" the scene was set.

Sophie had been excited all week about her debut for Claws. I had trouble spotting her when she was dancing, because the majority of the girls look alike. Amanda said she had done brilliantly, although the short shorts and crop top didn't seem appropriate for the middle of February.

Our mascot 'JT' has grown, standing at about 6 foot 7 inches in his stocking feet. One wag asked if ex Tiger, Barrie Jon Mather had got a new job.

Another sign of getting old is the number of layers you need for an evening kick off at the start of the season. Cold feet must be avoided and 2 pairs of socks were essential. There were still people there in their shirt sleeves. My mam would have said, "they will suffer in later life!"

Summer rugby? Not yet.

The pre match fire-eater and half time sumo racing were throw backs, if not exactly entertaining. One comical event at half time was when a bloke blasted tee shirts from an air gun into the crowd. To the amusement of everyone, it took him ages to find his range. A tee shirt came spiraling towards me, but with tomato soup in hand I unforgivably knocked on. Luckily it ricocheted off a little girl's head into the grateful hands of Janet Simpson.

The game itself was something of an anti climax. Hull didn't get out of third gear and seemed to be able to score at will. We made too many mistakes early in the tackle count and missed vital tackles on the line.

There were some positives and we scored some great tries.

As a club we had gone up a notch. Amanda thought that last years team would have conceded a 'cricket score'. The pace and ferociousness of Super League are a world away from the National Leagues.

10 debutantes and a lack of a play maker and we were on the end of an 18–42 defeat. It was still hard to swallow and our one and only chance of being at the top of league had been and gone. We were back competing with the big boys and that was all that mattered.

Of the debutantes, the 3 Dannys all went well and Gray Viane chipped in with a couple of well deserved tries. We had the chance to watch the game again on video, but I couldn't do it straight away. It was saved in the video library but never watched again.

The first weekend of fixtures threw up some remarkable results, such as Salford defeating the much fancied Warrington Wolves, and Les Catalans marking their debut in the competition with a home victory against the Wigan Warriors. Who said that the French would finish bottom and pointless?

Next on the agenda for the Tigers were St Helens and our first trip of the season across the Pennines. Who said there aren't any easy games in Super League?

Game of two halves

Our first journey of the season across the Pennines was on a Friday teatime, meaning that we missed another Friday tea.

I wondered how many Cas fans would actually make the journey. At Knowsley Road the Saints are formidable. Added to the likelihood of a nightmare journey on the M62, I was guessing that a lot of people would decide that this was a good game to miss.

On the way over we called in at the Birch service station, which is situated on the red rose side of the Pennines. Unbelievably, St Helens had gone to the trouble of sending a couple of players out, to put the fear of God into the travelling support.

There was Leon Pryce and Nick Fozzard having a bite to eat. They were joined by Leeds Rhinos Shane Millard and on our way out, we walked straight into Rhinos skipper Kevin Sinfield. The Rhinos were on their way to the JJB in Wigan.

As we were getting back into the car, the Tigers team bus pulled up. Full back Michael Platt got out of his car and jumped onto the bus.

Platty might not have felt comfortable sat with the more illustrious players in the public café.

We set back off but had to wait for Leon Pryce to cross the zebra crossing heading back to his car. He never looked twice at us, despite the fact that the car flags were flying and we were all donning our colours.

Similarly to the Jungle, Knowsley Road is a proper rugby

ground and we received a warm welcome from Saints supporters and staff.

We were taught a lesson in the first half, going into the
changing rooms looking down the barrel of a heavy defeat after
conceding 32 points without reply in the first 40 minutes.

Saints are a lot of supporters favourite 'other' team. They
play a style of rugby that most clubs aspire to. Wellans, Pryce,
Long, Cunningham and Sculthorpe are players that would get
into any team in the world. Jamie Lyon is one of the greatest
players to have played in the summer era. They are all world
class performers. If a couple of them have off games, so what?
The others will compensate.

Not one of the Cas team would get into the Saints first 17.

With long platted hair, they even played a prop forward
that looked like Manchester United and England defender Rio
Ferdinand. That was taking the biscuit. This Rio happened to be
new signing Jason Cayless, who was consistently good all
season.

The question of the support on the night? No worries there.
In a crowd of over 13,000, the loyal Tigers supporters were
fantastic. We out sung the home team and wondered why with
10 minutes to go, Saints fans were already leaving the stadium.
What is that about? What time do they leave when their team is
getting beat?

We were winning the second half, 8–6 until a last minute try
led to a full time score of 44–8 to the Saints. If we were to be
truthful, we would have settled for that before the kick-off. We
would certainly have settled for that at half time, when conversation turned to the possibility of losing by 60 or even 70 points.

At half time the then number one in the music charts, the
2006 remix of 'Thunder in my heart' by Meck and featuring Leo
Sayer was playing. Sophie said that she loved this song. Fleeceman said "It's not as good as the original by Leo Sayer".

"You're not singing anymore" echoed around after Andy Kain had sliced through to make it 38–4. "Here we go, here we go, here we go" soon followed and the team cannot have failed to be lifted by the supporters.

Saints will beat most teams. They will pile up the points and will be there and there abouts at the business end of the season.

The second half performance gave us the lift we needed going into the next game against Les Catalans Dragons at the Jungle. Looking at the fixture list, this was a must win game. It was vital that the supporters turned up in their thousands.

It would probably be the lowest attendance of the season and we had to lift the team to our first victory. News had come through that the Catalans inspirational skipper Stacey Jones had a broken arm. A blow to them, but a tonic for us, despite denying us the chance to see a world class performer at the Jungle.

Heading back home from St Helens, the M62 was awash with Tigers and Rhinos fans, who were celebrating after beating Wigan at the JJB stadium. Good luck to them, but the right to fly car flags declaring 'world champions' now belonged to the Bradford Bulls.

Name dropping

Being in the Prison Service for so long has given me the chance to meet one or two famous people along the way. I am not sure what makes someone a celebrity, so I will stick to famous.

One of the smallest people I have ever met was singer Toyah Wilcox. She did a performance at Leeds Prison in the early 90's and I had the pleasure of carrying some of her equipment to the chapel.

The chapel at Leeds is part of an amazing building. It is now known as the multi faith centre. It used to double up as the prison cinema, before televisions were introduced onto the wings and long before in cell T.V.

Our wing used to go to the movies on a Monday morning. Imagine 300 prisoners sat watching the latest flick. The only time I ever remember any bother was when we showed 'Bill and Ted's bogus adventure'. If you have seen that film you will know why there was almost a riot that day.

England cricketer Darren Gough, more famous now for his dancing ability, turned up on E Wing one morning. It was a charity ruse, which saw Goughie arrested and locked up inside until enough money was raised on the outside to secure his release. The TV cameras were in that day to show Goughie being 'banged up' and looking out of his cell window. The truth on that one was that the cell he went in was cleaned out to a royal standard, the cameras rolled for a few seconds and then Goughie was on his way. I am sure the stunt raised a lot of money, but we watched from afar and cringed as Goughie looked really uncomfortable in his prison uniform.

I have met a few Home Secretaries, Members of Parliament and Ministers. Another little person was Anne Widdecombe who turned up on ITV's 'celebrity fit club'. I had to meet and greet her as she arrived on E Wing. "Good Morning Minister, welcome to E Wing. I am Mark Hudson", was what I was supposed to say. When she eventually arrived, almost an hour late, she got a "hello". Stood on the end of a wing waiting for someone to arrive was not my idea of fun and I guess she meets so many people she wouldn't recognise me again anyway.

One person I did like was HRH Princess Anne. Again she was also smaller than I expected, but she seemed genuinely interested when I was talking to her on Leeds Prison's First Night Centre. About 6 staff had to line up, similar to a line up before a Cup Final and introduce themselves to the Princess. As I was waiting to speak I thought should I do something risqué like asking her for a kiss or an autograph? I bottled it and decided instead to do the noble thing by just shaking her hand, bowing my head and smiling. As we were speaking, I couldn't stop thinking about the time the Princess was on 'A Question of Sport' with Emlyn Hughes.

I am not a Royalist and actually have no real opinion on the Royal family. Amanda does. She knows all of the comings and goings that they have been involved with over the years. Amanda and I went to London to stand on the Mall when Andrew married Fergie. I never saw a thing all day and my only souvenirs were 2 sore ears after balancing Amanda on my shoulders for most of the day. She saw everything. I did like Princess Diana and remember putting the news on T.V the morning that she died. Amanda was devastated and at work that Sunday morning there was a sense of loss from both the staff and the prisoners.

Diana seemed to be one of the Royals that people could relate to and the outpouring of emotion at a funeral will never be repeated.

We took the girls to London on the day before Diana's funeral. It was a Friday and they were both off school. We took a book of condolence that their school had made with the intention of handing it in at the gates of Kensington Palace. When the Officer on the gate invited us to go up the long driveway and hand it in at the side door, it was a bit surreal.

Even more surreal, that on the day of the funeral, Diana's coffin was brought out of the same door where we had been stood less than 24 hours earlier.

What we saw in London that day was hard to take in. We were at Westminster Abbey reading the cards on the flowers, when a car pulled up and a gentleman got out dressed in a full dinner suit. He was carrying a single red rose. He just walked up to the Abbey gates with a tear rolling down his cheek, bowed his head, placed the flower down and got back in his car without saying a word to anyone. It was Bruce Forsyth.

The capital was silent that day. There were flowers everywhere and it was a fitting tribute to a person who gave a lot to those less fortunate.

We were sorting out our LP's recently after clearing out the clutter from the loft. There it was. A LP of Charles and Diana's wedding. Why would you buy that?

When I took Amanda to New York in 2000 to celebrate our 15th wedding anniversary, we did all of the touristy bits including a trip to see 'Cats' on Broadway. As usual I fell asleep. I am renowned for falling asleep at the cinema during the previews and now it was the theatres turn. A chance to watch a top quality show on Broadway and I slept through the first half. During the interval I had to go out and get some fresh air and wash my face. The second half of the performance was fantastic, but I didn't have a clue as to what was going on and had to keep asking. That annoyed Amanda even more than me being asleep. A group of Chinese people slept from start to finish and had to be woken up to leave. I am not a big theatre goer but have been to see Willy Russell's 'Blood Brothers' a couple of times. If you come out of that without shedding a few tears, then there must be something wrong with you.

On our trip to New York, we also had a meal at the top of one of the twin towers in the 'Windows of the world' restaurant. The views from the top of the Manhattan skyline were unbelievable.

I was at work the day of 9/11 and watched events unfold on TV.

I asked to go home, because that place meant something to us. We just sat and watched the news all night, not believing that we had actually been in one of the buildings not that long before.

As a family we have been back to New York and went to Ground Zero. It was very similar to the day before Diana's funeral. In one of the noisiest cities in the world, there was quiet as people of all nationalities looked at the scene of one of history's greatest atrocities. People had left messages of support from all over the world.

As a venue, there is nothing to touch Madison Square Garden. The greatest artistes in the world have all played there. Whilst in New York, we took in a game of basketball at the Garden, featuring the New York Liberty, who are the female equivalent of the Knicks. As a spectacle, it was very different with all the razzamatazz, but the game went on for hours to allow for commercial breaks during the T.V coverage. We bailed out in the 3rd quarter when the boredom set in. It was the first time I had ever seen basketball live. The best was when the crowd shouted "deeee-fence, deeee-fence", as the Liberty were defending. That chant would be great if it caught on at the Jungle.

New York Liberty are a talented team, but they wouldn't stand a chance against the Harlem Globetrotters. Every year around Christmas time, the Globetrotters were always on the T.V demonstrating their range of skills and pranks. My favourite players were Meadowlark Lemon and a guy who was bald as a coot, called 'Curly'.

One of the most genuine people I have met was current Glasgow Celtic manager Gordon Strachan. In 1994, a few of us decided to channel our running energies into doing something different.

'Circuit 22, premier challenge' was born. This was a 72 hour challenge to visit all of the Premier League football grounds and complete a 10km (6 mile) run around each pitch, Since Crystal Palace and Wimbledon were ground sharing, we also threw Wembley Stadium in for good measure.

Gordon Strachan was a patron of the charity we had chosen to run for. He invited us down to Elland Road for a photograph for the local press. We duly invited him to our end of challenge celebrations in Leeds on the Saturday evening when we finished. Our last run was at Elland Road just before the Leeds United game against Coventry City.

Gordon and his wife came for a drink with us in Leeds that night. The following Monday he left Leeds and signed for Coventry without even dropping us the slightest hint that that was going to happen. He was our Saturday drinking mate after all.

One of our back up team on that challenge was an Officer

from Leeds called John Shaw. He was driving us around in a borrowed mobile home. John was a cracking lad to have on the trip to keep your spirits up, but he was completely clueless about football. He came out with a few belters, like "who plays here then?" at Upton Park in front of the Bobby Moore stand.

"There are H's" which described the posts, when we thought we had arrived at Leicester City only to find that it was the Leicester rugby union ground.

In a petrol station in North London, John asked an attendant "Can you tell us where the Tottenham ground is please?" The attendant duly came out of the petrol station and pointed upwards. One of the stands at White Hart Lane was right above our heads.

Back at Upton Park, and sat in our mobile home, an identical vehicle pulled up alongside. The enthusiastic driver asked John, "What do you think of your mobile home?" John replied in his best Cleckheaton accent "Shite!"

The camaraderie on that trip was fantastic and we got to do a lot of things you wouldn't normally get to do. This trip was a pre cursor for the jaunts up to the North East for the Great North Runs. We enjoyed it so much that we did similar challenges in 1995, 1996 and again in 1999.

By 1999, Placey was the back up. Although he had more knowledge about football than John Shaw, he was useless at navigating and useless at driving. He came into his own at eating and drinking though.

One of the last legs in 99 was at St James's Park home of Newcastle United. We picked Astleys lad, Mark, 'young Astle', up in Leeds en route. It was his 12th birthday on the same day we were due at the 'Toon' and as a Newcastle supporter we couldn't think of a better present for him.

All of the runs made a few pounds for various charities. We got some great coverage in the press, on the radio and even on teletext. There is the story about the time Astley was live on Radio Teeside. He was cut off for pronouncing couldn't as another 4 letter word, but that story is too rude to share with you.

Our best running days are probably behind us now, but I still have an inkling to do one final challenge around the rugby league grounds, particularly now Les Catalans are on the map.

Steve Mardy joined the Prison Service in 1992. He is another top lad who got into the running and became a good friend. In June, 2004, tragedy struck his family. The Mardys son, Callum who was 5 at the time had gone down with chicken pox whilst on a family holiday. Within hours of having to return home early, Callum was admitted to St James's Hospital in Leeds. He was there for 6 months and to ultimately save his life, Callum had to have both of his legs amputated. He had been struck down with a rare virus.

We decided to help the family by organising various fund raising events, such as the usual raffles and sponsored runs.

The Prison is full of rugby league supporters and I decided to organise a rugby league event to raise money, but also to give the staff that had supported the Callum Mardy fund with an evening of entertainment.

It started off small scale and went massive.

When Sky Sports were at the Jungle covering a Tigers match, my youngest, Sophie chased the then Great Britain manager Phil Clarke half way around the pitch after the final whistle to give him a letter about our intentions. The day after at work, somebody said there had been a phone call for me from somebody called Philip Clarke. I didn't know anybody called Philip Clarke, and then suddenly it dawned.

Phil had called the day after not only to give his full support to the evening, but to show genuine concern for Callums well being.

We exchanged calls over the next few months and 'A question of rugby league' was born. By this time the 2004 Tri Nations had crept around and Phil was with the Great Britain team. He invited Astley and myself to the teams training camp in Manchester to go over the finer points of the evening. Phil had agreed to compere the event that would include a raffle, auction and an opportunity for the audience to ask questions of an invited panel.

The evening was staged at Leeds Rhinos social club and was supported by Barclays Mortgages. We managed to get signed shirts, balls and other memorabilia from most clubs and on the night we raised over £5,000.

The Social club is managed by former Leeds player Graham Eccles and we even managed, begrudgingly on my part, to have the Rhinos Grand Final trophy on hand for people to have their photograph taken with. We were asked to make sure Graham was handed the trophy back in its case at the end of the night.

No worries. That was until I got a call the following day asking, "What have you done with the trophy?" It had got mislaid somewhere along the line and the Rhinos were on stand by to dispatch the Police, to find out what the prison staff had done with their prized possession.

There were supporters there from Hunslet, Bramley, Wakefield, Batley, Wigan, Bradford, Hull FC, St Helens and Leeds, all united on that evening to support a family less fortunate than themselves.

The Leeds captain from the 1968 Challenge Cup final, Mick Clark was also there and impressed when I told him that I had played in the same Clapgate school team as his son Andy.

As for Phil Clarke, well he did a sterling job. It was the Tuesday after Great Britain had been hammered by Australia in the Tri Nations final at Elland Road, Leeds on the previous Saturday evening.

Remember that Phil had been Great Britains manager. 72 hours later and he was facing the rugby league public for the first time since that defeat. He also brought along Danny McGuire and Keith Senior who had both been part of the British squad as well as the legendary Barrie McDermott and other Sky Sports personalities. Barrie Mac spent the night dropping in plugs about his book, 'Made for rugby'. Every time someone asked him a question, he said, "you can see the answer on page 88 of Made for rugby"

Phil donated a signed Great Britain shirt for the auction, which was the last item in the auction. By that time the beer had been flowing and the shirt went to a Wakefield diehard Wayne Colbeck. At one point an officer called Yosser Hughes was bidding against himself for a signed Saints shirt. It is amazing what a few beers can do.

British coach Brian Noble had donated a Bradford Bulls Grand Final shirt and back at the teams hotel, Phil had asked kit man, Stan Wall to get the shirt signed, assuming that Stan would know who the Bradford players were. Stan obviously did not know, and got the whole British squad to sign it.

I later took Callum and Steve Mardy to Headingley where Sky were covering a Rhinos game. Phil and the rest of the Sky crew gave Callum a wonderful couple of hours. He ended up having a game of cards and a slice of gateaux with Mike 'Stevo' Stephenson in the crew bus

This is typical of what rugby league people do, and they never ask for anything in return.

I saw Phil Clarke at Headingley at the end of the 2005 season when England were playing France. The first question he asked was "How's Callum?"

Phil left his role with Great Britain at the start of the 2006 season. He had frustrations about how the international game was going in this country. He gave a very public interview on where the problems lie and I think that most supporters would have agreed with everything he said and appreciated his honesty.

The Sky commentators often come in for criticism about their possible biased opinions and slant towards certain teams. Their coverage is second to none and better than any other sport.

Luke Robinson joined the Tigers on loan for a while during the relegation season. I wrote to Luke to tell him about Callum's plight and the rugby league evening. A couple of days later a package arrived in the post with a note attached. It was from Luke and was a signed Wigan shirt from the Challenge Cup final. It was the 18th mans shirt and was something that you cannot buy in the shops. That gesture was remarkable. Again, Luke asked for nothing in return. What he did get was our utmost respect and hope that his career takes him to the level that his talent deserves. Luke is now doing great things at Salford.

The Mardy family has now come to terms with how their lives have been affected by such a terrible tragedy. Callum is back in full time education and looking forward to living his life to the full.

People often say "there's always somebody else worse off than you". Callum was in St James's hospital, Leeds for 6 months and was in the high dependency unit for much of it.

Throughout that time, I cannot imagine anybody been in a worse state than Steve Mardy and his family were. Our lives were touched by the tragedy, whilst their lives have been turned right around. They are heroes for coping with the adversity life has thrown at them.

The Prison Service like it always does stood up and closed ranks for Steve. This also included considerable donations from some of the offenders in our custody. This is a side to prison life that is seldom seen or acknowledged by the outside world.

As part of the fund raising, we also organised a football match between Leeds Prison F.C and a Leeds United X1, made up of old professionals who had plied their trade for the Whites.

Similarly to Phil Clarke, former United captain Brendan Ormsby couldn't do enough. Brendan is now a postman and also does a bit of presenting on a local radio station. The game was played at Garforth Town F.C, a club made famous after Brazilian legend Socrates turned out for them for a few minutes a couple of seasons ago.

Callum led the teams out in his wheelchair followed by proud dad Steve. Steve, never a natural footballer came on for what you would call a 'cameo' performance 10 minutes from the end. That's where any similarity between Steve Mardy and Socrates starts and finishes. Both played for 10 minutes at Garforth Town.

In goal for the Prison team was my mate Paul Mahoney who is tall by anybodies standards, so for obvious reasons people know him as 'tall Paul', 'Lofty' or 'Loftus'. His stature didn't help him on a couple of occasions when he was chipped from outside the box by Scott Sellars. He did to his credit make several fine saves to keep the United attack at bay. Paul is a Prison Officer by trade. That day he was a star, facing opponents with hundreds of international caps between them.

The old boys goalie was Leeds United manager Kevin Blackwell. After the game, I asked Kevin if he would go into the prison changing room and have a word with our lads.

"No problem", he said. Their faces were a delight when he came out with a torrent of abuse. "You set of w***ers! I train you all week and you put in a f***ing performance like that!" Then without another word he about turned and walked out. After a brief silence the prison staff just erupted in laughter. They knew that they had been part of something special that day. Something to tell their grandkids about...The day I played against Kevin Blackwell, Brendan Ormsby, Scott Sellars, Tommy Wright, Neil Aspin, John McClelland, Peter Lorimer etc.

Being part of the fund raising efforts for Callum was a pleasure. People were united for the cause and although there were a few sleepless nights along the way, it was great to be part of something that had brought people together.

Highs and lows

We were promised a French theme for the visit of the Catalans Dragons, with stilt walkers, uni-cyclists, a French market
stall selling popcorn and our ever popular mascots in Tiger
Town with the KFC Claws adding the 'can-can' to their dance
routine.

God help us if the French had gone for a 'Yorkshire mining
town' theme for the return match. We even laid on a French
Canadian lady, from Allerton Bywater, to read out a welcome
message to the Dragons supporters.

What made it amusing was when their team was read out in
French. Hughes, Murphy, Wilson, real French pedigree there.

Perhaps themed days could catch on. Fish related events
when Hull FC are in town and pie related events when Wigan
are the visitors?

The venue for the return game had still to be decided.
Would it be in Spain or France? I smiled a few weeks earlier
when I heard that the Wakefield Trinity Wildcats game had
been moved at the last minute, putting supporters who had
already booked transport and accommodation into limbo. Now
it was our turn. Our game was heading for Carcassonne in
France or Figures in Spain.

On the car park before the game, I recognised a familiar face
and someone I hadn't seen in over 30 years. It was Harry Jepson,
'Jeppo' the president of Leeds Rhinos and more famed in my
eyes for his discipline at primary school. When I introduced

myself to him, Mr. Jepson's first manoeuvre was to try and clip me around the head, saying, "It never did you any harm, did it?" No it didn't and it's a pity there isn't discipline in today's schools like there used to be.

The Tigers discipline in the first two games had been poor. In this one, it was excellent.

Looking at the next few fixtures a win was vital.

At 16–0 and 26–10 up, we were cruising to that first win, but with 6 minutes to go we were trailing 26–28. We had that sinking feeling, that sick in the stomach feeling that we had grown accustomed throughout 2004. Snatching a defeat from the jaws of victory.

The Tigers of 2006 didn't give in though and 2 late tries sent the crowd at the Wheldon Road end into raptures. A thoroughly deserved 34–28 victory and another 3 tries from the popular Gray Viane.

When the Dragons full back Mark Hughes was sin binned in the first half, there was a chorus of "au revoir, au revoir, au revoir" instead of the usual "bye-bye, bye-bye, bye-bye, byebye". Brilliant. Who in the crowd thought of that?

Afterwards coach Matterson spoke about the confidence that this victory gave the team. At the post match press conference there were 15 men and women of the press, all incidentally dressed in either black or grey jackets, which were not in keeping with the spirit of the themed day and more in keeping with going to a funeral or a wake. If we hadn't hung on for our first 2 points that dress may have been appropriate.

As I have previously said, the Dragons 3 year exemption from relegation may haunt the powers that be at some point. They are likely to win a few games at home, but on their travels they had already suffered back to back defeats at Salford and now at the Jungle.

3 rounds in and all 12 teams in the competition had points on the board.

We were up and running and looking forward to the next challenge, the little matter of facing former world champions Leeds Rhinos at Headingley.

There had been negative vibes coming out of the Jungle all week prior to that game. The news on the injury front wasn't promising, with doubts over forwards Danny Ward, Ben Roarty and Richard Fa'aoso. It made obvious sense to rest anyone who wasn't 100% fit for what is one of the toughest games in the calendar.

An interview in the local press had full back Michael Platt quoted as saying that the Tigers were targeting winnable games.

More worryingly, was a suggestion that this all ticket game had been boycotted by some of the Tigers faithful. Due to ongoing building work at the stadium, the capacity had been reduced with away teams being offered 1250 tickets. Surely we could sell those easily? Apparently not. A few days before the game only 600 had been sold.

We were going to Leeds on the back of our first win and although we were on a hiding to nothing, the team deserved more support than 600 people. We took more to Barrow and Whitehaven in 2005, and a Friday night jaunt across Leeds wasn't too difficult a journey to make.

I suspect historically that some Tigers fans do not like going to Headingley. It is a difficult ground to get any atmosphere going at from the away end. There were also the long distance games at London and against Les Catalans coming up. News came through that the Catalans game had been moved from Spain to Carcassonne in the South of France. The message from the Rugby League was basically 'tough luck' on those who had already booked hotels and transport, but that coaches would be put on to get spectators to the new venue.

I am all for Les Catalans joining the ranks this season, but moving games around at their convenience is well out of order. Other clubs would be fined or penalised points if they did what the French were getting away with.

The week of the Leeds game was also the week when Britain was expecting the 'big freeze' and first real signs of winter weather. We were now at the start of March and typically the snow came on the afternoon of the Rhinos game.

Local radio said the game was definitely on, so we set off, still wearing 2 pairs of socks, in good time for the 2000 hours kick-off.

The ground was half full when we arrived, with the Tigers squad having a casual walk on the frozen pitch. 10 minutes later, A Leeds steward came along and started saying that the game was off. Unbelievable. This was confirmed shortly afterwards over the tannoy. The referee was blamed, when the Leeds club needed to stand up and admit it was their fault. Just 45 minutes before the game parts of the pitch were deemed unplayable.

Luckily the game was all ticket. How would the Rhinos have administered refunds otherwise?

The match was rearranged for the following Sunday, which was all well and good for the supporters who were able to attend at the weekend. What about those who couldn't go? What about the people who hadn't bought tickets for a Friday night kick-off, but would have done for a Sunday game?

Again, I guess the message was 'tough luck'. The game really knows how to look after the people who are its lifeline.

Regardless of where your colours are posted, spectators deserved a better deal than what was served up by the Rhinos on that occasion.

One good thing that came out of the postponement was that on the way home, we heard an interview on BBC Radio Leeds between Barrie McDermott and our very own Andy Henderson. This was part of a 'on the spot' feature that is on every week. Obviously if you are at a game you do not get the chance to hear it, which is a shame because Barrie Mac is one of the funniest guys in the world. If he wanted to Barrie could play to sell out audiences.

Barrie asked Hendo, "Who has the best nickname at the Tigers?"

Hendo said it belonged to Luke Dyer who is known as 'Dish' or 'Dishy'. This came about after a few players were invited to the Gala Bingo club in Castleford. The Clubs manager who Hendo claimed 'batted for both sides', introduced Luke Dyer on stage, saying "Ladies you will like this one, he is a real dish". Hendo said he couldn't wait to get back to the club to tell everyone else. Dish stuck as a nickname.

Results on that Friday evening saw us back on the bottom of the league. Harlequins pulled off a fantastic win at the KC stadium against Hull FC.

After being hammered at home by Wakefield the previous weekend and sitting at the bottom of the ladder with 1 point from 3 games, I wondered if the Londoners had travelled to Hull thinking that that game was winnable?

Besides Danny Ward, Ben Roarty and Richard Fa'aoso, another injury doubt for the Rhinos game was Amanda. She had been suffering all week with a sore neck and shoulder. This meant that I had to do something I have always hated, super-market shopping. I think most blokes are the same, although my good friend 'Loftus' Mahoney takes delight in being able to tell you which vegetables are the best value and at which supermar-ket. He is a good mate, but come on?

Being in charge of the shopping does have some benefits in

that you can slip things into the trolley when the wife isn't looking. Supermarkets are good places for bargain C.D's and I was delighted to spot at £2.97 a compilation of Spandau Ballets 12" singles. Classics the lot of them.

The majority of the tracks were released 25 years ago, in the early eighties. This makes you realise that the years are rolling by. In 1981, when I was our Jessica's age, coming up to 18, songs that had been around for 25 years were brought out in 1956, long before the Beatles and Elvis entered the hit parade. I am not even sure that the hit parade had even been invented.

Reluctantly we all trooped back to Headingley for the hastily rearranged Sunday afternoon fixture. Amanda had passed a late fitness test.

The Tigers faithful sang "Is this Wembley in disguise?" recognising the ongoing build of a new stand. This was the best thing about a dreadful day,

At half time we were once again looking down the barrel as we went in 8–42 down. The Rhinos never seemed to get out of second gear throughout. Their physical size and presence made it a 'man against boys' classic and the final hooter couldn't come soon enough. To think that we had to go back to Headingley again later in the season was a daunting prospect.

Nobody hates losing to Leeds more than Castleford Tigers fans. Nobody more than a Tigers fan from South Leeds. You can't help but take it personally.

The final scoreline of 66–14 to the Rhinos actually flattered us. Their triangle of playmakers, Sinfield, McGuire and Burrows were conspicuous by their lack of involvement. Sinfield kicked 11 conversions to 11 tries, but did little else!

We were outplayed and out enthused in every department and our points against tally now read at 180 after only 4 games.

The doom and gloom merchants were already sounding the call of relegation being a cert.

Terry Matterson said he was embarrassed. He was not the only one. People had to go back to work and to school on Monday and be the butt of their colleagues and classmates jokes.

A word for the famous Southstanders at Headingley. You are by far the most polite spectators in Super League. A gathering of thousands whose team were hammering their local rivals and you never sang once throughout the whole 80 minutes. How sporting of you or is this just sour grapes on my behalf?

The lack of atmosphere they reckoned was something to do with to the game being played on a Sunday afternoon. I think it had more to do with the spectators being complacent and used to success. A season in the National League cures the complacency.

The Rhinos car flags say 'be part of the passion'. What passion is that then?

A mention also to the Rhinos forward Ryan Bailey. Learn a lesson from a true professional Barrie Mac. You are a big lad, big enough to take the taunts of the away support without having to give it back. Or again, is that just sour grapes on my behalf?

Enough of the sour grapes.

Looking at the fixture list, we now had a few 'winnable' games coming up. Harlequins away next. Before leaving to go to Headingley, we also booked 5 places for the trip to Carcassonne.

The 13 mile drive home from Headingley was bad enough after being thrashed. What would the journey home from the south of France be like in a few weeks time?

A Capital gain

We made the decision to travel to London on the club coach. At £15 a seat, it is reasonable value and means that you don't have to drive a 400+ mile round trip in one day.

Our numbers were depleted for various reasons, including the loss of Amanda who this time failed a late fitness test. Sophie also had to stay behind for Claws rehearsals for the next home game. Claws are a great dance squad, but very few of them are staunch Tigers.

Their absence meant that I had 2 seats on the coach, which was a Godsend going all that way. Accompanying me on the journey south were Jess and niece Naomi.

There had been good news throughout the week on the injury front. Forwards Ward, Fa'aoso and Fletcher were now fit and back in the squad.

Going to London is not an adventure or exciting. It is an away game miles away from our normal surroundings, and is a real inconvenience to the normal weekend routine. You see nothing of our capital city and I suggest that the majority of Londoners don't even know that their city has a Super League team. There are however some people who have followed the Londoners throughout all of their name and ground changes and it is interesting to see Harlequins supporters still wearing Fulham and London Broncos attire.

It is a long way to go, but these supporters make the reverse trip every fortnight. Who are we to complain at having to do it once or twice per season? When supporter of the year awards are dished out, the diehard London / Harlequins people should always get a mention.

British people are great at queuing. There were 5 coaches leaving the Jungle at 0900 hours for the trip to the Twickenham Stoop. At about 0845 hours the jostling for position started. This was before the coaches even arrived.

There were enough buses and enough seats to accommodate everyone, but you can't take a chance. We managed to muscle ourselves onto bus 5, taking up a position near the front.

There are times in most peoples lives when you spot a stranger in the distance and keep your fingers crossed that they do not end up next to you. This could be at the cinema, on the train or at the airport.

I had one of those experiences on that Sunday morning, but as it turned out for the benefit of research for this project, it couldn't have worked out any better.

At Headingley the previous week, we were stood next to a Tigers supporter who resembled the Peter Kay character Max, of 'Paddy and Max' fame. Max is the bouncer who first came to our attention at the Phoenix Club in 'Phoenix nights' and ultimately ended up on the 'Road to nowhere' with his mate Paddy.

Our Max was the spitting image complete with his black bomber jacket, skinhead and goatee beard.

As our coach loaded up, Max plonked himself right behind me with his mate who on this occasion was not Paddy.

Despite having Sophie's I-pod on and the coach's radio playing, I could still hear Max coming out with some classic lines.

His use of the English language was a treat throughout and despite it being a Sunday and the coach being full of supporters of all ages and genders, his use of the F word was not tempered.

The coach hadn't even left Castleford when the sound of

the first can of the day opening was heard. 0905 hours and the first of many John Smiths on the day.

Sophie's taste in music is excellent. For a 15 year old, she likes everything from R&B to the Kaiser Chiefs who are very much local heroes. A couple of years ago there was a band in the charts and on 'Top of the pops' called 'The Music'. They were local lads from Kippax and you still see their lead singer out running or in the shops. They once supported Coldplay on a world tour.

By the time the Tigers convoy had reached Leicester Forest services for a break, the hunger pains had obviously got the better of our Max. Without further ado he set his picnic out on one of the tables located outside the services. All that was missing was a candelabra.

By the time we reached the fringes of London on the M25, Max was warming up nicely.

"Hey up, ramblers brigade, Southern doggers!" was his observations on a group of elderly walkers.

"Salad, what's tha washing that down wi'? 6 pints ur John Smiths?" was what Max asked the lad in charge of the bus after he dared to have a healthy option for his lunch.

"Tha's only avin' that cos yerr lass is on't bus", Max declared

The Stoop is a great ground for watching the game. It is right in the shadows of Twickenham and is probably the only ground in the country where you will see spectators with a glass of white wine, or a hot chocolate with fresh cream and floating marshmallows.

Summer rugby still seemed like ages away. It was cold and windy and you couldn't ever imagine watching a game in your shorts and T-shirt.

The takings over the bar must have been at record levels, as Max seemed determined to drink the ground dry. Although he wasn't sat near us in the ground, we saw him more than once heading off to the Gents.

The atmosphere in the away end at the kick off gave us a sense of optimism and I really fancied us for a win.

The team news had the Quins captain Mark McLinden making his first start of the season. Unfortunately for the Londoners, their star man aggravated an injury warming up and had to sit-out another game. Great news for us.

Ryan McGoldrick dropped the kick off and all thoughts of an easy win had gone after only 15 minutes when we had already conceded 3 unanswered tries, to trail 14–0.

Mark Tookey had cult status during a short spell with the Tigers during our relegation season. Tooks has got the belly of an old fashioned prop forward. He got a magnificent reception from the Tigers 'barmy army'. "Tookey, Tookey give us a wave" was followed by a Tookey wave to the crowd.

"You fat bastard", followed and Tookey just smiled and took it all in the spirit it was meant. His colleague Thomas Leuluai was lapping it up and nearly bust a rib when "Ee's got a pineapple on his 'ead" went up, to acknowledge Karl Temata's unusual hairstyle.

Pineapple 'ead was totally oblivious or was it that he was focussed on the job in hand?

All this was going on as the Quins players lined up after scoring another try.

Suddenly the tide began to turn when Waine Pryce raced in at the corner to open our account. Ryan McGoldrick made amends and out sprinted the cover to close the gap further and when Danny Sculthorpe powered over right on half time, we were within striking distance at 16–20 down.

With a sense of what was to come, I sent a text home at half time to say that if we didn't win this game, we would not win another game all season.

"You're supposed to be in France" was sung to suggest that the Quins fans should really have been on the continent watching the England rugby union boys get walloped by the French.

One Tigers fan kicked a 40–20 to win the half time competition. The prize? A voucher for the local wine shop that had to be used by 5 o' clock that afternoon. Without doubt a prize that ranks alongside a chocolate fireguard or an ash tray for a motor bike.

Our second half display was awesome and a magnificent response to the previous weeks hiding at Leeds. 18 unanswered points and tackling that meant the home team barely ventured into our half let alone threaten the line.

The icing on the cake came with an Andy Henderson try in the dying minutes. Our first away win, 34–20.

The weekend results saw us off the bottom of the league. After 5 games we were up into 8th position.

This team had now played together in only 5 competitive games, winning 2 of them. No mean feat and with Willie Manu due to return from Australia at any time, the confidence in the camp going into the next 2 games, both at the Jungle, was certainly greater than it would have been if we had lost and gone into those games rock bottom.

The authorities would have an interesting situation to resolve if the Catalans Dragons finished bottom and the Harlequins finished 11th. Would the RFL relegate the Quins?

Questions about relegation would be answered as the season unfolded. All we knew as we got back on the coach was that there were some distinguished teams below us in the table, including our next opponents from the JJB.

The atmosphere on the coach heading north was always going to be good if we were returning victorious.

As the darkness set in, the bus got quieter with the exception of Max, who by this time was getting to what you would call 'worse for wear'. Totally pissed would be another good description.

"£10.80. If ad known it wud be that much, I wunt ave ordered 4", led me to believe that Max thought alcoholic beverages at the Stoop were expensive.

His displeasure at the cost of ale was soon forgotten as he fell into a deep sleep. Remember I had the I-pod on and the coach's radio was blasting out the weeks top 40. With all that noise you would think it would have drowned out the sound of Max's snoring. No chance. He was driving them home right up to pulling in at the services for the stop on the way home.

Naomi although only 12 years old, observed that when he woke up Max didn't know where he was.

He soon came back to life when he spotted a Marks and Spencers, asking his mate "D'ya think they sell ale?"

After a quick look around, Max declared "It's an alcohol free Marks and Spencers".

Max headed straight for Burger King and we watched him from afar, a bit like David Attenborough watching prey in the Jungle from behind a bush.

Ready to get the Cas fans singing, Max broke out the loudest "Nar, nar nar," and then took a large bite out of what was obviously a double whopper burger (no doubt topped with cheese and bacon).

Back on the bus and within minutes he was back asleep and snoring his way back home. We got back to the ground some 12 $\frac{1}{2}$ hours after our departure. 2 points in the bank and optimism for what lie ahead.

I sent coach Matterson a congratulatory text from the motorway. He replied asking me to thank the fans for their support. On this occasion, you were more than welcome Terry. A few of the Tigers squad of 2006 earned their stripes that day at the Stoop.

Thanks also to Max for giving us some memories that will last longer than the duration of the 2006 season.

Just before the coach pulled into the Jungle the Arctic Monkeys song 'When the sun goes down', came on the radio. It was a real flashback to that night in the Omnibus when Meat Loaf's 'Paradise by the dashboard light' came on. Everyone, young and old, sober and blathered started singing,

"Said who's that girl there?
I wonder what went wrong so that she had to roam the streets,
She dunt do major credit cards, I doubt she does receipts,
It's all not quite legitimate"

Not exactly Lennon and McCartney, but a brilliant rendition of a brilliant song and the perfect end to a winning day.

Latest news was that any chance of former Tiger, Danny Orr returning to Castleford from Wigan now seemed highly unlikely. Would we find that halfback we were looking for now that the Australian season had commenced? And how much longer would the Tigers fans be shouting for assistant coach Brad Davis to get his kit back on?

Hunslet Hawks were also in the headlines. One of the worlds greatest ever sportsman, 'Iron' Mike Tyson was going to be at their next game against the Doncaster Lakers. A legend kicking off the game at the South Leeds stadium. Whoever arranged this deserved a large pat on the back, for bringing the name of the Hawks to the attention of the worlds press.

Perhaps the stadium should be renamed the 'Mike Tyson stadium'? Apologies for this sarcastic line, which is in response to a ludicrous decision made by Leeds City Council to rename the South Leeds stadium, home of Hunslet Hawks rugby league club, the 'John Charles' stadium in memory of the late Leeds United and Wales footballer. John Charles was one of the greatest footballers the world has ever seen, but he had no affinity with Hunslet.

On the day, Tyson never showed up, but at least the Hawks had the decency to announce it rather than conning people into turning up and being disappointed on the day.

The fourth round Challenge Cup draw was also made. For some reason the RFL rolled out Shaun Edwards and Martin Offiah to do the draw. They are 2 of the best players to play the modern game and 2 players who have both scored 10 tries in a match. Was there nobody more appropriate than the current London Wasps rugby union coach and an ex player from another generation who is more famous now for his dancing exploits to front the draw? I guess that the BBC who broadcasted the draw live on Radio 5live had some influence. There was some confusion when Les Catalans appeared to be drawn at home against Toulouse. When the draw was re-read, it saw Les Catalans at home to Thornhill Trojans.

I was not really sure what went on with that one, but it was a great tie for the amateurs of Thornhill.

It's difficult to know who you would want to be drawn against at this stage of the competition. A trip to Leeds or Saints are real no-no's. You also want to avoid possible banana skins and a home draw against a team that is on a 'hiding to nothing'

The Tigers got the reward of a trip to Widnes, a potential

banana skin, but it gave us the chance to return to the scene of one of our greatest days, 9th October, 2005, to face a Vikings team containing old war horses Barrie McDermott, Terry O'Connor and Mick Cassidy.

Super Leeds 1970. In a fancy dress
competition at Butlins in 1970

Mick Jones. A Leeds United legend.
I named my pet rabbit after Mick

Star jumper. Don't laugh, we all used to wear them and one day they might make a comeback

Hunslet Schoolboys 1975–76. In the shirts of legends.
Never a prouder moment. (Back row, in the centre)

With the legendary cricketer Geoffrey Boycott

At Wembley with Amanda in 1986, in our
Hunslet jumpers but supporting Cas.
The Charlie Nicholas lookalike on the end is brother in law, Bram

Out for a run with Gordan Strachan. Looking at his face,
my fitness level was obviously too much for Gordan.

Another cricketing legend and former England captain Michael Atherton with (L to R) a young Sophie, a young Jess and young Astle

Jess and Cal Simpson. Young Tigers

Former Tiger Mark Lennon receives his end of season flag

After the Leeds Half
Marathon in 1999, with
my good mate Placey

Having a breather in the 2000 New York City Marathon

Jess Tiger

Rhinos, not one of my favourite animals.

Relegation night in 2004.

Callum Mardy with the Sky team. (From L to R) Phil Clarke,
John Kear and Eddie Hemmings

Nephew 'Rhino' George with Keith Senior

Blackpool, 2005

With Waine Pryce on promotion night in October 2005

Moon with Stacey Jones

Fleeceman at the JJB sampling a local delight

The girls and young Josh Gibbo on the big screen

Head coach Terry Matterson

Sophie as a claw

Claws Sophie and Katie Gow with
Richard Fa'aoso

Danny Brough celebrating in front
of the Wheldon Road faithful

Scully gets refreshed

Amanda with Willie Manu

Whilst Fleeceman, Jess and Cal share a joke,
everyone else looks worried

The crew minus my dad
(Back row from L to R) Fleeceman, Janet, Amanda, Me and Sophie
(Front row from L to R) Cal, Jess, Young Josh Gibbo (with ball) and Naomi

As honest as the day is long

Some people are too honest for their own good. Amandas ongoing neck/shoulder/back trouble caused her to miss yet another match and I had the feeling that her enthusiasm for the 2006 season was waning. That was until I rang her at half time during the Wigan game, to find that she had been 'watching' the first half live on ceefax. She said that she couldn't bear to listen to the game on local radio.

Amanda had been off sick from work for 2 weeks. She had never had any time off work for years. She works as a teaching assistant at Brigshaw School, looking after children with learning difficulties. It's a job the majority of the population wouldn't be able to do. I certainly couldn't do it. It is more of a vocation than a job and she is ideally suited for it.

She has always been honest and never tells lies. She is so honest that she won't even go to the dustbin when she is on the sick, so trying to convince her that she would be okay going to the Jungle was a waste of breath. Physically she wasn't fit, but she was more worried that someone would see her leaping about at the rugby on the Sunday and then off sick again on the Monday.

There are some great examples of honesty beyond the call of duty.

Several years ago we were in Orlando Airport waiting to fly home after a holiday. We had an international phone card with some credit left on it, so decided to call the families to let them know when we were due to take off and land back in the U.K.

We made the calls and seemed to be on ages without the credit going down. We decided to make a few more calls to friends and then a few more until we couldn't remember anymore telephone numbers. When I put the phone down, it rang immediately. I picked it up and the operator said, "you owe 16 dollars 50 cents for those calls". I said, "okay, thank you". Amanda asked who was on the phone and what they had wanted.

She said, "we are going to have to pay it". I said, "what are they gonna do, come down the phone and arrest us?"

She wouldn't have any of it and headed off to get some change before standing and feeding $16.50 into the payphone.

About 2 years ago, the postman delivered what looked like a birthday card. It had our address on it, and the name of a person we didn't recognise. The card was on the side for months. Amanda eventually opened it to find a £10 note enclosed. 2 years later, it is still there, because although it is never going to be claimed, Amanda is too honest to spend it.

Our squad for the Wigan game was depleted again. Amanda is as passionate as you can get. She loves throwing paper confetti as the team runs out and possesses the highest pitched "boo" which is usual reserved for St Helens forward Nick Fozzard and/or Rhino, Ryan Bailey.

This was Wayne Godwin's first return to the Jungle in a Wigan shirt and he got a mixed reception as the teams were read out.

You can always guarantee that at one point or another during the season there will be a group of people waiting to accost you as you enter the ground. "Can I interest you in a Tigers credit card?" they ask. "No thanks, I do not want one of those baseball caps that you are trying to bribe me with". Alas, several people are up for the bribe and parade proudly in their new headgear despite the caps not being in the club colours.

Claws did their routines and lined up in the usual guard of honour as the teams ran out. Sophie said that when Waine Pryce ran past her, he came out with a really loud "Wooooo-hooooo!!!!". Time will tell if that was one of Prycey's pre match rituals.

Wigan are a great club with a proud history. Their team on paper had creativeness in Danny Orr, Dennis Moran and the under rated Mick Higham.

We were 0–12 down in no time. London, sorry Harlequins all over again?

Wigan scored 2 tries in no time. Would we be capable of turning another game around?

Well about an hour later when the score was 30–12, the answer was an undoubted YES. This was the best display by any Tigers team in years and the scoreline actually flattered our illustrious opponents. We had 2 tries disallowed in the first half after a touch judges intervention, but as usual the referee took the flack as the officials trooped off at the interval, when we were 6–12 down.

I wonder if the authorities will ever consider video referees at all Super League games. There are only ever 6 games per weekend and at least 2 of these are always on live TV. How much would it cost to have the technology available at all games? Rugby league has always been at the forefront of innovation. One example is letting play continue whilst an injured player receives treatment.

For supporters, it is really frustrating when a footballer feigns injury, gets the play stopped and then has to go to the side of the pitch only to be allowed back on within seconds. A pointless exercise.

Another example of innovation is putting incidents on

report. It is like trial by video and sometimes allows the referee to avoid making contentious decisions. A lack of consistency in placing an incident on report instead of using the sin bin option annoys spectators. Everyone is looking for consistency in every game. Neither the sin bin nor putting incidents on report is in football, but might be one day.

Refereeing in any sport is a thankless task and the speed of games means that the officials have to be super fit to be able to keep up. Poor decisions cost games and lost games cost people their livelihoods. I wonder if the RFL will invest in officials and let Super League lead the way again by having the same technology available for every game?

The final scoreline of 38–18 saw us up to seventh in the table (or joint 5th according to Willie Manu). There had been some outstanding performances by the forwards, led by fans favourite Danny Nutley, who made almost 30 'hit-ups'.

Ex Wiganer, Danny Sculthorpe must have been looking forward to the game since the fixtures came out. Unfortunately Scully's season was brought to a temporary halt after picking up a hand injury that would subsequently lead to several weeks absence.

It was great to see Willie Manu back from Australia. Coming off the bench, his addition to the squad gave everyone a lift.

As the Tigers acknowledged the supporters at the end, David came out with a classic and knew immediately that it would feature in this book. "Who's that bloke with the beard? I've not seen him before". It turned out that 'that bloke' was none other than coach Terry Matterson sporting a new look.

It was standing room only at the post match press conference and really noble for visiting coach Millward to concede that the best team had won. There was only one team there that day Mr. Millward.

Tuesday 21st March 2006

Some days come and go without anything significant happening. This day wasn't one of them.

After a nationwide hunt going back almost 30 years a man called John Humble was jailed at Leeds Crown Court after admitting to being the hoaxer 'Wearside Jack' who had had the West Yorkshire Police believing that the Yorkshire Ripper was from the North East. In the late 70's and early 80's, the female population in Yorkshire could not go out for fear of being the next victim. Those were dark days when the Police came into work places to play the tapes Humble had sent to them, in the faintest hope that someone would recognise his distinctive voice.

On the same day and in the 5th round of footballs F.A Cup: Birmingham City 0, Liverpool 7.

A remarkable score that would never happen in Super League.

It would be the equivalent of: Hull F.C 0, St Helens 46 or Harlequins 0, Leeds Rhinos 60.

Results you would never expect to get in our game, but we did.

On the same day and a bit nearer home, the Castleford Tigers Supporters Club played host to 'an evening with the coaching staff'. Terry Matterson and his team were the panel in front of an audience of a couple of hundred.

MARK HUDSON

I tried to persuade Amanda to go with me, but because she was still on the sick, I knew I was wasting my time. It's a good job she didn't go. Her boss was in the audience and actually won the raffle. It's another British trait that when anyone wins a raffle, they immediately wave their tickets in the air and continue to do so until they have collected their prize. Mrs. Jones was no different.

The evening started with the focus on the junior set up. Coach, Tony O'Brien (T.O.B) can talk for England, and amusingly sometimes gets a bit mixed up. He said that one junior who would be a star of the future had an 'inept' body for his age, when I think he meant his body was awesome for his age. He also said that Richard Fletcher had a 'head the size of the moon', when he returned for pre season training. T.O.B might not be the greatest speaker but he certainly got the Tigers squad fit and competing against the best for the full 80 minutes.

The current scholarship schemes we were told would produce Super League players of the future and that we had already signed several local lads who were being courted by the top teams.

Another message was that the club had been in the mire in recent times but that we wouldn't be returning to that position. That got a massive round of applause. Time would tell on that statement.

Terry Matterson had been at a rugby league disciplinary that day after Richard Fa'aoso had been cited for a dangerous tackle in the Wigan game. Fa'aoso received a 1 match ban. In the car going to the hearing, Terry asked Richie what his disciplinary record was like. Richie said he had only ever received 1 previous suspension. When the guilty verdict and previous convictions were read out, it turned out that the popular Tongan had had a few bans that he thought didn't count, when he was playing junior and reserve grade football. A fine and a 1 match ban were accepted and Fa'aoso missed the next game.

This was the night I met Stuart Barrow, who had recently joined the coaching staff as the player performance manager. Stu is the son in law of Mick Wormald. Remember Mick from chapter 1? The lad who takes photos for Bramley and collects RL memorabilia. Rugby league is a small world.

Terry Matterson moved into new surroundings close to the Jungle, yet a million miles away. There are some picturesque villages and hamlets in and around Castleford and Terry had found one of them. All he needed now was for his wife and children to join him. It is testament to the man that he came half way around the world to do a job many thought was a thankless task, without the support of his nearest and dearest.

Matterson is an unassuming character, professional in every detail and a winner. The team and management had come in for plenty of back slapping after 3 wins out of 6. Terry had to get their feet back on the ground and ready for the next challenge. Players like Michael Shenton, Craig Huby and Andy Kain were performing consistently in the elite league, on the big stage less than 2 years after starring for the Tigers Academy team. If we could produce more like these three, our future would certainly be in good hands.

We were almost a quarter of the way through Super League X1. There hadn't been an inkling of summer rugby. The clocks were due to change and the lighter nights were upon us. It always amazes me that nobody ever remembers which way the clocks go. Do they go forward or backwards? Do we get an extra hour in bed or lose an hour?

We lost an hour, but in the space of a week seemed to gain a hint of summer rugby. The parka and several layers of previous weeks were back in the wardrobe for another year. We were even down to a single pair of socks. How long would it be before we are wearing shorts to a game?

Huddersfield were back in town. They are a team with a bit of an enigma surrounding them. Very much established in Super League, attracting quality players, yet still unable to break into the top 6. After the previous 2 games in which we gave 12 and 14 point starts we really had to get out of the blocks early.

11 minutes played and we were losing 0–22. 4 unanswered tries against a team playing some of the most scintillating offensive football you would see anywhere in the world. It was like watching the Aussies from 1986. Credit where it's due, the Giants were fantastic for 11 minutes. We didn't have an answer and looked like we were heading for a heavy defeat. Brother in law Bram who had used Amanda's season ticket in her continued absence commented that "they could run in 'undred ere".

This Tigers squad knew how to fight and boy did we fight. A couple of scores late in the first half and we were back in it.

Huddersfield have giant forwards in Eorl Crabtree and Wayne McDonald. Crabtree could one day play for Great Britain if he fulfills his potential, whilst McDonald has never been a favourite of mine, but he certainly takes some stopping and has the ability to offload despite 4 or 5 tacklers hanging on to him.

We were never going to compete against their size, but we did muscle up and get back in the game. Just after half time we were back on level terms at 22–22, and looking capable of sneaking an unlikely victory.

When Michael Shenton collected a high cross-field kick, all he had to do was fall out of the sky and land over the try line to put us in front. He took the catch magnificently but in the wet conditions dropped the ball in the act of scoring. Without the big screen and with unsighted officials our own supporters gave the game away. If we had all started cheering and jumping up and down perhaps we could have influenced referee Ganson to award the try. Instead we all groaned and held our heads in our hands.

The Giants went back in front with a penalty kick and scored a couple of late tries, making the final scoreline of 22–36 a flattering one. It would have been one the great comebacks.

There were some positives. We were a quarter of the way through the league programme. This was only the 7th time our team had played together. There were 7 players who had brought us up from the National League in the starting 13. They have all 'upped' their games as individuals since Matterson took charge.

The new home kit had been available in the club shop for a few weeks. Young Josh Gibbo was the first of our crew to get one and appeared in a number 7, Kain shirt. He had Dyer printed on his away shirt. Josh is a little fella and having McGoldrick on his shirt would have been impossible. He would have no chance if he was a Harlequins supporter and his favourite players were Bradley-Qalilawa or McCarthy-Scarsbrook.

Before the game I witnessed a really disturbing incident. The 'credit card for a cap' brigade had had the audacity to return for a second time and Danny Sculthorpe, even with a pot on his hand, was selling his soul and signing up for one.

There was an old fashioned punch up in the junior curtain raiser. Everyone piled in with the faithful shouting, "Get inta 'em". Brad Davis who was preparing for the pre match warm up was enthralled.

The league table a quarter of the way through made good reading and I think we would have settled for mid table at that point of the season when we kicked off back in February. There was now a week off for the Challenge Cup. Terry Matterson returned to Australia to wrap up some unfinished business, leaving Brad Davis in charge for the trip to Widnes. The question was whether Terry also going scouting whilst back home?

I have never been a fan of open bucket collections at matches. My dad told me how him and his mates used to 'divvy' up when they did similar collections at the old Parkside stadium, when they were lads.

The sight of a bucket collection at Widnes had me moving at the rate of knots, whilst side stepping and swerving ala Waine Pryce. Unfortunately on this occasion, I got tagged by one of the lads and my excuse that "I had no change until I got in" didn't hold any sway, One of the adults with the group said in a great Scouse accent, "No worry mate, we will see you inside" Hearing the scouse twang at a rugby match is always amusing. Didn't Liverpool's right on any ownership of a team go the day Huyton folded?

It was so cold at Widnes that I had to swap the baseball cap for my woolly hat the minute we got in the ground. After only 1 weeks lapse, winter rugby had returned with a vengeance.

I heard the Scouse accent again. "There he is. He promised to put something in when he got in". I thought, "No, how have I been caught?" Luckily and due solely to my timely exchange of headwear, the young lad went and got a donation from another unsuspecting Cas supporter sat near us in a Tigers baseball cap. My woolly hat had saved the day and my 10p was safe for another week.

I have a thousand and one excuses for never putting in collections, including, "I am sorry I am like Prince Charles when I come out, no money".

They say Yorkshiremen are miserly. I prefer 'careful with their money'. I have seen Prison Officers wear poppies that they bought 20 years ago for a pound. £1 for 20 years wear is obviously good value.

Yorkshiremen are very much in their element at the 'eat as much as you like buffets'. Astley, now an adopted Yorkshireman is the champion on the Pizza Hut lunch time buffet. 20 slices of pizza as well as salad and fizzy drinks takes some beating, but at least he gets his fivers worth, so good luck to him I say.

Talking of Yorkshiremen, Chris Place (Placey) was telling me that one of his sons, Shaun, was working for the company sponsoring Featherstone Rovers. This brought along the 'perk' of access to the hospitality suite. Placey said that the rugby at Post Office Road wasn't great but that the hospitality was first class despite (and in the true tradition of being tight) having to buy your own drinks. On one occasion, whilst enjoying the proceedings, a club official asked Shaun to pick a Rovers man of the match. Shaun didn't have a clue, so asked his dad to bail him out. Placey said that he just picked a number off the top of his head. It is to be hoped that he chose wisely. You can imagine the Rovers fans in the family stand wanting a piece of him if he had chosen wrongly.

It was pleasing to hear that Placey was still enjoying his running and that he was contemplating entering the Leeds Half Marathon. I asked him if he had got an I-pod yet to keep him company on the long weekend runs. He said that he hadn't, and still relied on a walkman cassette player. I am not sure again if this is a sign of being careful with his money or simply that he hasn't joined the I.T revolution yet. He also confessed to wanting Neil Sedaka's greatest hits, which is inexcusable.

The trip to Widnes for the cup game had an air of inevitability about it. I am not sure that the great love affair with the Challenge Cup is there anymore. It was years since a real underdog had been to Wembley, in fact it was years since anyone got to Wembley. The RFL had announced that the 2006 cup final was going to be played at Twickenham.

On the day and after a treacherous 75-mile trip, we were soundly beaten by a Widnes side that played to their strengths and eliminated our qualities. In full back David Peachey, they had a world class performer. Peachey had a great game but returned home to Australia a few weeks later. He was a loss to the British game and I was surprised that no Super League teams were interested in his signature. It is always eventful when Barrie Mac plays and Terry O' Connor will cart the ball forward until his body gives in. Barrie Mac was hogging the media spotlight in the build up to the game. There was a 'blinding' interview on Radio 5live, live on the Saturday morning before the game. Barrie described footballers as 'puffs' for the way they dive about. The interviewer reminded Barrie that this was a family show. I just thought 'good on you' Barrie for saying what the rest of the nation thinks.

When Widnes scored the decisive try towards the end of the game, Terry O' Connor was ribbed by the huge Tigers following about his rather large size. Terry just smiled, lapped it up and promptly patted his 6 pack. He then turn around and rub both of his backside cheeks. We got the message Terry. On the day, McDermott and O'Connor were outstanding and Widnes deserved their victory. I bet it was a bit of sweet revenge for their coach, Steve McCormack who coached Whitehaven to defeat in our success at the 2005 Grand Final.

We slipped on the banana skin. It was the first time a Super League club had been beaten by a team from the National League since Huddersfield were dumped out by a magnificent Hunslet Hawks performance in 2003.

We were without several key players and as Brad Davis said afterwards, "If we stay in Super League, who will care that we lost in the cup at Widnes?" Fair point, no-one will care.

Once again we shared the M62 motorway going home with the Leeds Rhinos fans and their 'feel the passion' car flags. They were returning from a victory against Leigh. Another potential banana skin well avoided. It's fair to say that the Rhinos are in every competition to win them. Our priorities this season were different.

Attendances were poor in all of the cup games. Leeds had the sold out signs up at Headingley with 17,000+ in the ground. There were less than 4,000 at Hilton Park, Leigh for their game.

Coach John Kear left Hull F.C by mutual agreement after a run of poor results and performances. This was the first coaching casualty of the season. Kear had brought the Challenge Cup to Hull in 2005, but similar to the Tigers, they fell at the first hurdle against Bradford.

7 league games in and Hull were on the lookout for a new man. John Kear always strikes me as a really genuine bloke and one who will always look for the Tigers result first. He was born on Wheldon Road. There are only 12 head coaches jobs in Super League, so where would he go from here to find alternative employment? He may decide to develop his fledgling career as a presenter on TV and radio.

We welcomed Terry Matterson back from his visit to Australia and got everyone fit for the flight to France. A trip to Carcassonne in early April had been eagerly awaited. It was a chance to sample the Catalan culture and a chance to don the summer gear.

Stacey Jones was still missing from the Catalans squad.

From France to Franze in a week

We had been looking forward to going to France since seeing the Wigan fans over there in round 1 of the competition. The feedback from everyone who had been since had been that it was a trip not to miss. We were heading to Carcassonne for the game via Perpignan, both apparently lovely regions of Southern France.

We had all been practising our pigeon French to get us by. At school, I had never grasped the idea of speaking another language, but I admired anyone who did. It is a bit like learning to swim in your pyjamas, a case of 'just in case'. We had to learn to read and write in French just in case we ever went to France. What if you went somewhere else like Croatia? How would you get by then? The same way you would get by in France if you couldn't speak a word of French, by speaking English!

We had to have a French name at school to encourage you to speak French. I liked the idea of being Marc. Unfortunately you weren't allowed to choose your own name, so Davids couldn't be Daveed and Marks couldn't be Marc. I chose Nicholas instead. That sounded manly enough.

"Ja mapelle Nicholas". Unfortunately the 's' was a silent 's' and for a year I was "Ja mapelle Nichola", which wasn't manly at all and another reason I dropped French and every other language at the first opportunity.

We did some net surfing to come up with the best package and even contemplated travelling independently of any organised trip.

After missing 5 weeks, Amanda was declared fit to travel. She went back to work for 3 days to prove her fitness and to prove to the rest of the world that she wasn't being dishonest catching a flight to France.

Fleeceman, Janet and Cal were going to Disneyland, Paris for a short break. They would be in France the day after the game. They were celebrating Janet's birthday. It was the next big birthday after her 40th.

We were due to fly out of Robin Hood airport near Doncaster on a chartered flight early on the morning of the match, spend a night in Perpignan before flying back home on the Sunday evening.

We were all set. Passports out, luggage labels written, the house hoovered so it was tidy when we got home, clean bed sheets on and enough clothes packed for 2 weeks let alone 1 night.

Amanda is a good organiser and she had everything in hand by the time we had lights out at 2200 hours on the Friday night and alarm clocks set for 0400 hours on the Saturday morning. Niece Naomi made up our party for the trip that would be our last family holiday together before Jessica headed off to university in the autumn of 2006.

When your phone rings in the middle of the night, you generally know that something is wrong.

When I answered the phone at 2316 hours precisely I somehow knew that it would be bad news. It was the tour operator. There had been a mechanical problem with our plane and it was too late to charter another. The trip had been cancelled.

That news was devastating. The promise of a full refund wasn't what I wanted to hear at the time. When your car breaks down on the morning of a game, you borrow another car or cadge a lift. What do you do when your plane breaks down?

Everyone was gutted. This was going to be a trip of a lifetime. A chance to see the Tigers first game in that region of France. We would never be able to say that we were there that day. Listening to the game on the radio, watching it on teletext or seeing updates coming through on Sky Sports were not the same.

At the end of the day, we accepted that the operators were trying to do us a favour by not having us travel to the airport in the early hours. That would have been even worse. Having to come home from the airport knowing the trip was off would have been unimaginable.

The team would be running out with some support there, but certainly with a plane full less. They would probably never even know that a big following went to bed early that Friday evening looking forward to being part of something special.

Amanda declared, "Av even shaved mi legs". Sophie said "We should go somewhere else for the day". Naomi asked, "Like Cornwall?" Well it was nearly midnight and she does live with a Rhino brother.

I was hoping to say that just like Cumbria and Venice, Carcassonne is a lovely place and somewhere we promised ourselves to visit again one day. Alas not.

Saturday, match day, came and it was like getting up on Christmas morning knowing Santa hadn't been.

News filtered through that the local radio reporter was also booked on our trip, so radio coverage would be nil. We had to watch the Bulls v Wolves game on Sky and wait for score flashes to appear. It was difficult to resist the "we would have just been getting into the ground now" or "they will be out warming up now" lines.

It hurt us all not to be there.

The first score came in. 6–0 to the Catalans after 2 minutes. Then 10–0. Here we go again. Lets give every team we play a start.

By half time we were behind 10–20. Sky always shows the first half highlights straight away from the games in France. Our defence looked appalling. We had to score first in the second stanza to make a game of it, but we didn't. We let in try after try after try and went down to an embarrassing 14–51 defeat. The tackling had gone from appalling to none existent. This result put the Catalans on the map even without the mercurial Stacey Jones.

Were we glad we didn't make it? Yes and no really. To be part of the trip, the atmosphere and the event would have been something else, but to be in France all day waiting for our flight home, with the disappointment of that defeat hanging over us would have been painful.

Terry Matterson's comments said it all. He described the performance as pathetic, and the last 20 minutes as disgraceful. He said that we were very poor.

Our thoughts were with the supporters who had managed to get there by hook or by crook. It was bad enough coming away from Headingley a few weeks before after a hiding. We were back in the house that night 30 minutes after the match finished. How do you react to a hiding when you are stuck in France?

The next few weeks were vital if we were to mount a realistic challenge to stay in Super League.

The bottom of the table at the end of week 8 and with 20 games to go, read:

	P	W	D	L	PTS
Hull	8	3	0	5	6
Catalans	8	3	0	5	6
TIGERS	8	3	0	5	6
Wakefield	8	2	0	6	4
Harlequins	8	1	1	6	3
Wigan	8	1	0	7	2

Next up were our closest geographic rivals the Wildcats for a Good Friday encounter.

It took a few days to get over the disappointment of not making the trip to France. It is hard to read a match reports when you're not at the game and even harder when you cop a hiding like that one. The first rumblings of a Brad Davis comeback were heard in the build up to the Wakefield game. 8 matches in and we were looking at the prospect of assistant coach Brad, aged 38, coming out of retirement to steer us around the park. Imagine what Brad would be worth if he were 15 years younger. There were also rumblings about some new blood coming into the squad.

They say a week is a long time in politics; well a week is certainly a long time in Super League. Ian Millward wouldn't be bringing new blood into the Wigan camp. He became the second coaching casualty of the season, leaving this great club at the foot of the table and without a leader going into their Good Friday fixture against unbeaten St Helens, a match that the Saints won 48–10. There was a Warriors start for Jordan James, a player deemed to be not good enough for us this season and someone who was plucked from near obscurity at Swinton

MARK HUDSON

to go to the JJB. Few people were shedding any tears as the turmoil continued at Wigan. A club that ruled the roost for years was now having a reality check.

Paul Franze joined the Tigers squad on the day before the Wakefield game and made his debut off the bench at Belle Vue. Apparently Franze was a promising youngster back home in Australia. He had lost his way in the game and was signed from union side, London Irish from the Zurich Premiership.

Belle Vue, a bit like the Jungle has seen better days. It's a 13 mile trip away and isn't a bad ground to watch at, but unlike the Jungle, there is never any atmosphere, and despite it being a bank holiday and a local derby under the floodlights, the atmosphere was still average. There was a comeback to the terraces of epic proportions by Amanda. She was back with a vengeance and several weeks of frustration were taken out on referee Ashley Klein, the majority of the Wakefield team and the one or two Wakefield fans dotted around us.

The Tigers faithful outnumbered our hosts who had gotten into the Easter spirit by handing out a free Cadbury's crème egg as you entered the ground. A real bonus when you pay £16 to get in. Is there anybody out there who actually likes Cadburys crème eggs?

Fleeceman said his favourite chocolate bar was the chunky kit-kat, claiming that they are the only product to have made a successful transition and have reinvented themselves into a better model.

Wakefield had been getting off to some real flyers in recent weeks. They were 21–0 up at home against Warrington and lost. Taking into account our slow starts it wouldn't have been a surprise if we had gone in at half time chasing the game. Remarkably we went 10–0 up in no time. Brad Davis was back and marshalling the troops and all looked promising.

Wakefield have some quality and are an established Super League outfit. Players like Rooney, Jeffries and the 'King', David Solomona would get into most teams. At half time we were trailing 16–24, but we were still in with a shout.

This was the first of 3 games for the Tigers in 8 days. An unbelievable ask of a newly promoted team, with the smallest squad in the competition. How could players put their bodies on the line without having the opportunity of any recovery period?

We were still missing Danny Sculthorpe and he was joined on the injury list by Michael Platt and Craig Huby. There was an early injury to Michael Shenton, so Paul Franze was thrown in at the deep end.

We just couldn't break down the Wakefield defence. I don't really know if it was how good they were defensively or how poor we were at creating chances. Everytime we scored, they scored soon afterwards and we were always chasing the game.

Unashamedly, Amanda blamed Wakefield's dirty tactics and referee Klein's inability to spot everything for aiding to our downfall.

Wakefield certainly had one tactic that caught us out every time and that was keeping the ball in the scrum under the loose forwards feet, whilst our pack broke up to take their place in the defensive line up. It led to penalty after penalty. It caught us out more than once.

The match ended in a 26–34 defeat. It was our 4th defeat on the trot. We were on a rollercoaster and heading downhill at a rate of knots.

On the way out of Belle Vue, 12 year old Naomi said "Trouble was we tried to offload t'many times and knocked on. Its tekken 5 years, but I know mi stuff, me".

That analysis of our performance summed it up in a nutshell.

Another sign of getting old is when you actually look forward to being able to get into the garden to cut the grass. Growing up, grass was for playing sport on. The first cut meant that the decent weather was around the corner and summer rugby was finally on its way.

Holiday fixtures come around thick and fast and we had the chance to bounce back almost immediately against the Warrington Wolves at the Jungle. Sophie had been dancing around the house for weeks to 'Material girl'. The game was televised live on Sky, and Claws would be in the spotlight dancing to a Madonna classic. This was our chance to show the competition that we were here for the long stay.

Wigan were still marooned at the bottom, but a new coach was heading for the JJB, some bloke from Bradford who also coached Great Britain and was leaving the world champions to go to a team at the bottom of the league. Why would he do that?

There was a letter published in the 'Rugby Leaguer' on Thursday 22nd May 1980. It was titled 'Wigan's hope in decline', and read

'Although it is sad to see a club full of tradition get relegated, the sudden deterioration of Wigan must provide hope for some of the lesser rugby league clubs. Clubs struggling for survival must now believe they can come through while others like Wigan are falling. Of course the blame can and I'm sure will be pinned on various parties – the board, coach, players and even the fans, but I say to all these people forget about this season and re-build into the great side you once were'

I was really proud to have a letter published in a world renowned rugby league newspaper, especially on my 17th birthday.

Wigan went down and came back up the following season.

The rest they say is history. Didn't they then go on to win the Challenge Cup 7 times on the trot?

Who would have thought that 26 seasons on and the threat of relegation would be looming for Wigan?

The darkest day

When you go down to a club record home defeat there isn't much to say. In front of the nation on live T.V, we went down to a 6–64 defeat that saw the Tigers faithful supporters leaving in droves long before the final hooter sounded. The players walked off to resounding boo's at half and at full-time.

This was one of the lowest points in the clubs history. Warrington Wolves are a half-decent side at best with a couple of world class performers in Lee Briers and Martin Gleeson. They generally lose as many as they win and I fancied our chances of a victory to ease the disappointment of the defeat at Wakefield less than 72 hours earlier.

It was a disaster. Trailing 6–28 at the break, it was men against boys throughout. We conceded 36 points without reply in the second half. We moved to the railway end of the ground for the second half. It is not one of my favourite places to watch rugby league from, especially when your team loses the half 0–36 and all the points are scored at the opposite end.

To console myself, I began texting a few mates as soon as I got home. Shaun McCabe a mate from work and a Middlesborough supporter sent one back saying, *"The scoreline is something u must put in your book! A warts and all account. U can also mention that u turned down my kind offer of a Boro season ticket 2 watch cack!!"* I wasn't sure if Shaun was describing the Tigers or his own team as 'cack'.

Bradford Bull, Russell Hanwell had watched the game on Sky and said, *"65 missed tackles said sky. They think poss a record. No defensive line. Have a beer n 4get about it".*

The day started with the Tigers squad hurling miniature rugby balls into the crowd. One caught Cal Simpson a beauty on her leg. She failed to gather the ricochet and the trend was set for the rest of the day.

There was a minutes silence before the game for a Tigers fan who had died whilst over in France watching his team. The deafening silence was only broken by the posh rotating advertising boards that only come out when the cameras are in town. It would be interesting to find out how much business Qatar Airways got after advertising at the Jungle. I bet their switchboard was jammed with season ticket holders looking to flee to Qatar to avoid watching their team get any more hidings.

Wigan lost again on the day, but we were now second from bottom, still 4 points clear of the cherry and whites, but with a points against tally of over 400 against in only 10 games.

We had now conceded 50 points in 3 games, twice against teams that on paper we should have been looking to beat.

What we didn't need after a game like that was another trip to Headingley in 4 days time to face the Rhinos. All we could hope for was a frozen pitch and a postponed fixture. At least we could go there knowing that the Leeds Tykes had just been relegated from the top flight of English Rugby Union. Did anybody actually care about the fortunes of Leeds Tykes?

A wag was heard to say that Leeds Rhinos were looking into the possibility of using Yorkshire's cricket score board for our game.

Would coach Matterson be able to turn it around and instill the much needed shot of enthusiasm?

Did the Tigers squad know what it meant to their supporters to come away from Headingley with pride still in tact?

In the bigger picture of things, our dismay with the performance against the Wolves was short lived. We were all there at the next game willing our team on. That is what supporters do. It is about supporting through thick and thin.

To accuse the players of not trying and being gutless doesn't help the situation, but the Tigers supporters now had a vehicle to vent their frustrations to. The club had relaunched its website and the fans forum returned. It's a place where people generally moan and gossip about new signings. I guess it's also a place where the players look to see what their supporters are saying. Negative talk and personal attacks don't help anybody, but you can understand the fans frustrations at seeing their teams apparent lack of pride in the shirt.

Realism checks are essential in life. One supporter who went to see the Tigers game in France will never see another game. The Warrington defeat also occurred on the day before the first anniversary of when my mam died. We had been at Oldham's Boundary Park watching the Tigers scrape home when I took a call from my sister to say that my mam had taken a turn for the worse and that we should go and see her as soon as we got home. She had been in St Gemma's Hospice, Leeds for a few days as respite for herself and my dad, when the Doctors suddenly told the family that her condition had deteriorated and she was now gravely ill.

We did see her on that Sunday evening, and she died the following day.

She was 68 years of age and left behind a husband of nearly 47 years and 3 Grand daughters.

This was the first time either Amanda or I had lost a parent. We still think we are young and if we are young, so are our parents.

It is very difficult to put such a loss into words and life somehow will never be the same again. My dad had lost his soul mate and best friend and the girls would one-day graduate and get married without their Grandma Maureen being there.

I have a feeling that she will be looking down on their every move.

Losing a rugby match to a record score happens, but we get over it and will be there for the next game. Sport is all about the celebrating the highs and wallowing in the lows. It was only a few weeks earlier when Max was keeping us entertained on the coach home from London. We were world-beaters then.

When you lose someone close you never really get over it, but readjust and brave it out in support of others.

My mam had worked hard all her life. She never complained about anything and never asked for anything. It was a difficult thing to do, but I had no hesitation in speaking on behalf of the family at her funeral. It made it more personal. People laughed and people cried. She had some funny ways, such as thinking that all motor cyclists were 'nutters'. Everytime a plane went overhead, she would say "Bet they're coming home skint" and she called people 'tuppence, ha'penny snobs' if they pretended to be something they were not.

Despite being well into my forties, she still treated me like a dependant child. It always made Amanda and the girls laugh the way she fussed over me and I guess, like most sons, I used to lap it up. I got treats for birthdays and Christmas, such as a box of jaffa cakes.

Her illness was short lived and she died of cancer less than 3 months after being diagnosed. She suffered in silence throughout and said she had no pain, when we probably knew that she did, but that she wasn't going to start complaining now.

Parents put you on the road in life and guide you when you come to the crossroads on what is right and wrong. They influence you in being grateful for what you have and to appreciate what others do for you.

My sister Bev and I couldn't have had a better upbringing and I hope it has rubbed off on us both as parents ourselves.

Pride in the shirt

Only 4 days after the Warrington defeat we headed back to Headingley for the 3rd time this season, the second game and the time we went and the game was called off. The computer that worked out this seasons fixtures needed an overhaul. Hull and Wakefield had already played each other 3 times in the first 10 fixtures. We were playing the Rhinos for the second time despite not playing either Salford or the Bulls yet.

We were on a hiding to nothing and most people around us weren't too bothered about the result. This game was all about restoring the pride in wearing the Tigers colours.

The support that was at Headingley was magnificent. It didn't stop nephew, Rhino George texting from the South Stand that Cas had 'more players than fans'. We had a few more than that, but not that many. The ones that were there did create an atmosphere that made this game a proper derby match.

There was another boycott of the game by some Tigers supporters who were probably sick of getting beaten and expected another thumping. Headingley is the worse place in the world to suffer any type of defeat. This is when loyalty counts for everything.

We were 11 games into Super League and we had lost a few games heavily. 11 games into the toughest competition in world rugby league and some of our fans had had enough. Loyal supporters? Loyalty counts for everything. This time a year ago we were going to places like Batley and Barrow and no disrespect to these clubs, but we were now playing in a different

competition and a different game. If ever the team and supporters needed to be as one, it was there at Headingley that night.

The match was supposed to be on Sky, but during the week,
they had announced that they would now be televising Salford's
home game against the unbeaten Saints. They cited the fact that
Salford were flying high and that they hadn't had much coverage. Everyone knew that nobody would watch another Tigers
mauling. Viewers must have been turning off in droves during
the Wolves debacle. This was the ultimate insult.

Seeing the Tigers warming up really lifted the spirits. Ben
Roarty plays hard and takes no prisoners. As he warmed up in
front of us, there was a glance towards the Tigers fans and a
smile. He knew what this game meant to everyone.

"6–0 after 10 minutes" was the cry from the Tigers fans and
we were really getting into the faces of our more illustrious
opponents. Leeds are a quality team and would be around at the
business end of the season. Their success didn't come overnight.
Despite been one of the worlds biggest clubs, their trophy cabinet had been empty for years. They were now one of the worlds
best teams and we gave them a right game. The final scoreline
flattered Leeds. 6–42 doesn't look great on paper and some of
the missing Tigers fans will have thought 'glad we didn't go'. The
response of the team and the supporters was brilliant and at the
final whistle we reacted as if we had have won. The looks on the
faces of the Rhinos supporters sat on the wall surrounding the
pitch were priceless. They spend the whole match staring at you
and cannot understand how you can get over excited when your
team gets beat. They are also probably wondering where the
passion comes from.

The Rhinos don't do things by half. There are more stewards at Headingley than spectators at some National League
games. There ought to be a salary cap on the wages of stewards.
This would leave Leeds at the start of the season at −20 points.

David 'Fleeceman' Simpson was on top form. He is after Amanda one of the most honest people in the world. He does however have a dark side that has seen him having some brushes with the worlds law enforcers. Without doubt 'big brother' will be watching David and the FBI, CIA and Scotland Yard will all have files on him. He got into trouble in Spain after parking illegally and had his vehicle towed away. He also received a £50 fine in Leeds City Centre for dropping litter, so when he lit up a cigarette at Headingley, he couldn't put it out quick enough when I pointed at that we were in a no smoking stadium. One of the 6,000 stewards on duty would have been sure to see him.

David also entered the Tony O' Brien school of using big words to impress. He described a young Rhino fan as 'incredulous', which is apparently a real word and a real word used in the right context. I am not sure that there is room for such talk on the terraces at rugby league games.

Pride had been restored. 4 games in 14 days was a tough challenge. We now had a week off and time to prepare for a home game against the flying Salford Reds.

One worrying aspect was our inability to get over the white wash. In 3 of the last 4 games, we had scored 4 against Widnes, 6 against the Wire and 6 against the Rhinos. 16 points and 3 tries is not a great return in 240 minutes of rugby. The Rhinos scored 9 tries in 80 minutes and Warrington ran in 11. Our attacking flair needed to be rediscovered if we were to climb away from the lower reaches of the league.

Wigan had a new man in charge. Brian Noble coach of the most successful club in the summer era had swapped the world champions for the Warriors. Without doubt Nobby would turn the Wigan around. His first game ended in a 46–10 away victory against Fartown. The Warriors looked awesome and were now only 2 points adrift at the bottom of the table.

Aaron Smith who joined the Tigers prior to the 2005 season

was forced out of the game with a persistent neck injury. At 24 years of age, this must have been a crushing blow. He must have been looking forward to a long career at the highest level. It's another reality check that careers are short lived and players are only passing through the club. The club will always be there, but the management, players and supporters are only caretakers. Who will care about what happened in 2006 in another 50 years time? How many people care what happened in the 1956 season?

Losing Aaron Smith became Whitehavens gain several weeks later when he came out of retirement to play for the Cumbrians.

Wigan legend, Kris Radlinski had also announced his retirement from the game earlier in the season. He played at the top level for years and was one of our most consistent performers on the international stage. A great player and another massive loss to our game.

Towards the end of our relegation season of 2004, there were comings and goings of playing personnel in an attempt to stave off the inevitable. It was worrying therefore when not even half way through this campaign, new players were still arriving as others were leaving. The Australian club season was in full swing but none of the other clubs in Super League were going to release quality players to their competitors.

The recently arrived Paul Franze left the club and one Tigers fan in our household was heard to comment, "d'ya know what? Good!" The pen picture we had of Franze before his arrival made it look a really good signing. In reality it was a poor one. Franze looked over weight and sluggish and to be fair to him, he did the club a favour by leaving when he did. After 2 full appearances and 1 as a substitute, Franze returned to Australia and signed for Newcastle Knights for 2007.

"Everyone's doing summat about it. Wigans got Brain

Noble, Londons got Henry Paul and who do we get? Peter Lupton. Never heard of 'im", was how Amanda took the news that we had at last recruited some half-back cover. It wasn't Craig Gower but Peter Lupton from Hull FC.

Lupton had been a fringe player at the KC and the arrival of their new coach Peter Sharp, had seen his immediate departure for a loan spell at the Jungle.

Henry Paul was one of the greatest players to have played our game, but when he left 5 years ago to play rugby union, he left his best days behind him. This signing will either be a masterstroke by Harlequins or will backfire and thrust them into the relegation dogfight.

Salford were one of my second favourite teams growing up. David 'Dai' Watkins was a legend and Keith Fielding was a flying winger who was more famous for his achievements on BBC TV's 'Superstars'. They were a flair team. This 2006 team also had some flair. They were one of the surprise teams of the season so far. Coached by Karl Harrison and the former Hunslet man James Lowes, the City Reds were establishing themselves comfortably in the top 6. There was a rumour going back a couple of years that Karl Harrison was about to become a Prison Officer at HMP Leeds. His career path took a different route however when Salford got promoted to Super League. Having Karl at the side of you in a prison wouldn't have been a bad thing.

Half-back, Luke Robinson is a player you would always pay to watch. With ball in hand, he is a magician. He may be too small for the international arena but he is quality. His half-back partner was Andrew Dunnemann, a Rhinos cast off and another who got away when we were looking to recruit a top class half-back.

Added into the equation were Malcolm Alker and Karl Fitzpatrick. The Reds had the craft players to damage any team. Alker, like Luke Robinson may never play for his country, but after signing a new contract for the Reds that will probably see out his career, the Salford fans unfurled a massive banner naming their legends and Alker's name was on it. Imagine running out and seeing that?

The first half was really competitive. We went in trailing 8–16. It should have been closer. Ryan McGoldrick had missed 2 very kickable conversions. This wasn't a win or bust game, but was a game we were capable of winning. I was looking for a win; Fleeceman was looking for an improved performance. News was coming through that Hull were beating Wigan, 42–0 at half time at the KC. What would the score have been with Peter Lupton playing?

What an opportunity to put a marker down. It was not to be however and half way through the second period, we were looking down the barrel again. 8–26 down with some eliminatory mistakes such as kicking the ball dead on 2 consecutive kick-offs (1 which led to a sin binning for dissent for McGoldrick). In another moment of madness prop forward Danny Nutley had the ball on the last tackle and with no other option he ended up putting in an unimpressive bomb, which is an old fashioned up 'n' under. We were heading for another damage limitation exercise. The doom and gloom merchants were joining the 'Matterson out' brigade.

With only 13 minutes left on the clock, something magical happened. Danny Nutley scored, but Brad Davis missed the conversion. That made it 12–26. Richard Fa'aoso scored and Craig Huby added the extras. Making it 18–26.

Then Gray Viane (looking a lot like Lesley Vainakolos little brother, with platted hair) crossed in the corner. Huby again converted with a great kick off the touchline. 24–26 and game on.

The South Sea islanders, Fa'aoso, Viane and Willie Manu were still settling into their new surroundings. The culture shock and cold weather were bound to have had an affect and none of the 3 had played to their full potential up to then. When Willie Manu received the ball 20 metres out, he had it all to do and boy did he do it all. Skittling defender after defender Manu wrote himself a place in the 'heroes of 2006' book with a fantastic try to nudge us in front 28–26. What made it better for us was that he scored right in front of where we stand. We, along with the rest of the Wheldon Road end went mad. Amanda's neck injury had comeback, but she didn't care. We were going to win this one and make the rest of the league stand up and take notice. Huby missed the conversion and despite some last minute Salford panic attacking, our last minute panic defending held up and we had notched our 4th win of the season in the most bizarre fashion. I bet Sky wish they had been in town for that one.

It was a classic and it produced a great result. Salford played their part in a game that was as exciting as they come. The team celebrated and we celebrated. Was this to be the pivotal moment of the 2006 season, or a false dawn?

Hull hammered Brian Noble's Wigan 54–12 and we headed to the JJB with a chance of stretching the gap between us to 6 points. Our victory also had Wakefield, Huddersfield and Harlequins looking over their shoulders.

Sister in law, Helen Bramley, like the impressive Peter Lupton made her debut in a different arena. Helen had trained long and hard to be able to compete in a local 10km run. It was her first race after taking up running a few months earlier. We were all out in force to cheer her on, with a 3-stage strategy to see her at the start, half way around and finally at the finish. She looked great at the start and great at the finish, half way around she looked as though she would rather be somewhere else. Most people who enter any sort of road race will tell you that whatever distance it is, you will always hit a patch when you wonder why you are doing it. Credit to her for digging deep and believing in herself. She now has the T-shirt to prove that she got around. She has a personal best time and talked immediately about her next race. Helen is similar to a lot of women who run or go to the gym. For whatever reason, she always wears a tracksuit top or sweatshirt tied around her waist in an attempt to hide her bottom. Why are females obsessed with doing that?

"Has anyone got any Rennies?"

It was the start of May and we had another jaunt on the M62 on a Friday night, but at least summer rugby had arrived. The game at the JJB Stadium would go along way to shaping the rest of the season. My dad made his first trip to Wigan's new surroundings, but it didn't stop him mentioning Wigan legend Billy Boston at least 10 times. From passing Tesco's where Central Park once stood to "Imagine Billy Boston playing at a ground like this?" once we entered the arena.

Going to the JJB is like going to Widnes. You are never sure how you actually get there and you certainly never go back the way you came. It is one of my favourite grounds with great car parking and a warm welcome from the stewards. The car parking is great but it takes you hours to get away at the end of the game.

On the way over whilst driving through the outskirts of Wigan we witnessed something that belonged in the TV programme, 'Shameless'. A group of people were having a few beers and a barbecue on some grass in front of their houses. In this country, the barbies come out the minute the sun comes out. On this occasion the party goers were able to enjoy their food and drink with home comforts after the 3-piece suite out was carried out of one house.

There were all sorts of distractions to stop Tigers fans travelling in numbers to Wigan. The game was live on Sky for starters. Leeds United were involved in their Championship play-off and their game against Preston North End was also live on Sky. The play-offs meant that the football season was almost over, although we had the World Cup to look forward to. The flags of St George were already flying from cars and bedroom windows and World Cup fever was about to sweep the country. It wouldn't be long before the newspapers had the World Cup supplements with fixture charts for you to plan your days off and sweeps so you had an alternative team to support in the works competition. Winner takes all for a £1 a team gamble. The sweep is usually more interesting than the competition itself, unless you pull out Trinidad and Tobago or Togo. You can write your quid off for another 4 years.

Credit to the Cas fans. They turned out in numbers and regardless of how many there are of you, you always seem to make more noise than the Wigan fans at the JJB.

We took last seasons 'It's not the size of the Tiger....' banner with us. It had been in the boot of the car for the last 7 months. For some reason, we decided that this occasion demanded that it needed another airing.

Fleeceman, again without his fleece for the duration of the game, entered into the Wigan spirit by sampling the delights of a stadium pie. 5 minutes later, he was asking for the Rennies. Some people want to walk the Great Wall of China or visit the Vatican in their lifetime. Downing a pie in Wigan nailed an ambition for one brave supporter.

There is a group of Tigers supporters who would have been in their element at Wigan. We call them the 'pie family', for no other reason apart from the fact that at least one of them is always eating a pie no matter where you go.

Danny Sculthorpe had been absent for weeks through injury, but he was a visible figure at Wigan. Perhaps it had something to do with him having the opportunity to tread the turf at his former ground or perhaps it was a chance to convince his coach that he was nearly match fit. Danny was the water carrier and despite wearing the smallest T-shirt possible, he spent more time on the pitch than he would have done in a match. His return was a welcome boost.

Keith Mason left the club. It became obvious that Mason didn't have a future at the Jungle. Whatever had gone on, and we will probably never know, Mason headed to Huddersfield after only 2 substitute appearances in 12 rounds. He made his debut for the Giants in a game that ended the rather subdued St Helens unbeaten start to the season.

This was Brian Noble's first home game as Wigan coach and he got a rousing reception from the home fans. The Tigers old boys didn't get much reception at all. Danny Orr had been gone for what seemed like years and it was as if he never played for Cas. Wayne Godwin would have been a legend if he had stayed after relegation, but he didn't. Once Noble got his feet under the table, we all wondered how many more games Jordan James would play for Wigan. The last time we saw Jordan at a Cas game, he was donning Mr. Purrfect's head after the Grand Final victory at Widnes.

The Wigan squad contains some great players. It was Noble's job to get them playing as a team.

We knew that we had to back up the previous weeks effort with another victory. Over the years the JJB has been a home fortress. How could we seriously expect to beat a team coached by the Great Britain boss and containing high quality performers like Moran, O' Loughlin and Higham?

The difference this time was that we were going there with confidence and they were rooted to the bottom of the league and coming off a hiding at Hull. The pressure was on them and we would never have a better chance to beat them on their home patch.

Sophie got a text before kick-off to say that she had been spotted on Sky. That made her day. The girls also got excited when they appeared on the big screen and like everyone who appears on the big screen they all nudged each other in a fit of excitement and proceeded to wave at the wrong camera.

This was the night when some of the Tigers played their best game in the shirt and a win was never in doubt. We went in at half-time 22–12 in front after scoring 2 tries just before the interval.

A half-time rendition of the Arctic Monkeys 'when the sun goes down' brought back memories of the trip to London. It lifted the spirits and ensured the Tigers traveling army where in good voice when the team returned to the battle field. We were 40 minutes away from putting us 6 league points in front of Wigan.

It was vital that we scored first in the second half. A victory would then be in touching distance. We didn't and all of a sudden the Wigan fans woke up as we teetered at 22–18. We didn't teeter for long though. Tiger Handforth scored from a scrum after another crunching tackle saw a Wigan player lose possession from the kick-off. 26–18 and game over?

Willie Manu had written himself a place in Castleford folk-lore against Salford. There are not enough descriptives to explain what the feeling was like when Willie repeated the feat and crashed over skittling defender after defender to score right in front of us to make it 30–18.

Craig Huby had a bad day at the office with his kicking, but he had a great game with ball in hand and tackled everything that moved. Would the inability to turn 4 points into 6 prove costly?

An attempted Peter Lupton drop goal missed by a couple of feet. That would have clinched it.

With the clock ticking, Mick Higham scored under the posts and the conversion made it 24–30. The score line was beginning to flatter Wigan. Surely we weren't going to blow this? There was still time for Wigan to have a final set of 6 and for the first time in 80 minutes there was doubt. The final play of the game saw a big bomb defused comfortably by full back Michael Platt and the 2 points were ours. Platty had played a blinder throughout, scoring twice and marshalling a defence that on the night was nothing but awesome. So that was it.

Wigan 24 - Tigers 30.

This was a great game. We had redeemed ourselves with Sky and for a neutral this was the best game of the season so far. A vital 2 points and the best performance of the season. We were a team growing in confidence and playing with the passion and commitment for the cause that the supporters demand.

Celebrations at the final whistle were fantastic. Willie Manu sneaked the man of the match award and a new chant was born. Going back to the 'hardest car park to get away from in the world' was magic and our celebrations seemed to be well received by the disappointed Warriors supporters. They knew that that was our night and that they would have their nights before the season was over. Too good to go down? We were not really bothered. All we were looking forward to was avenging our recent hammering against the Catalans and a chance to record 3 consecutive victories. We were nearly half way through the season and had recorded 5 victories. Other results meant we were now up 8th. The top 6 seemed to be away and the bottom 6 knew that they would all have to fight to avoid the bottom spot from here on in.

Terry Matterson said that as long as we continued to improve relegation would not be an issue. That was a good point, but it didn't stop the majority of Cas fans looking at everyone else's fixtures and calculating week by week, month by month if we would gather enough points to stay up. Throughout any other season I can never remember been interested in who was playing who, but after the hurt of relegation there was now a different thinking.

Sophie received another text telling her that she had appeared on the Sky credits and we had heard that Leeds United had drawn 1–1.

The girls were soon asleep as we hit the motorway going home. A long wait in the car park letting the traffic get away added to their sleepiness. There was still time for my dad to delight in telling us that he had bought some toothpaste for 21p. "It'll do for me, it's only for cleaning mi gums!" he said proudly.

The game was repeated on Sky at 0030 hours and try as I might, I couldn't keep my eyes open to watch it. We were still euphoric on the Saturday morning and the car flags flew all weekend.

The Leeds Rhinos were at home that same night and there were obviously split loyalties with Leeds United playing their biggest game at home in years. There were almost 50,000 supporters at these 2 matches in Leeds that evening and every one of them will have been looking forward to the games all week. Sport throws up winners and losers and as I have said before whatever happens people still come back. We now had a feel good factor at our club after 2 wins on the spin. This was only a few weeks after suffering the heaviest away defeat in the clubs history and after suffering the heaviest home defeat in the clubs history. It's amazing how these games were now forgotten and how things turnaround. Players who looked slow and lethargic were now pacy and world-beaters. Supporters who booed their team were now singing from the rooftops.

Willie Manu made the headlines. 'Willie's the Manu', reported one daily.

The bottom of the table at the end of week 13 and with 15 games to go, read:

	P	W	D	L	PTS
Huddersfield	13	5	0	8	10
TIGERS	13	5	0	8	10
Harlequins	13	4	1	8	9
Wakefield	13	4	0	9	8
Catalans	13	3	0	10	6
Wigan	13	2	0	11	4

This was also the week when 'Lost' returned to the small screens. It is a programme that I got into late. Amanda and the girls had watched it from the start. I picked it up when the girls got the first series set of DVD's for Christmas. It is different from anything before and like most things you either like it or you don't. It's an American programme about a group of people stranded on a mysterious island after a plane crash. The first series had ended with a typical cliffhanger and the eagerly awaited first episode of series 2 didn't disappoint. Whether the survivors are rescued before the end of Super League X1 remains to be seen, and whether Lost has the potential to displace my favourite American imports, 'Hill Street Blues', 'Friends', 'NYPD Blue' and the 'West Wing' also remains to be seen.

Like our plight in the Super League and the question of survival, it was too early in the season to tell.

After 93 years, Arsenal FC played their last match at Highbury Stadium. They went out with a bang and a great party. Before the game, supporters were given T-shirts in the club colours. Some wore red whilst others wore white. The red ones sat in certain areas of the ground and the whites sat in other areas to produce a colourful spectacle.

Let's hope the powers that be at Castleford saw this event and kept it in their memory bank for our last game at the Jungle. There was a post match parade of the clubs greatest ever players and the Who's Roger Daltrey blasted out a song called, 'Highbury days'. Who would be singing 'Wheldon Road days' when we have our farewell party?

Leeds United qualified for the play off final after defeating Preston 2–0 in the second leg of the semi final, to win 3–1 on aggregate. They were now only 90 minutes away from a return to the Premiership. There are a lot of loyal United fans who are Tigers fans as well. Leeds would be taking an estimated 40,000 supporters to the final when their attendances have often been around 20,000 this season. Glory supporters?

Of course there will be a lot of people there who will not have been to a game in years. They will wear their colours with pride and sing along like everyone else. Marching on together? Yes, loyal supporters alongside the glory supporters, but at the end of the day, they would be united.

Amanda announced that she was going to be part of a world record attempt. Girl Guides from all over were doing a sleepover for charity. This brought back memories of the T.V series 'Record Breakers' that was fronted by the late Roy Castle along with Ross and Norris McQuirter who were twins I think and who worked for the Guinness Book of Records. Every week there was a world record attempt in the studio and every week Roy would finish the show with the same song:

"If you're the fattest, the thinnest,
if you beat them all,
then you're a record breaker"

Every Christmas I would get a Guinness book of records. I used to memorise the most obscure records and was always on the look-out for a record to break. Blowing up hot water bottles like blowing up a balloon was one I always fancied having a go at, but as a 10-year-old, I could never get the lid off the water bottle!

In my 20 years with the Prison Service there have been many celebrities come and go on fact-finding missions or publicity stunts. I have also come across some celebrities on the wrong side of the bars. When anyone with a hint of fame ends up in custody, the press generally has a field day. The press certainly had a field day in following the progress of Sheffield boxer, Naseem Hamed when he commenced a 15 month prison sentence for dangerous driving. There is the possibility that the 'Prince' will be out before the end of our season, because a 15-month prison sentence doesn't actually mean that. This was a fall into disgrace beyond all recognition. Hamed is one of the greatest boxers this country has ever produced. For him to get to where he got to in his profession he must have made sacrifices and trained harder than anyone. All that was forgotten now as he started a different life. His wealth, championship belts and celebrity status counted for nothing. He was now a number in the system.

The next home game and another win guaranteed. This would see us with 6 wins out of 14 games at the half way point of the season. All we had to do was turn up to beat the Catalans to record our third successive victory.

The result, Tigers 18, Catalans 40. Enough said. We didn't turn up and were soundly beaten.

It was a poor performance and instead of pulling well clear of the drop zone we were once again looking over our shoulders.

The game wasn't memorable at all, but there were a few memorable moments. Brad Davis went off after 17 minutes with a dislocated shoulder. He would be out for up to 8 weeks. It looked like the end of his career. If it was, then what a loss to the game and what a sad way to bid farewell.

Post match, I was anxious to get the Catalans injured captain, Stacey Jones's autograph. Jones is in my top 10 of greatest players I have ever seen. Maybe that's why I had to get one of Sophie's mates, Sam Holmes (Moon) to get the prized signature on the match day programme. Sophie's generation have best friends who are girls and boys. Sam is a lad and another best friend is Chris who is also a lad. It is good of the lads to have names that could be either boys or girls and thinking about it, it was fitting that either Sam or Chris got Stacey's autograph. I have worked with prison officers called Val and Tracey and both had beards at one time or another.

Driving home from the Jungle the mood in the car was subdued after that defeat. That was until we hit a queue of traffic which was being held up by a lone swan walking in the middle of the road. There are not many grounds in the rugby league world when a swan would hold the traffic up. There is generally a good citizen around to do their bit in such circumstances. On this occasion a lady was marshalling the swan back into a nearby field. Unbelievably the swan reacted to the lady when she pointed to the field. It amused everyone and cheered us up albeit temporarily.

The Tigers squad was given a week off.

Their efforts in the first half of the season deserved it. Most thought that their efforts in the Catalans game demanded double training sessions.

The blank weekend was due to the next round of the Challenge Cup being played. Once again the crowds were down with less than 5,000 at Headingley to see the Rhinos play Rochdale. It was the lowest gate at Leeds in the summer era. The Hornets may not have the same pull as some clubs, but where were the other 10,000 Leeds fans on the night? No doubt they will be out in force should their club get to the final.

One final played that weekend was the championship play off between Watford and Leeds United. This gave the Tigers / United fans an opportunity to don their football shirts for United's biggest game since the night Howlers was made an 'alien of France' some 31 years previously. It was estimated that the game was worth £40 million to the winners and it is quite simply the biggest club game in the world. I had the offer of a ticket for the match, but at £65 each, politely declined. Leeds lost 0–3 and in the local paper the following night there were loads of photographs of dejected supporters.

"Dad, there's Max", shouted our Jessica. There in glorious black and white tucked away on page 2 of the Yorkshire Evening Post was Max, more famous for being a Cas fan and for keeping us amused on the coach trip to London.

I wonder how much Max drunk that day in Cardiff?

Leeds now had to contend with another season in the Championship. They did take an estimated 40,000 supporters to Cardiff. How many would be at their first home game when the new season kicked off in August? It is hard to imagine how their supporters must have all felt on the way back home after such a defeat. Not too long ago, Leeds were one of the best teams in Europe. Their fans now had the prospect of going to the not so glamorous surroundings of Colchester and Southend.

That eventful week ended with a new arrival in the family. Nephew, Callum Kirk Torvill arrived as a 6th Grand child for the in laws, almost 18 years after their first, our Jessica was born. Jessica also left 6th form. Her last day at school made me realise that life was ticking by. I remember her first day at school as if it was yesterday. I celebrated my 43rd birthday, if your 43rd birthday is something to celebrate.

With 14 games gone, we were now entering the business end of the season. It is the time when champions are decided and the threat of relegation would loom nearer and nearer for someone as the weeks rolled by. If only we had beaten the Catalans then we would have been 8 points clear of the bottom club with just 14 games to go.

Two weeks later and that defeat was still wrangling. How much of our confidence was shot after that performance? Would we be starting from square 1 again? There was no real time to feel sorry for our situation as a trip to the Warrington Wolves was looming. We had only been to the Halliwell Jones once before. It is a great ground and hopefully when the 'new Jungle' is built, it will look pretty similar. It is not exactly a fortress, but it is a difficult place to go to and win. In Paul Cullen, the Wolves have a young British coach capable of going all the way in the game. His team are inconsistent and can be as bad one week as they were brilliant the week before. We hoped that they would have a bad week and that we would avenge that record 6–64 defeat at the Jungle just 6 weeks previously.

The run in starts here

A Sunday afternoon trip across the M62 is much more pleasant than the Friday night trips and yet another Bank Holiday came around. The Halliwell Jones is a great arena with decent access and excellent from a spectating point of view. I am not sure who or what is Halliwell Jones. If he isn't a legendary Welsh winger from the 50's, then he ought to have been.

There are 2 stands for standing and 2 stands for sitting. I will never understanding why we call stands with seats in, stands.

We occupied a stand behind the goals. The last time we were there, the ground hadn't been open long and there was a bad atmosphere throughout because of the mix of home and away fans in the same area. Don't get me wrong, this is what our game is built around, but on that occasion the good natured bantering was overtaken by verbal abuse from both sides, to leave a bad taste. This time it was different. Once again there was a magnificent away support to do any club proud.

Questions were asked when Warrington brought over Andrew Johns from Newcastle Knights for a few games towards the end of Super League X. Their investment paid off looking at how Lee Briers played in 2006. Briers seems to have been around forever. He is pivotal to everything the Wire do. He had another blinder against us and although we were in the game for a good 20 minutes of the first half, by the interval we were heading for a mauling, going in 6–26 behind. An example of the magic of Lee Briers was a kick out of his own quarter that led to a try under the posts from flying winger, Richie Barnett. A move perfectly executed from the training field. Briers has that half a second that most players can only dream of. John Wolford had it for Hunslet in the late 80's. Iestyn Harris had it at Leeds before he went to rugby union. It is frustrating when you are the opposition because you generally cannot lay a hand on players like that. It is like chasing shadows at times. They are that good.

Would we go under in the second half or come out fighting? Whatever Matterson said at half time worked. We played some good stuff and with 10 minutes to go we were behind 28–40. Another score then and it would have made it really interesting. It wasn't to be however and when Danny Sculthorpe, back after several weeks out injured, threw out a speculative pass, there was our friend Lee Briers accepting the interception. He ran in from 40 yards out to score under the sticks, once again without a finger being laid on him. So it finished 28–46. We won the second half and I suppose we would have settled for an 18-point defeat at the start of the game. It was actually a decent game with some questionable decisions by the referee. I am not one to call the officials, but if there was ever a need to bring in video technology to every game, then here it was.

For one of our tries in the second half, Danny Ward must have ran at least 80 metres leaving Warrington defenders in his wake. He received a standing ovation as he returned to our end. He would though since we were all stood up to start with. Being so close to the pitch means you can make eye contact with the players and 'gee' them up when their heads seem to be down. Amanda certainly did that with Ryan McGoldrick and I did it with Waine Pryce. Pryce and Michael Shenton were magnificent on the day, marshalling Martin Gleeson and Henry Fa'afili. Those two would get in any side in the world. Shenny and Flash I mean.

Towards the end of the game when the Cas faithful were enjoying events like Wardy's run and Gray Vianes crunching tackles, they decided not to give the ball back every time Briers converted a try. This led to great amusement amongst the travelling support. It is not a clever thing to do, but when it leads to the cavalry arriving in the shape of several stewards and supervisors it is very funny to watch. At one point a steward was heard to say, "He's got it, the bloke up there in the orange". There could have been a riot or a streaker and the stewards wouldn't have cared, as long as they got their ball back. Whatever happened to streakers?

As we left the ground the stewards were all 'eagle eyed' looking for the culprits who had kept their balls. It's a wonder they didn't search everyone as we left. Somebody will have got home with a souvenir, no doubt with the inevitable Warrington Wolves written on the side of it.

We came home without the points but with hope for the remainder of the campaign.

On the way home Salford coach Karl Harrison was on local radio saying that he thought we only needed 2 more wins to survive. Let's hope so. We competed well for an hour against Warrington. They have a ground, a club and a team that we should be looking to model ourselves on in the future.

We also heard on the radio that Cheltenham Town had won promotion to Football League Division 1. Their victory at Cardiff was inspired by team captain John Finnigan, from our street.

Results elsewhere that weekend meant that we were now second from bottom of the league. Harlequins went to Salford and won with a priceless last minute drop goal by Henry Paul. That could prove invaluable in the long run.

There was another weekend off and time for the Tigers to do some more recruiting. 22 year old, Adam Fletcher arrived

from the Redcliffe Dolphins from the Queensland Cup competition in Australia. He is of Greek origin, and didn't count on our
overseas quota. It was that time of season when clubs recruit to
either seal trophies or fight off a disaster. We were in the latter
bracket. We were still short of a quality half back with less than
half the season to go, with the name of Danny Brough
mentioned as a possible signing. Brough won the cup with Hull
FC in 2005 and we hoped against hope that the Tigers could
offer him a deal that would see him signing for us before it was
too late.

Any aspirations to be like Warrington soon disappeared on
our weekend off, when they went to Hull KR and lost in the
quarter-finals of the Challenge Cup. One TV commentator
described Rovers ground as a picturesque. I am not sure about
that, but one thing was for certain, that Rovers deserved their
victory and a semi-final shot at the Saints. Leeds came through
against Harlequins in front of another poor crowd at Headingley. Their reward was a semi against the Giants. No surprises
with the draw then and it was all set up for a Saints, Rhinos final.
Call me cynical but not for the first time you could have put a
years wages on the outcome of the draw. It would have pleased
the majority of the rugby league public to see Huddersfield and
Hull KR drawn together with Leeds drawing St Helens.

'A desire to achieve.....'

When I was growing up, dandelion and burdock was always sold in small bottles in the fish and chip shop. As kids, we were never allowed to have bottles of pop from the chippy. "You can wait till you get home for a drink, there's plenty of water in the tap". I am glad to say that I have instilled the same philosophy with our 2 girls, only this time it's with bread cakes, which are sold in chip shops at an exorbitant price.

When the world club champions, the Bradford Bulls came to town, it was a red-hot day in the middle of June and week 15 of the competition. The match was sponsored by dandelion and burdock. The Bulls had quality throughout, although their season had been a stop-start affair has they adjusted to life without Brian Noble. They were now under the leadership of Steve McNamara.

The D&B was flowing before the kick off with supporters obviously aware that throughout a game in stifling conditions you are liable to lose up to 10lbs in weight. So chips, ice cream and several bottles of fizzy pop were just what the doctor ordered.

The football World Cup had begun and the country had gone mad with flags flying from literally everywhere. Nothing that happened during the duration of that competition will match up to events at the Jungle that afternoon.

Amanda and Naomi were away on a camping weekend, but kept in touch over the mobiles. I also had a word with my long time friend, best man and Bulls supporter, Russ Hanwell, who turned up in a Newcastle Knights polo shirt. Russ has never worn his club colours to any match. It was interesting to hear him say that he wouldn't mind if they lost this one, if it helped send Wigan down.

The Claws danced in their new outfits. Sophie had been modeling hers all week and couldn't wait for match day to come around. I may be biased but Claws are the best dance outfit in Super League by a country mile.

Within 5 minutes of the kick off we were behind 0–12. A typical Tigers start with a hint of a couple of dubious refereeing decisions. The crowd sang, "12–0 to the referee". We were like rabbits in the headlights again and against the world champions we already feared the worst. The energy we had after a zillion bottles of D&B was wearing off and it looked like another home drubbing. However, there was something special in the air that day and what followed was one of the greatest games of any season.

Ex Tiger Andy Lynch was off loading the ball at will and looked everything like a Great Britain prospect. With the quality of Hape, Vainikolo, Deacon, Fielden and the rest, the Bulls are capable of hammering any side on their day.

We lost Deon Bird early on with what turned out to be a serious shoulder injury. This meant that new signing Adam Fletcher was soon in the thick of it. It also meant that we played the majority of the game with only 16 players in the hottest temperatures imaginable. Innovation in our game has been mentioned before and it was pleasing to see that both coaches had agreed with the officials that there would be a 'time out' after 20 minutes of each half to allow the players to get some fluids on board. The game is hard enough without risking illness due to dehydration.

The Tigers response to falling behind was magnificent. Had they been drinking D&B for rehydration purposes?

Our defence muscled up and kept the champions out for almost an hour. In between times we had crossed for 4 tries to lead 20–12. A shock result was in the offing. The Bulls were not champions for nothing and inspired by Terry Newton they went back in front after scoring 3 quick tries. It looked like game over for us at 20–26.

Had we once again snatched defeat from the jaws of victory? Our players had given everything and a bit more. Some had run their blood to water. The support had been in good voice throughout. We deserved something and we were going to get nothing.

From nowhere Andy Henderson, who had had a fantastic game in outplaying his younger brother Ian, made a half break and a few moments later, the impressive Michael Shenton powered over in the Willie Manu corner for a 4 pointer. We were scoring some vital tries in that corner of the ground and luckily for us, it was in our corner. That try made it 24–26. Our goal kicking for several seasons had been poor. We hadn't had a regular kicker and throughout almost every game we seem to have had 2 or 3 people having a go. The responsibility of taking this shot at goal fell to substitute forward, Craig Huby. Chubs never dwelt on the kick. He just placed the ball down and did his usual routine. If he missed, then we had done well to keep the Bulls to 24–26.

After 80 minutes in the intense heat, Huby stroked the ball between the uprights. The team and the crowd went berserk. It was 26–26. The Bulls kicked off and the hooter sounded. We reacted as though we had won the Grand Final. It was a great game, played in a great spirit between 2 highly committed teams. The Bulls were applauded all the way down the tunnel. The Tigers were cheered for what seemed like ages afterwards. They had achieved something special here and quite rightly lapped it up to the max. We all did. That point gained took us into the next game with a renewed confidence. If we had lost, then the next game at home to the Huddersfield Giants would have been win or bust.

To round off a great weekend, results elsewhere couldn't have gone any better. The Wigan Warriors were taken to the cleaners at Headingley and the Wakefield Wildcats lost at home to the Salford Reds. We were now 7 points clear of Wigan and 1 point better off than both the Catalans and Wakefield. The calculators were out and it wouldn't be long before we were safe from relegation and planning for life in Super League X11, in 2007.

At half time during the Bulls game, the local constabulary was handing out pen pictures of the players with messages about bullying and general safety issues on the back.

On the back of Craig Huby's card it read, '**Desire.** A desire to achieve will put you at the top of your game!'

I doubt whether Huby had even seen these cards, but his heroics that day at the Jungle, said it all.

Always gallant in defeat, although they had actually drawn, Russ Hanwell sent a text message to say that it was a fair result and he hoped it sent Wigan down.

Nothing about how well we had played and how he hoped it meant we stayed up, but that's rugby league fans for you.

'We're certain, nothings certain'

The best football anthem ever, 'Three Lions' was back in the charts. It was written by comic duo Baddiel and Skinner with music by Ian Broudie, the lead man from the Lightning Seeds.

There is a chorus in the Lightning Seeds 1992 song, 'The life of Riley', that summed up the season so far. There were that many uncertainties that nothing was certain.

"It's your life,
We'll find a way
We're sailing blind,
We're certain, nothings certain"

The draw against the world champions was just the boost the club needed going into the next game at home against the Huddersfield Giants. This was another quirk to the fixtures in that Fartown were back in town again before we had played them away. The rumour mill had been working overtime with the suggestion that the Tigers were about to get their man and to finally have a quality half-back. That man was Danny Brough from Hull F.C. Brough had been unlucky not to win the Lance Todd trophy in the 2005 Challenge Cup final, when Hull defeated the Rhinos. It was less than a year ago, but it seemed that he was another one out of favour with the new coaching set up at the KC.

When Brough arrived he had just 3 training sessions before

the Huddersfield game. He also joined a growing list of Dannys, with Scully, Nutley and Ward already in the ranks.

'Team full of Dannys,
We're just a team full of Dannys', wasn't good enough to get into the charts, but it did provide us with another song to sing.

From now until the end of the season, every weekend was going to be a big one. The majority of supporters across the country were fascinated by the situation at the foot of the table. The bottom spot was going to one of the bottom 6, or 5 taking the French out of the equation.

Huddersfield at home was a game we needed to win and in the end it was a game we won comfortably, 32–14. In a defensive effort of Herculean proportion, we kept the Giants scoreless in the second half. It goes without saying that the new man always wins the man of the match award. On the day 'Danny, Danny Brough' (sang to 'Daddy, daddy cool') showed what we had been missing all season. A sound kicking game and the ability to take us around the park and get better performances out of others.

This was a priceless 2 points, with both Wigan and Wakefield also winning. The Wildcats success was by one point at Warrington, which was one of the surprise results of the year.

Wigan won a poor game at home to the Catalans. The match was on Sky and at half time the Warriors owner was interviewed about his clubs plight and about an article that had appeared in the Sunday papers. It was suggested that Wigan would basically 'buy off' the team promoted from National League One in order to preserve their own Super League status if they finished 12th. Dave Whelan said that if Wigan finished bottom, then they would deserve to go down, would go down and come back bigger and stronger. It was a great interview but gave you the feeling that they were not going to lie down without a fight.

At the end of round 17, Wigan were still 6 points adrift of Wakefield and 7 points adrift of the Tigers.

Next and for the only time in the season we headed east, for a Friday night appointment at the KC stadium to play Hull FC. It is another quirk when a player leaves a club that he always seems to go back to that club with his new team straight away. The same thing happens with the coaches. The KC is, in my opinion the best rugby league stadium in the country. A few years earlier we had been drawn away at Hull in the cup. That Sunday morning I had gone out for a run and then decided to wash the car. As I reached down for the sponge from the bucket, my back went. I had to crawl into the house on all fours much to the amusement of everyone. I wasn't going to miss the game though and Amanda drove, with me clinging on to ease the pain and discomfort. It must have taken me half an hour to walk the short distance from the car park to the ground and I was in agony throughout. We got nilled on the day and exited the cup without a whimper. I think I made up for it by whimpering all the way there and all the way home.

On this occasion, we traveled to Hull with a renewed confidence. In fact it wasn't a renewed confidence. It was just confidence, although we couldn't have played Hull at a worse time. They had won their last 9 league games under new coach Peter Sharp. Former coach John Kear had been forgotten. A victory against the Tigers would have given them a record breaking 10 straight wins.

The prospect of winning at the KC had been over shadowed by the extra ordinary events at Wigan during the week. The Warriors had signed Stuart Fielden from the Bulls. Fielden had been the best forward in the country for years. He was the first name down on the teamsheet for Bradford and Great Britain. The trophy cabinet at Odsal was never empty.

"Gutted", was how my old mate Russ Hanwell described the news. We were also gutted. This was a marker being put down by the Warriors to say that they may have only won 3 games out of the first 18, but that they intended to win the remaining 10, to avoid relegation.

If we felt that we had got our man in Danny Brough, what must the Wigan fans have thought when coach Brian Noble secured the services of one of his former charges?

Everything about the deal gave me cause for concern. Why would the world champions sell their best player mid way through a season? Why would Fielden go to a team languishing at the foot of the table and with the threat of relegation hanging over them? Where did Wigan get the reported £450,000 transfer fee? And whatever happened to the salary cap?

To compare a similar deal is difficult. Sunderland struggled all season to avoid relegation from football's Premiership in 2005/06. To avoid relegation with a dozen games to go, they paid Manchester United £50 million for the services of Wayne Rooney. That would never happen, so how come it happened in our game?

Everything about the deal gave me cause for concern.

Not surprisingly, Wigan backed up their victory against the Catalans with a comfortable home win against the Wolves and not surprisingly, Fielden was named man of the match. Kris Radlinski had also come out of retirement to play for Wigan for free. If that was the case then credit to him. Putting your long term well being on the line for a club you love deserved a knighthood. Was this the start of their great escape?

On the night at the KC, we never played well enough to get close to Hull. We played well in patches and our defence was awesome at times. Hull are a top 3 team and a few weeks earlier we would have settled for conceding anything less than 50. It was a sign of our teams recent form that we fancied going to the East Coast and ending their winning streak.

We started well enough and scored after 16 seconds when Hull fumbled a towering Danny Brough kick off. A charging Danny Nutley collected the spills and Andy Henderson dived over from short range from the play the ball. A great start, but we never threatened to score again for long periods. At half time we were behind 6–18 and we went on to lose 10–28. Pride in defeat nonetheless, but for the very first time, I had the feeling that Wigan would survive, but not necessarily by catching us. We were down near the foot of the table and it was going to be a tortuous run in. 10 games to go, but still 5 points in front of the Warriors.

Over at Odsal, Russ texted to say that Terry Newton was not in the Bulls squad as they entertained the Giants. Was he to be the next big money transfer to Wigan?

We were well into summer by now and Fleeceman had long since discarded his winter wears. He did us proud at the KC by being the only Cas fan in the stadium to join in when the Mexican wave got going.

There is the option of taking a picnic with you when you go on the longer jaunts such as Kippax to Hull. I think it is about 53 miles door-to-door. One family sat near us in at the KC are now known as the 'smelly egg family'. Bringing stink bomb flavoured sandwiches into the ground is an arrestable offence. They smelt lousy and caused our eyes to water at one point. Thinking about it, the smell of rotten eggs could have been the reason for Fleeceman jumping out of his seat and waving his arms around like a mad man, whilst yelling, "Wayyyy".

Next on the fixture list was another home game against

Warrington, who hadn't won for ages. If ever there was a chance to gain revenge for 2 heavy defeats then this was it.

Before this game however there was the small matter of our Jessica's 18th birthday and another midweek jaunt across the M62, heading west this time.

"My ball"

The football World Cup was now at the quarter-final stage and England were surviving if not convincing. I never got into the tournament citing the fact that all of the 32 nations involved had players you see week in and week out in our Premiership. In previous competitions you saw players you had heard and read about, but had never actually seen play. Teams like Ghana and the Ivory Coast both had players that were household names and few of the players actually played in their own countries. I remember when Zaire played in the 1974 World Cup in Germany there was innocence about them.

The St George flags were still flying from cars and houses.

I think it is a sign of how well you have brought your children up when on her 18th birthday Jess asked if we could go to the Great Britain v New Zealand test match at Knowsley Road, St Helens.

We were back on the M62 again, and just 4 days after the KC on the east coast, we were heading for the west coast. Rough calculations suggest a 300 mile round trip every time Hull play in that part of the country. They are loyal supporters.

The British squad had a strong Saints influence. The game was arranged to get our boys together before heading off down under at the end of the season for the 2006 Tri Nations. The Kiwi squad was built around their best British placed players.

The marketing men got it wrong big style. The poster that said *'Stuart Fielden against Lesley Vainikolo. Same clubs. Different sides'* was a couple of weeks out of date, unless they knew something we didn't and big Les was on his way to the JJB.

Amanda was also puzzled as to why Saint Jamie Lyon wasn't selected for Great Britain until I informed her that it was because he was Australian.

Going to a ground like Knowsley Road and not supporting your club team is interesting in that you can stand where you wouldn't normally stand. We headed for the touchline stand near to the dug outs and had a great view. We were stood amongst a large Saints contingent and one chap in particular impressed us with his industry. He was one of those supporters who had been going for years and had been standing in the same spot forever. Not wanting to carry jackets etc, he decided to bring some coat hooks with him one week and fix them in a strategic position that allowed him to hang up excess clobber. Not just 1 hook, but 5, enough for all of his mates. Just like being at home and Knowsley Road was obviously their second home.

The match itself was a bit of an anti climax. The home pack was too strong and dictated from the off, allowing Cunningham and Long the time and space to run the show. We did at last see Stacey Jones play, but his team was never at the races and went down to a 14–46 defeat. The game was nothing like the Tri Nations encounter at Loftus Road 8 months earlier. It had an air of a pre season friendly about it although it was interesting to hear the reaction every time Stuart Fielden touched the ball. There was a hint that his move to Wigan hadn't been universally approved of by the Saints supporters.

It's difficult to get into a game when none of your own team is playing. New Zealand had Hull's ex Tiger Motu Tony, but he didn't really count.

3 of us all had our Tigers colours on. Sophie had borrowed a Great Britain shirt for the match. As we made our way to the

exit as the final whistle blew we were greeted by, "Have a safe trip home", "Good luck for the rest of the season" and "I hope you stay up". We all said thank you and left St Helens with a real feel good factor. We reciprocated with, "I hope you beat the Rhinos in the Cup final", which was a bit tongue in cheek since the semi finals hadn't been played yet.

One lasting memory about the test match was the extraordinary effort by yours truly to catch a Sean Long penalty kick to touch. As soon as it left his left boot I thought, "that is mine". It came spiraling down out of the night sky heading straight for me. As Amanda and the girls ducked for cover, I went for it and launched myself what felt like 25 feet up in the air. It was all to no avail as I unforgivably knocked on much to the delight of everyone around us. My fingers were still stinging when I got back to the car and I blamed the St Helens floodlights for me spilling the ball.

As for Jess, well I think she had an 18th birthday to remember. In the local evening paper we put a personal greeting which said, 'A desire to achieve will put you at the top of your game' along with the Tigers motif. Her favourite present? A framed Tigers shirt signed by the 2006 squad with a message from Andy Henderson. I suspect that this will go with her as she heads for university and with her wherever she ends up after that.

10 to go

The bottom of the table had taken shape and the team to finish bottom in 10 games time would be one of the bottom 6.

The Tigers points difference was considerably worst than all of those around us. If we were going to win games we would have to score plenty of points, because we were always likely to concede plenty.

The bottom of the table at the end of week 18 and with 10 games to go, read:

	P	W	D	L	Diff	PTS
Huddersfield	18	7	0	11	−84	14
Harlequins	18	6	1	11	−239	13
TIGERS	18	6	1	11	−257	13
Wakefield	18	6	0	12	−98	12
Catalans	18	6	0	12	−143	12
Wigan	18	4	0	14	−182	8

Every game was a must win for all of the sides at the bottom. Newspapers were beginning to print the fixtures left and then speculate who would be relegated. The bookmakers had Wigan surviving now that Fielden was on board. Some reporters also suggested that Wigan would win all of their last 10 games to force their way into the play-offs. If they won 10 on the trot, they would deserve to win the Grand Final. Winning 10 on the trot would be nigh on impossible after winning only 4 out of their first 18 games.

I had the opportunity of spending some time at the Jungle prior to the week 19 game at home to the Wolves. If you think that this game is just about turning up every Sunday for 80 minutes of rugby, then think again. What goes on behind the scenes at a top rugby league clubs is a real eye opener.

In years gone by, teams had their opponents watched before a vital game, in an attempt to find out who the key players were and what sort of moves they had up their sleeves. Nowadays it is slightly different in that clubs invest in I.T. If you thought that I-pods were difficult to operate, you should take a look at the Opta statistics and software package that accompanies it. Staff at the Jungle are able to analyse not only the individual Tigers performances, but also those of their opponents. In the build up to the Wolves game, they were targeting players to run at in the defensive line and looking at the positions Lee Briers likes to take before kicking. If our staff were looking at things like that then there was nothing surer than somebody at Warrington would be doing the exact same job. It is like chess. It is modern sports science, but cheaper and more effective than employing a coach with a function to go and watch a game and then to report back.

Behind the scenes is a workforce who prepares the ground for us all to occupy every other week. I always think how demoralizing it must me to see the ground after a game with the divots out of the pitch and the litter blowing all over the place.

Staff work in the community encouraging youngsters to be part of the sport. Meeting a player at School has a lasting impression on children.

There are staff who prepare meals for the players after train-ing. Ben Roarty told me that he would like to stay for lunch. I said, "No worries", but didn't have a clue what he was on about, just like he didn't have a clue who I was. I soon disappeared in case there was no lunch for him.

These are all roles that go on day in and day out. Throughout the length and breadth of the country similar roles will be performed by people with similar roles within their own clubs. The majority of us just turn up, pay our money, support the team and go home again. Castleford Tigers is a business. Super League is a business.

In week 10, the Wire had handed us a record 6–64 home defeat and in week 15 we travelled to the Halliwell Jones and lost 28–46.

Two games with the aggregate score of 34–110.

After recent and improved performances, confidence in the camp was extremely high and we all thought that this would be a 'great game to win'. Since defeating us 5 weeks earlier, the Wolves had lost 4 in a row. It was revenge time and time to set out our stall for the run in.

Sophie had been over excited all week. It was her turn to be the featured Claw in the match day programme. She looked a knockout, not on page 3, but on page 38, declaring in her write up that her hobbies were dancing, socializing and going to the gym with her dad. I love Sophie with all my heart, but her favourite part of going to the gym is looking at herself in the mirrors.

This game took place on 'orange day'. We didn't parade as the name suggests, but we were encouraged to wear anything and everything orange in front of the Sky cameras. The match had been switched from a Saturday teatime kick-off to the unusual time of 1230 hours on a Sunday. For a change it was not for the benefit of television, but because Jessica was having her 18th birthday party on the Saturday night. That was really thoughtful of Sky to accommodate us. England were also playing in their World Cup quarter final against Portugal on the

Saturday. Not for the first time, our football team choked once again and went out on penalties. Time to take the St George flags down. There were no tears in our house and 'three lions' wouldn't be heard for a few more years.

The measures of success at a party are usually how late people stay and how drunk they are when they leave. On this occasion, our Jess had invited her friends around and we had invited close family and some of our friends to celebrate her coming of age. This is the generation of boys and girls all being mates. They mixed together as one, with the party looking like the Kippax equivalent of 'The O.C', a popular teenage style soap that follows the lives of young adults in California. All the young and beautiful residents of Kippax were in our back garden that night. They were joined by some girls as well. The measures of success? How many breakages there were, how much was spilt and what level of bad language was used. There were no breakages, minimal spillages and just one naughty word that followed one of the spillages.

Football manager, Mick 'Robbo' Robinson sported a bright orange hair do for the Warrington game. I bet Robbo never imagined having orange hair at any point in his life let alone live on Sky TV.

Mick 'memorabilia man' Wormald, came down to the ground early to take some photographs. He was in his element as we were allowed access to the changing rooms and behind the scenes. Although they are far from luxurious, the changing rooms at the Jungle have an aura about them when they are empty, apart from the shirts hanging on the pegs. Some of the greatest players in the games history have been in those dressing rooms.

When you arrive early on match day you see exactly what

goes on behind the scenes. Everything is planned with military precision. The groundstaff are working on the pitch and the fast food caterers are preparing the food. It's a good job they were there early, as Warrington's injured troops were straight in the queue for a burger before the fit ones were even in the changing rooms.

Mark Gleeson was sporting an unusual contraption on a hand injury, but it didn't stop him walloping a burger down in record time.

On the day we were magnificent. Quickly out of the blocks we roared into a 16–0 lead before Warrington had touched the ball. We were never going to lose that one. 28–14 up at half time and tackling everything that moved. If we had played like that all season then we would be in the top 4 never mind bottom 6. We continued to pile on the misery in the second stanza, to record a memorable 52–26 victory. It was as convincing as it sounds and although revenge was never on the agenda, I bet it was a sweet victory for the boys who had been mauled in the previous 2 encounters.

At one point in the second half we were reduced to 10 men after Handforth was sin binned by referee Ganson for holding down. Gray Viane followed after putting Ben Westwood on his backside. Another song was created,

"Viane knocked Westwood out, Viane knocked Westwood out", to the tune of "Go west" by the Pet Shop boys.

The fighting didn't stop there. Ryan McGoldrick was shown a red card after an altercation with Paul Wood. It was what would be described as an old fashion punch up. Hand bags really, but sending both of them off calmed proceedings.

Our unsung heroes were magnificent. Our game winners were magnificent. The support and occasion were magnificent.

In a brief moment of madness, I persuaded my lot to stay put at half time and we watched the second half in the Wheldon Road end alongside the smaller than usual travelling support.

They had a go at Waine Pryce at one point for having a pineapple on his head. That wasn't nice. Their hostility towards the Tigers and match officials soon turned to hostility against their own team. One elderly Warrington fan summed it up nicely on the day when he said, "You deserved what you got, that Brough is a right player"

That was praise coming from a supporter that watches Lee Briers week in and week out.

We now had 15 points. Nobody had ever been relegated with 15 points and we were heading back to London, knowing that 1 more win would make us safe from the drop.

The club remained positive and players were signing contracts for 2007 and beyond. We were back and we were staying up.

"Do it for Prycey"

One character I have not mentioned so far in this book is the wife of my best mate Nick Astle, Lynn Astle. Lynn is one of the funniest people imaginable. Like Astley, Lynn hails from the North east and still slings in the odd "Whii eye man" just to prove that despite 20 odd years in West Yorkshire she is still very much a magpie. Lynn can eat for England and thinks nothing of getting up in the middle of the night for a snack of something like beans on toast. Most people like food, Lynn loves food.

We were once in York enjoying a picnic on the banks of the River Ouse when the rest of the party saw a St Bernard dog approaching. We all sat up to shoo it away, but Lynn was completely oblivious to its presence. As it got nearer, it had obviously seen the delights laid out on the picnic rug because its mouth was watering. As it got besides Lynn, it shook its head and what looked like 2 pints of slaver landed on the poor girl. Even that didn't put her off finishing what she was eating.

She loves food, hates flying and loves having a good time.

Lynn has the knack, after a couple of lagers, of calling people by the wrong name. She once described herself as looking like Andrea Undress when she was walking out of the sea on holiday. She actually thought that she looked like Ursula Andress from the Bond film, Dr. No.

Lynn has the worst technique known to man when ten pin bowling. She once launched her ball backwards towards the spectators. It had people diving for cover.

Lynn went to the Jungle just the once. She didn't like it.

One of the best nights we have ever had with the Astles was when we hosted a murder mystery night. These nights are a good laugh and an opportunity to get dressed up into character and play the game whilst consuming vast amounts of alcohol.

One of the 8 guests is the murderer and the game is about trying to guess who it is. Within 2 minutes of the game commencing, everyone knew that Lynn was the culprit because she couldn't keep her face straight. On this occasion, Astley was Rod Plant the gardener and the victim was a make believe chap called John Dosh. Everytime John Dosh's name was mentioned we had a rule that you had to finish whatever drink you had in front of you.

By the end of the evening, the gardener, still wearing his flat cap and wellies, was plastered. The following morning, Astley couldn't understand why he was still wearing his gardening gear. I had to put him into our bed and he never moved an inch all night to the point that his flat cap was still perched on the top of his head when he got up.

On another occasion, Astley played a randy vicar. Being part of the clergy came in handy when he went to collect the supper from our local pizza shop. If you ever want to negotiate a massive discount at a take away, then take a vicar with you.

Sister in law, Helen was 'Helen Melons' the buxom wench that night. She has always supported winners like Steve Davis at snooker when nobody else could stand him. I guess she was always going to become a Leeds Rhinos fan at some point. Luckily for me she couldn't make the Rhinos week 20 clash at home to Bradford. The match was a sell out and I always thought that Cas fans hated Leeds more than anybody until that night at Headingley. I stood with best man Russ and enjoyed every minute as the Bulls went in 18–4 up at half time. The Bulls fans were in great voice for the first 79 $^1/_2$ minutes. The last 30 seconds, when Rob Burrow converted a Scott Donald try from the touchline, probably spoilt their evening. The Rhinos triumphed 26–24.

The Bulls fans called Jamie Peacock a 'Judas'. The Rhinos fans called Iestyn Harris a 'Judas'. I wasn't sure what to make of the Rhinos new signing Jamie Thackray parading around in his new colours at half time. Thackray started his career at Hunslet and also had a spell with the Tigers.

That game took place on the Friday night. The day after we were at the Jungle boarding one of 6 coaches heading south to the Twickenham Stoop.

Would Max be on board or would he still be sobering up after the mammoth drinking session the last time we were in the capital? Alas he wasn't on our coach this time, but rest assured there is always an incident to keep you smiling on this mind numbingly boring trip. One young lad at the back of our bus was desperate to pay a call. "Can you stop the bus? I need a piss", he asked. Bearing in mind that we were on the M25 and already racing to be there for kick-off, he had no chance.

He even resorted to a pathetic, "pleeeeease, I need a weeeeee", which caused great amusement, but still got him nowhere.

I never got into that game against the Quins. We were late getting in and it all felt rushed. There was a great support that day but there was a sense as soon as we conceded our first try that we were not at the races. Like the Rhinos the previous night, we trailed 4–18 at half time. Although we did threaten a come back but it never materialised and we eventually lost 16–24. No last minute try and touchline conversion to win this one.

When Waine Pryce went down under a heavy challenge,

MARK HUDSON

"There's only one Waine Pryce,
There's only one Waine Pryce,
He used to be shite, but now he's alright,
Walking in a Prycey wonderland"

echoed around our end of the stadium as Flash was stretchered
off with what looked straight away like a serious leg injury. It
turned out to be an injury that brought an early end to his
season.

It is also one of the worst songs ever, competing for that title
with our 2005 classic, 'There's only 2 Watenes' sung to the same
tune of 'Winter wonderland'
"There's only 2 Watenes,
There's only 2 Watenes,
Walking along, singing a song.
Walking in Watene wonderland"

The singing continued with "Win it for Prycey". We didn't
and after Wigans victory against Wakefield, we were back in the
relegation dogfight. Wigan had now won 4 on the trot and were
off the bottom of the table.

With just 8 games to go, only 3 points separated the bottom
6. If it was tight before, it was even tighter after round 20.

It took 4 $\frac{1}{2}$ hours to get home, and I sulked for 4 $\frac{1}{2}$ hours.
The bus was quiet all the way back to the Jungle. I vowed never
to travel to London that way ever again. At least the lad with the
weak bladder did the noble thing and collected for the driver.

Just 6 days earlier we were celebrating one of our greatest
days after sticking 50 points on Warrington, but we now looked
like a team with the threat of relegation hanging over us once
again. As a family we were gutted. The trip cost well over £100,
but who cared? It was all about the 2 points. Our Jess was now

MARK HUDSON

in Ibiza with her mates, but she was straight on the phone to find out how we had got on.

This was her first trip away with her mates. She was all set to go to University and was also taking driving lessons. When your eldest is doing all of these, you know you are getting old. She had asked me to take her out driving, but the insurance premiums were far too expensive. I think I also had it in the back of my mind the time my dad took me out when I was 18. I crashed his brand new Lada. It was the first new car he had ever had. He got out and chased me down the road. I think I would have done the exact same thing.

That day finished with one of the loyalist servants to the club in a London Hospital with what could have been a career threatening injury. Waine Pryce is a professional rugby league player. Who were we to sulk when Pryce's career was on the line?

Italy duly won footballs World Cup, but with England's involvement a distant memory and not many people cared.

Next up, it was the Leeds Rhinos at home. If the Tigers couldn't get up for that game, they couldn't get up for any.

241

Rhinos derby woe

Flip-flops are an essential piece of warm weather footwear. It amuses me to see grown men wearing them at the rugby. Long gone are what we used to call 'J.C's', which stood for Jesus creepers. They were a sort of leather, open toed sandal that dads used to wear on their holidays, whilst still sporting a pair of white socks. I have threatened on a couple of occasions to wear socks with my flip-flops but I don't think the girls would ever speak to me again if I did it in public.

Flying winger Adam Fletcher had been spotted cycling down Wheldon Road wearing a pair of flip-flops. That is quality because walking in them is difficult enough.

In week 4, the Rhinos had handed us a record 14–66 away defeat and in week 11, we were on the end of a 6–42 reversal.

Two games with the aggregate score of 20–108

Similar to the 2 fixtures against the Wolves, it was payback time.

It was a long week leading up to the Rhinos game at the Jungle. We were still sulking after the disappointing journey to London. Victory against the Quins would have more than likely made us safe, but instead we were well beaten and back in the relegation dogfight. It looked like a damage limitation exercise against the Rhinos, who were a side sitting comfortably in second place in the table. Points difference might prove vital at the end of the season, so we if we were going to lose then we couldn't afford to lose by many.

Along with my dad and our Jess, we were the first spectators into the Jungle on a boiling hot mid July Sunday afternoon. The senior academy match was the prelude to the big one. Whatever happened we would always be able tell our grandchildren about the day "we were the first ones in the ground". In fact my dad could have told his eldest grand daughter there and then, but I never heard him say it.

The first 3 in out of a bumper crowd of 11,016, easily surpassing the opening night attendance against Hull F.C by almost a 1,000.

To their credit the 'public library branch' of the Rhinos supporters club traveled in numbers. Once again they were polite enough to remain silent throughout what turned out to be one of the greatest games of the Super League era.

Without inspirational skipper Kevin Sinfield, Leeds looked a different side. They still had enough quality across the park and with McGuire and Burrow in the ranks, they are a team that can strike from anywhere on the pitch.

They struck in no time at all. Burrow scampered over under the sticks and converted to make it 0–6. We had Rhino season ticket holder, sister in law Helen, stood with us in the Wheldon Road end. Helen changes colours when it suits and lo and behold, she was supporting the Tigers that day. She also hinted that the South Stand was nothing compared to the atmosphere at the Jungle. For that I do give her some credit, but after cheering the Rhinos on all season, how could she support the opposition for this 1 match?

The Tigers wore a one off kit for the occasion to commemorate the 80th anniversary of the Castleford club. The club could retire the shirt in the safe knowledge that it was worn in a classic match that produced some magical moments.

When Danny Ward sprinted his way over for our first try,

the immortal "Ee dunt go that far on 'is 'olidays" commentary was heard when BBC TV's 'Look North' showed brief highlights. Unsung hero, Adam Fletcher flew in at the corner to make it 10–6 and we never looked like losing.

I never doubted for one minute that we wouldn't beat the Rhinos. Others around me were on tenterhooks for the full 80 minutes. To a man, we were quite brilliant on the day. As bad as we were the week before in London, we were magnificent on this occasion.

When Danny Brough landed a drop goal in the second half, we never thought that in the end that 1 pointer would be decisive. This game went down to the wire. Adam Fletcher scored again on the 77th minute, with Brough converting to make it 31–24. There was still time for more excitement, when Rhinos hooker Shane Millard scored under the posts for Burrow to convert. 31–30 with seconds to go. All that was needed was a decent kick off by Danny Brough, a sold defensive effort and the spoils were ours.

Brough's restarts are a coach's dream. The hapless Ryan Bailey had earlier watched one kick off bounce majestically over his head. That made Amanda's day. I am sure she would have gone home happy at that point.

There was still time for an attempted McGuire drop goal to level the scores, but it was a daisy cutter and sailed harmlessly over the dead ball line. A couple of tackles later and the hooter went. Wayne, the Tigers entertaining 'MC' was heard to say, "here it comes Tigers fans" as the hooter was about to sound.

That was that, 31–30 and time for the Tigers fans to celebrate. The Rhinos fans in the Railway End demonstrated their appreciation of their teams performance by launching all sorts of debris onto the pitch. When we were on the end of that 6–42 defeat at Headingley, we sang as though we had won the Grand Final.

The result didn't balance up the aggregate score over 3 matches, but it was a very sweet victory. Any thoughts of that postponed game at Headingley in March were a distant memory. This was one of our greatest victories and testament to how far Terry Matterson had brought this group of players. A year ago, that very weekend, the Tigers lost to Hull K.R in the Northern Rail Cup final at Blackpool. There were just 5 survivors from that squad.

At the end of the day it was just another 2 points, but everyone knew it meant more than that. We had bragging rights for a while at work and school and the Tigers car flags flew with pride for several days. The placards for the Yorkshire Evening Post read 'Rhinos derby woe'. No mention of any credit to the Tigers for their outstanding effort. Post match Matterson said that his team loved playing in the hot weather at the Jungle.

The supporters who wore the 'one off' shirt will no doubt wear it again to add to the catalogue of colours that makes the Jungle a special place to be on a day like that. Fleeceman had another shirt to tally up.

Leeds are a great club but certain things they do border on arrogance. Weeks before their Challenge Cup semi final against the Giants, Leeds fans were invited to express their interest in cup final tickets. I guess the club would say that this was done to avoid large queues should they actually win the semi. The majority would say that it is really taking the biscuit.

Wigan defeated Salford to record their 5th successive victory.

We didn't care.

The bottom of the table at the end of week 21 and with just 7 games to go, read:

	P	W	D	L	Diff	PTS
TIGERS	21	8	1	12	−238	17
Huddersfield	21	8	0	13	−104	16
Harlequins	21	7	1	13	−239	15
Wigan	21	7	0	14	−154	14
Wakefield	21	6	0	15	−138	12
Catalans	21	6	0	15	−191	12

Wakefield fell into the relegation spot, which resulted in coach Tony Smith departing, by what is commonly known as 'mutual consent'. I always wonder how that conversation goes when a coach leaves in those circumstances.

"Do you think I should go?" asks the coach.

"I am not sure", says the Chief Executive, "What do you want to do?"

"I will go if you want me to", replies the coach

"Well, if that's what you want" etc, etc.

However the conversation at Belle Vue went, 'Casper' was unemployed, becoming the 3rd coaching casualty of the season.

We didn't care.

No doubt the new man coming in would inspire the same set of players to a win in his first game in charge. That always happens regardless of the sport and it makes you think, why they couldn't perform like that all season.

In the space of one week we had experienced the very reason for writing this book. To support is to follow through thick and thin, through good times and bad. The euphoria at beating Leeds and a wanting for the day not to end had replaced the disappointment and disillusionment from the London trip.

All we wanted to do was to read the reports on teletext, get tomorrows papers and flaunt our 2 points in the Rhinos faces. On the car park, I even had time for a tongue in cheek, "Good luck for the future" to Leeds departing centre Chev Walker who was heading off to Bath to play rugby union.

Walking away from the Jungle we had the pleasure of waving the Rhinos team bus off down Wheldon Road.

The 17 players were received as heroes. These were the same 17 men who I hadn't even bothered to applaud from the pitch after their efforts just 8 days earlier in London.

Was I has fickle as the rest?

This was the pinnacle and survival in the Super League was almost assured. There was even talk about Terry Matterson winning the coach of the year award for steering us to safety and the outside possibility that the Tigers would sneak into the top 6 and end of season play-offs.

My dad has always had the knack of bumping into people he knows in the most unlikeliest of places. He sees people he went to school with and ex work colleagues everywhere he goes. It was Amanda's turn at the Rhinos game. One of my first trips to Castleford from Belle Isle was in 1981, when it seemed to take ages to get there on the 2 bus journey. I had just started going out with Amanda when she was the chief Bridesmaid at a wedding for a friend from work. I was invited to the evening reception in Glasshoughton. I must have set off at about 4 o' clock to get there for 8. It would have been quicker walking. Amanda had not seen the girl she had been a bridesmaid for, in almost 25 years, until that day at the Jungle, when she bumped into Karen whilst on the way to the ladies. Of all the places. Amanda came back and asked, "Guess who I have just bumped into?" After throwing in a few pointless guesses I gave in. She pointed Karen and her husband Don out in the crowd. It turns out that they stand near us and have done for years. It's a small world. It is Karen and Dons silver wedding anniversary in 2006, to be celebrated where else but in the Tiger bar at the Jungle.

The week ended on a real high when the Tigers announced that they had signed Shaun Timmins and Awen Gutenbeil for the 2007 season. This was great news all round.

At that time I wouldn't recognise either of them if they were sat in the back garden, which is exactly what I would have said a year ago if someone had said "Look out for that Willie Manu and Rich Fa'aoso, they are great players". The club was demonstrating a confidence that they believed we were staying in the top flight and the Board were backing the coach by getting the prized signatures of 2 star players from Australia's NRL.

This was for next season, but I was already worrying about how many pronunciations of Awen's surname name there would be?

Guttenbeal, Guttenberg, Battenburg, the list will be endless.

7 days hence.....

"Do ya know, am thinkin' of not even goin'
It's doin' mi 'ead in.
1 week superb, the next week rubbish,
1 week superb, the next week rubbish,
1 week superb, the next week rubbish"

These were not the lyrics to the next Arctic Monkeys single but Amanda's reaction to the game that followed the euphoric scenes at the Jungle.

We headed off to the birthplace of rugby league for a win that would take us 7 points in front of Wakefield Trinity, who were still leaderless and who had hit rock bottom after a home defeat against the Bulls. Their supporters had resigned themselves to the National League, which seemed extraordinary since they were only 2 points off safety with 6 games still to play. 2 of those games were against the Tigers. When we beat Huddersfield we would be safe.

Tigers fans turned up at the Galpharm Stadium in their thousands. As always, we arrived earlier than most, got the rug out and enjoyed a picnic in the stadium car park. This gave 'Fleeceman' time to explain and show that he had discovered what he believed to be a varicose vein. There is nothing in old age to look forward to and I hope this ailment does not restrict his ability to launch into the Mexican wave in future seasons.

He could always try some old fashioned remedies that I

have fallen foul of over the years, such as drinking dried eggs shells crumbled into powder and mixed with milk to get rid of boils. What about raw steak rubbed onto warts and then buried in the garden. Would you believe me if I said that both remedies actually worked?

Huddersfield never opened the ground until exactly 1 hour before kick-off. That didn't stop Cas fans queuing outside in typically British fashion and chuntering at each other when someone dared to sneak in front of them.

The support on the day was once again magnificent. The performance on the pitch was like Harlequins revisited. Despite going into an early lead through a smartly taken Adam Fletcher try, from a quite brilliant 'Lyonesque' pass from Michael Shenton, our forwards didn't win what is now known as the 'go forward'.

Robbie Paul and Brad Drew were inspirational for the Giants and they thoroughly deserved their 34–10 victory. It was in fact a right pasting. We were taken to the cleaners by a Giants team who had a Challenge Cup semi final to look forward to the following week against the Rhinos. Any thoughts of them taking it easy were wishful thinking on our behalf.

Highlights along the way included Paul Reilly getting felled by a Fa'aoso stiff arm that knocked the Giants full back out. The referee missed the shot and said it was a tackle around the shoulder. Reilly left the field with blood pouring out of a head wound.

The officials came in for a lot of stick from the Tigers support. Some decisions were baffling and obviously got to the players. So much so that Danny Brough said something out of turn and was given 10 minutes in the sin bin. He must have then thanked the ref for that, which duly earned him a red card. Brough had been outstanding since his arrival. For that show of dissent, he received a 2-match suspension and a £400 fine.

I am all for players being punished for hurling verbals at the match officials, but when indiscriminations like head high tackles go unnoticed and unpunished there has got to be something wrong. In every game there are loads of head high shots. Some get put on report and some go unseen. To be suspended for verbal abuse seemed harsh, but at the end of the day why should the referee take abuse from a player in any sport?

Even Mr. Reliable, Adam Fletcher let in a try and when that happens you know it is not your day. The Huddersfield crowd, and there were a few more than normal to be fair, sang their usual, "Fartown, Fartown".

It was a hot day again, with my dad explaining that a cooling fan he had in his bedroom made the noise of supporters singing, "get into 'em" as it rotated. Perhaps this is where 'fans' come up with the songs they sing!

The Giants supporters could now prepare for a trip to Odsal to see their team challenge for a chance to get to their first Cup final in years.

We headed off back home on the M62 with another week off to look forward to. We rued those lost 2 points for 13 days. On local radio ex Hull coach John Kear was the studio guest on the post match phone in. It was obvious by what he said that he hadn't been approached by Wakefield to fill the coaching vacancy at Belle Vue. There was even talk of Hull K.R's assistant Dean Sampson getting the job. All this did was get the pesimistic Trinity fans phoning in to say that the club was doomed. No coach, no support and they were going to be out of existence within a year.

All we could think about was that Trinity were heading to our place in 13 days for what was without any question would be the biggest game of the season so far. A win would more or less guarantee us safety. A loss would bring Trinity to within 3 points, with us still having to go there on the last day of the season.

It wasn't over by a long chalk and the fat lady hadn't sung yet.

Just a week after the greatest win in years, we were in the gutter once more. Amanda said she couldn't stand the tension and that we were bound to lose against Wakefield.

"Do ya know, am thinkin' of not even goin'
It's doin' mi 'ead in.
1 week superb, the next week rubbish,
1 week superb, the next week rubbish,
1 week superb, the next week rubbish"

The greatest sporting event on the planet concluded on the same day as the Giants defeat. I had followed the Tour de France, 'Le Tour' on T.V for years. This years race was won by American, Floyd Landis, but it lacked something in 2006 because Lance Armstrong wasn't there after his retirement from competitive cycling.

Lance Armstrong is the greatest living athlete. To win the event once takes a feat of extraordinary fitness, skill and stamina, but to do it 7 times in 7 years is beyond comprehension. There is nothing in the sporting world to compare it against. Taking into account Armstrong's personal challenge of fighting cancer along the way and you have a true legend.

He also had to contend with the finger of suspicion pointing at him for years. The suspicion was that he was a cheat. There was still a hint that some people still believed that he had taken performance enhancers in winning the 'Tour'. This has never been proven.

If you ever feel sorry for yourself, read a few chapters from his autobiography, 'It's not about the bike'. It is inspirational stuff. I wear with pride one of Armstrong's 'livestrong' yellow wrist bands. My mam had it on the day she passed away, which I guess is a bit ironic.

One day Floyd Landis may also write his autobiography and include a chapter about how he failed a drug test and was stripped of his 2006 yellow jersey. How disappointing for the sport and it's supporters around the world.

There is no room in any sport for drug cheats.

I would love to see the Tour live one day. It's a bit like a visit to the Middleton Light Railway, I wonder if I will ever get there?

The teenage word of 2006 was 'minging'. Its pronunciation rhymes with singing. If the girls didn't like something, they described it as minging.

If they thought somebody looked less than attractive, then they would be described as a minger, rhyming with singer.

A local supermarket had the idea of producing 2006 versions of the ever popular 'Love heart' sweets. Minger was chosen to be on one of the sweets, which makes a change from the 'you're gorgeous' or 'I love you' of yesteryear. If you gave a girl a love heart with one of those messages, it meant that you would end up getting married, so you generally ate them all to yourself.

Even Sophie surpassed herself and created a new word in 'minginger' (pronounced ming-in-er). This described a sandwich that was more minging than another one.

Words or sayings do the rounds, like 'cool' or 'that looks mint' which both suggest that something is okay. 'Sorted' is another way of saying thank you.

"Ya do mi 'ead in", means "you really get on my nerves"

Other ones doing the rounds were, "That's proper good", and "That's well good". Both mean "That's good"

There are some great sayings in prisons, such as "bari".

"I will sort that out for you". "Thanks boss, bari". Bari basically means, sorted.

"Alright cho?" means, "How are you my friend?" in prison speak.

Ones we used to use as teenagers, included, 'I wouldn't dare' or 'Bet ya felt half', which described an embarrassing moment.

On the Monday after the Giants game, I bet John Kear felt half when it was announced that he was the new coach at Wakefield. His appointment was made just over 12 hours after he had said that he hadn't been approached. Whatever. John Kear seemed to get a raw deal at Hull, so good luck to him. He had 6 games to save Trinity from the drop and as fate always dictates the first one of those was against his old team down at the Jungle.

Our weekend off brought the cup semi finals.

Hull KR 0, St Helens 50

Giants 30, Rhinos 12

The authorities may not have got their dream final, but they did get a Yorkshire vs Lancashire, David against Goliath occasion, which might guarantee a full house at Twickenham. A Rhinos vs Giants semi final at Odsal and just over 12,000 people turned up. That was a puzzle.

As an outsider, it was egg on the face for the Rhinos who had encouraged their supporters to pre order tickets for the final. There was even a suggestion that some had already booked hotel rooms and transport for the trip to London. On the day, Fartown were quite brilliant and did the same job on Leeds that they had done on us a week earlier.

Poor Rovers got a real pasting and a reality check. They were nearing the business end of the domestic season and have swept aside all before them. They had one eye on Super League, with promotion looking a real possibility. I wasn't overjoyed to see them embarrassed on the big stage, but it put our achievements for this season into perspective. A year ago we were Rovers, sweeping all aside and having one eye on Super League. The difference now was that we were there and holding our own, without actually receiving the recognition we deserved.

Amanda was very, very nervous as the Wakefield game approached. She was still talking about not going, when we all knew that she wouldn't miss it for the world. "What if they beat us? The gap will only be 3 points". Her glass was half-empty. "When we beat them, we will be 7 points clear and that will be enough". My glass was half full, although I was also nervous as hell and putting a brave face on for everyone else's benefit. Post match, would we be on the car park celebrating our survival, or with only 5 games to go, would we be seriously contemplating relegation?

Best job in the world

In the week leading up to the Wakefield game, our Jess had gone and got herself another job to assist in the saving up process before going to University.

After her first day, I asked. "How did it go?" She replied, "I've got the best job in the world". That is saying something for an 18 year old that would rather be in the pub with her mates.

Some people have several jobs in their lifetimes whilst others go on to collect gold clocks for years of loyalty. I was fast approaching my 20 years in the Prison Service. Some might say that people commit murder and do less time. I have enjoyed every minute of it and have never get up on a morning thinking that I didn't want to go to work. People who moan about what they do for a living, need to have a good look at themselves. If they dislike their job so much, why not go and get another one? Do something that you want to do.

I was now working at the Yorkshire and Humberside Prison Service Area Office, as part of the resettlement team that has the task of reducing reoffending. It was a great job. The sort of job when people ask, "He's got a good job, how do you get a job like that?"

If you ever ask someone what their dream job would be, they will tell you allsorts. Very few will tell you that it is actually the job they are doing. In that scenario, my dream job would probably be working as a sports journalist or as a painter and decorator. I still think I am lucky to have a job that I really enjoy.

The only thing wrong with my job was the lack of enthusiasm in the office by my colleagues for any kind of sport, but in particular for rugby league. At Leeds Prison, there are that many people involved with the game that we would still discussing last weekends fixtures on the following Friday. At Area Office, there was no interest at all.

How can people survive in life without being hooked to a sport and supporting a team? What do these people do with their time? They would reply by saying, "how said is it to be hooked on rugby league and following Castleford Tigers".

I didn't have the best job in the world according to Jess, who had got herself a nice little number working at none other than Castleford Tigers.

She was working part time in the club shop, the Tigers den.

On her first day, she said that someone who had never been to the Jungle before, had rung up enquiring about tickets for the Wildcats game. "I've never been before, but I've heard that the Barmy Army stands in the Wildon Road End".

The Tigers Den at the Jungle must rank as one of the smallest souvenir shops in the league. When Amanda worked in the Hunslet shop at Elland Road, in the late 80's, we had to load all of the goods for sale into our cars and deliver them to the Leeds United ticket office on the car park, which then doubled up as souvenir shop on a match day. It wasn't too bad before the match but when the side was beaten, the last thing we felt like doing was loading the car back up and storing the gear away, particularly in the depths of winter.

When you buy anything from the souvenir shop, you are buying something with the clubs name and crest on it. Everytime you pull on a replica shirt, T-shirt, vest, sweatshirt or even fleece in Fleeceman's case, you do so with pride. The Tigers emblem on your chest is something to be very proud of.

'Ending up with egg on your face' is not something to be proud of. Leeds had it when the Giants beat them in the cup semi-final. There is in all sports a balance between winding opponents up and a real arrogance and expectation that you only have to turn up to win.

The weekend of the Wildcats game was also the first weekend of the new football season. Hundreds of thousands of football fans up and down the country were dreaming of success again. It didn't seem that long ago when the 40,000 Leeds United fans were in Cardiff to see their play-off defeat in May. United started the 2006/07 season with a win in front of 22,000 people at Elland Road. Losing 18,000 fans in 3 months takes some doing.

'This is a real 4 pointer' is another great saying and never more apt than the Tigers home game against bottom side Wakefield Wildcats.

In the lead up to the game Wakefield's new coach, John Kear was a constant media figure. The right messages were coming out of their camp, namely that the players were in the fight together, that one win would lead to another and that with 6 games to go, and despite being adrift at the foot of the table, Kear had every confidence that his side would retain their Super League status.

I suppose he couldn't say much else. His team was bound to be up for the Tigers game. If this was a big game for us, it was probably one of the biggest games in their history.

Without the suspended Danny Brough, this was always going to be a close game. Rumours were rife leading up to the game that Brad Davis would make another comeback. The comeback never materialized.

With a real smack of 'egg on the face', somebody had hired

a light aircraft to fly a banner over the ground just before kick-off. It read 'No fear, It's only Kear. Go Tigers'.

With another smack, someone decided to play Status Quo's 'Down down' as the Wildcats ran out. With a final smack, the Wheldon Road end sang "Going down, going down, going down".

All 3 smacks bordered on arrogance and demonstrated a real lack of respect for the opposition. If Wakefield and their supporters needed anymore encouragement, then there it was. It left us with egg well and truly on our faces. I say 'us' and mean the club as a whole. Victory would have made us safe. We lost 0–18 and with 5 games to go we were in big trouble. Without Brough we had nobody good enough on the night to open up a magnificent defence. We lacked any creativeness near the line with the no. 28 Davis shirt back in the draw for another week. Perhaps that would be that for Brad.

Since the Rhinos victory our form had taken a real dip with probably the worst 2 performances since our return to the top flight.

0–18 sounds convincing. It was. It was also the first time since 1961 that Castleford had been nilled at home. That happened before I was born. If we went another 45 years before it happened again, we would be in the year 2051, and I would be 88. I wonder when I am 88 if I will say "I was at the Jungle the last time we were nilled". The nurses in the care home will probably say, "I bet that was proper good".

We got exactly what we deserved. To make matters worse, we played the whole of the second half against 12 men after the Wildcats skipper Monty Beatham had been sent off for attacking Ryan McGoldrick. A second Wildcat followed late on when Ned Catic was given his marching orders for attacking Danny Sculthorpe. No-one could accuse Wakefield of lacking fight.

Suspensions of 2 and 3 games followed. Danny Brough got 2 games for verbally abusing a referee. Beatham got 2 games for an all out attack on a defenceless Ryan McGoldrick, witnessed live by Sky sports viewers. Just desserts?

To rub salt into the wounds, the Wildcats had Tigers old boys, Saxton, Elima and Adam Watene in their ranks.

Credit where it is due, Wakefield did a number on us and played as though their livelihoods depended on a victory. Their livelihoods wouldn't hinge on the 2 points they collected at the Jungle, but the confidence of beating their closet geographical rivals and keeping us scoreless in the process got everyone associated with the Wildcats believing that they would not could survive.

We were thinking the opposite. A rapid decline in performance and confidence could see us returning to the National League. This was unimaginable only 3 weeks earlier after the victory against the Rhinos.

Everyone faces pressure situations in their day to day lives. The pressure we were putting ourselves under as a supporter of the Tigers was all self inflicted. We didn't have to go. No-one forces you to walk through the turnstile every week for 28 weeks between February and September. Looking at the faces of the others in our group, I could see that they were all suffering. Some of the supporters left the Wakefield game early whilst others booed the team off. We did neither and just stood in silence looking as miserable as sin as the final hooter sounded. I think this may have been done in an attempt to register another appearance on Sky. The feelings were genuine though.

As the final hooter sounded the 'Wildon Road' end was nearly empty. I wonder if the first time visitor ever came back for a second dose?

Amanda said that she couldn't stand it anymore and that she

wouldn't be going to the next game. This was the little matter of St Helens the current league leaders at the Jungle. I knew how she felt. Our dream of survival was fading away and witnessing it was tortuous. The Wakefield defeat came on her birthday weekend and I am sure that her special day was ruined by the performance and result against the Wildcats.

In National League 2, Gateshead Thunder's Chairman, Bill Midgley had to don a stewards vest at a home game against Featherstone Rovers. The attendance was just 282. In 1983, Featherstone Rovers were winning the Challenge Cup final at Wembley. Talk about pressure. Everyone in the game was feeling it as end of the season approached. At the South Leeds stadium, the Hunslet vs. Workington game attracted just 338 spectators. In 1999, Hunslet won the right to play in Super League. The names, Featherstone Rovers and Hunslet are known all over the world of rugby league. Both clubs were now playing in front of pathetically low attendances. Their loyal supporters deserve a massive pat on the back. Who were we to complain about the situation we are facing?

The bottom of the table at the end of week 23 and with just 5 games to go, read:

	P	W	D	L	Diff	PTS
Huddersfield	23	9	0	14	− 128	18
Harlequins	23	8	1	14	− 271	17
TIGERS	23	8	1	14	− 280	17
Wigan	23	8	0	15	− 120	16
Wakefield	23	7	0	16	− 142	14
Catalans	23	7	0	16	− 207	14

We now had to contemplate wanting the Leeds Rhinos to win their next 2 games, at home to Wigan and away at Wakefield. Cheering the boys from Headingley never comes naturally, but there are exceptions to every rule. For us to survive, it was vital for the Rhinos to put the opposition away big style in their next 2 matches.

Beating the Warriors was even more crucial after the Rugby Football League announced that Wigan were being deducted 2 points and fined £50,000 for a breach of the salary cap in 2005. The salary cap breach was in 2005 and they were penalised by losing points in 2006. How fair is that system? What would happen if a club avoided relegation by 1 point and 1 year on, they were before the RFL for a breach of the salary cap in 2006 and deducted 2 points? The penalty of losing points should be made in the current season.

All it meant for us was that instead of being just 1 point behind, Wigan were now 3 points in arrears of the Tigers. It was just a pity that they weren't deducted a few more points. If the Rhinos could beat them, it would leave Wigan 3 points adrift with just 4 games to go. There were all sorts of permutations. 5 games left and any one of 5 could still finish in the relegation spot.

With 5 games to go would we swap positions with sides below us in the table? Everyone always says that you need points in the bag. After 23 games we were still 3 points better off than both Wigan and Wakefield.

As supporters you live and breathe the game with all of its ups and downs. I still felt that there was enough quality in the side to keep us in Super League. Others, particularly Amanda felt that we had blown it. "I've never, never, never felt like this", she said. The Saints and Bulls were next up. If we were to survive we would have to get something from these games. No-one wanted us to have to go to Wakefield in week 28 to have to win to survive.

News broke that our inspirational captain, Danny Nutley was leaving the club at the end of the season despite signing an extension to his current contract some weeks earlier. Personal reasons were cited. Nuts can rest assured that his performances on the field throughout the season had already elevated him to a legendary status down at the Jungle. His style of play and willingness to run his blood to water every week set the standard for commitment.

On his impending departure, Nutley said, "I would like to thank the Tigers fans, the best in the world of rugby league, and the people of Castleford for the welcome and support they gave me and I wish you much success in the years ahead. I can assure you that my remaining time at the club will be devoted to ensuring that the Tigers stay where they belong, in the Super League."

The timing of his announcement wasn't great. We were on a low anyway, but to find out that skipper was heading out of the door at the end of the season was a body blow.

Nutley's future was now with the Sydney Roosters.

Who needs Daniel Anderson?

The world was not a happy place. There was trouble brewing in the Middle East and the intelligence forces in this country had managed to avoid the possibility of several aeroplanes being blown up over the mid Atlantic. This led to increased security and inevitable delays as people checked in at the airport. In typically British fashion, holiday makers were complaining that they weren't allowed to take hand luggage on the plane with them and that it was chaos at the check-ins. I never heard anyone thanking the authorities for ensuring that they arrived safely at their destination.

All we cared about was the future of our rugby league club. That was the only thing on our minds leading up to the Saints game.

Like I have said previously wanting Leeds to win doesn't come easily. I would normally support any other team when they were playing the Rhinos regardless of whether they came from the other side of the Pennines, Australia or indeed from another planet. Their Friday night encounter at home to the Wigan Warriors was different. Leeds were in the middle of a worse run of form than us. 4 defeats on the trot, but they wouldn't lose at home to a team languishing in the bottom 3, would they?

As usual on any match day, the mobile phone texts were flying around, including one from my best man Russ who was in Dublin for the weekend, obviously drowning his sorrows prior to the Bulls hearing at the RFL to look into their 2005 breach of the salary cap.

I received a classic text from niece Naomi, who is a massive Cas fan, but also has the unique distinction of being a Rhinos season ticket holder as well. Perverse I know, but at 12 years of age, what can she do?

'It read,' *'Oh no leeds r crap n im missin big brova!'*

I guess this translates to:

'Oh no. Leeds Rhinos aren't playing too well and I wish I was at home watching that dreadful programme about those people locked in a house like goldfish in a bowl'.

I have never been into Big Brother myself, but millions are and it was a case years ago of someone having a really simple idea and making millions from it. The characters who have appeared in every series of the show have long since returned to being unknowns. I think most viewers in a perverted sort of way are looking for housemates to just get it on with each other. I might just have to take a look if that ever happens.

Even worse than Big Brother is 'I'm a celebrity get me out of here'. Celebrities from years ago tucked up in the Aussie outback and made to eat Kangaroos testicles. Classic television? I don't think so, but there again millions watch it.

Back at Headingley, Wigan played magnificently. Amanda went away from wanting Leeds to win and I have got to say, that so did I. The cherry and whites performance on the night deserved 2 points. They won 20–18. A last minute conversion attempt from Rhinos skipper, Kevin Sinfield came back off the upright. The Rhinos didn't deserve anything from the game. The Wigan fans went mad at the final hooter. We watched Tigers old boy Wayne Godwin celebrate and remembered that he did exactly the same for us when we put some wins together in the relegation season of 2004. So, it was 5 losses in a row for the poor Rhinos. Their worst run for 10 years, when they were called plain Leeds.

To make matters worse for the Tigers, the Harlequins beat the Bulls, 28–26.

Wigan beating Leeds and the Quins beating the Bulls. 10th beat 2nd and 8th beat 4th. Could 9th beat 1st? Could we overturn the 8–44 reversal from week 2 of the competition?

The omens were not good. The team news had Brough still out suspended and there were injury doubts over Viane, Dyer, Lupton and Ward. Youngsters Payne, Boyle, Knowles and Edwards were drafted into the 20 man squad to face the league leaders. They had a total of 1 appearance and 8 as substitutes between them.

"Imagine them lot facing Ava Gardner", said Amanda. I think she had Ade Gardner in mind, but I got her point.

Saints were coming off a 56–8 victory against their cup final opponents, the Huddersfield Giants. To say we played them on a day when they were red hot is a possible under statement.

Fleeceman and Janet had even left the country to avoid the game, which in hindsight was probably the best thing to have done. Winter rugby came back and the shorts and T-Shirt were swapped for jeans and several jumpers. David would have been disappointed to miss the opportunity of donning his fleece for this game. For the second week running, we had an addition to our crew. Young Josh Gibbo's dad Barry Gibbo came to the Wildcats game and must have enjoyed it so much that he returned for a second helping. Or was he just a glutton for punishment? Barry bears an uncanny resemblance to the Wolves and England coach Paul Cullen.

It is difficult not to like the Saints. They have been there and there abouts for years and have always played a style of rugby that has branded them as the 'entertainers'. This season they were close to being the best club side I had ever seen. Someone commented that they could play in the NRL in Australia and win that comfortably. From 1 to 17 they run hard, pass the ball out of tackles, support each other and in 2006 have demonstrated a meanness in defence not normally associated with a team playing free flowing rugby. In short, they are awesome.

In the end, Jason Payne did make his debut and Grant Edwards came off the bench. Payne was such an unknown that he didn't even have a squad number in the programme. Men against boys? Lambs to the slaughter? The omens were not good and when the senior academy were beaten 6–52 by their St Helens counterparts, I think we knew it wasn't going to be a good day.

One good thing about the academy matches, that are played as curtain raisers, is that you can hear everything said by the players. The players can also hear what is being said by the crowd. The majority of the crowd are usually related to the players anyway.

There was a really annoying woman supporting the Saints youngsters who let out a loud "woo-hoo" every time the announcer gave the score out when the Saints had scored again. If she did the same during the main attraction, then her throat must have been sore by the time she got back home.

There was a strange atmosphere in the ground before, during and after the game. Before it was really subdued, with a sense of the inevitability about what was going to happen. During, we watched with utter admiration as a world class outfit did a professional job on us. There was a nice moment when the Wheldon Road end applauded after St Helens had scored one of their tries. It wasn't done sarcastically, but in appreciation of seeing one of the great sides of this generation and certainly of the Super League era.

The lack of respect shown to Wakefield a week earlier was more than made up for by this gesture. In these times when sportsmanship and appreciation of the opposition is a rare commodity, it was fitting for the Tigers fans to applaud some world class players. Kieran Cunningham may just about be the best British born player I have ever seen and his retirement from the international game will be a massive blow for Great Britain's chances of winning the Tri Nations.

The Saints coach Daniel Anderson said afterwards that his side was on fire and that their style of play and determination to keep the ball alive wasn't down to his coaching, but down to how the team wanted to play. He also had the luxury of leaving out current Great Britain internationals, Lee Gilmour and James Graham. Neither made the first 17.

Half way through the second half, I was thinking that I would have to change the line in the previous chapter about it being another 45 years before we would be kept scoreless at home. At 0–56 what else would you think? At 0–72 with just seconds to go, Grant Edwards put Gray Viane in at the corner and we had registered our first try in 222 minutes.

The last one was scored by Deon Bird at Huddersfield in the first half of that defeat.

The supporters who had stayed until the bitter end resisted the obvious, "you're not singing anymore". It was one of those days that you just wanted to end, but didn't because the opposition were a joy to watch.

It ended in another record home defeat. 4–72 defeat against a side that would hopefully go on to win all before them. This was the Tigers record defeat in their history.

'I'm a Tigers fan, get me out of here' would have been an apt title for this performance. Were we that poor or were the Saints that good?

Youngsters Payne and Edwards did not let themselves down. They would remember that experience for years to come.

If we thought we were in trouble before the game, then we were in deep trouble as the weekend fixtures ended with a Wakefield victory at home to the Catalans Dragons. With 4 games to go, we were now the bookmakers favourites for the drop. Things changed around so quickly in this competition. A few weeks earlier, Coach Terry Matterson was in the frame for coach of the year and the Tigers were heading for the top 6 play-offs.

Barry Gibbo was the worst lucky mascot ever. He had witnessed 2 really poor performances. If we went down because of those results I think Barry would be in the firing line to take some of the blame.

We had lost the last 3 games with an aggregate score of 14–124, scoring only 3 tries in 4 hours. The Saints ran in 12 tries in 80 minutes,

How would the side respond from here on in? There was no going back and the reality was that we were now relegation fodder. We had come so far and on paper had the makings of a really good team who were capable of challenging and beating the best on our day. We needed at least 2 more of those days if we were to avoid the tag of being the best team ever relegated.

In and around the ground afterwards the mood wasn't as glum as it had been after the Wakefield defeat. There was an acceptance that the Saints would have blown most teams away playing like that. The atmosphere was strange. It was as if the supporters had witnessed something really special and that this unwinable game was now out of the way and we could look forward to the run in with some optimism.

Jess managed to have her photograph with the legendary Paul Sculthorpe, who was far from his best but was far too good for us. Amanda had a word with Sean Long, wishing him all the best for the rest of the season.

On hearing the result, Fleeceman sent a text from Spain saying. *'Devastating. You must be gutted'*. Just a bit.

The bottom of the table at the end of week 24 and with just 4 games to go, read:

	P	W	D	L	Diff	PTS
Harlequins	24	9	1	14	− 269	19
Huddersfield	24	9	0	15	− 142	18
TIGERS	24	8	1	15	− 348	17
Wigan	24	9	0	15	− 118	16* deducted 2 points
Wakefield	24	8	0	16	− 122	16
Catalans	24	7	0	17	− 227	14

Les Catalans looked certain to finish bottom with the relegation spot going to 1 from 5. The French newcomers have done themselves proud, but by finishing bottom they really ought to go. Their 3 year exemption from relegation may come back to haunt the RFL. Sour grapes? I think so.

Whoever went down in 5 weeks time would do so with a record points tally for a relegated team. The RFL had finally got a competition where everyone was capable of beating everyone else and where every match, every week meant something. One side would be gone in a few weeks and whoever that was going to be would be a massive loss for the competition. I just hoped to God that it wasn't us.

It was time to close ranks and come together as one for the final 4 games. The supporters had a massive part to play. We were all up for it and ready for Odsal to face a Bradford Bulls team who like Wigan had just been docked 2 league points for a salary cap breach in 2005. They went on to win the Grand Final in 2005.

It's a 4 game season

The Saints defeat took some getting over. The fans forum on the clubs website was full of postings bemoaning the result and performance. Heroes after beating the Leeds Rhinos were now villains.

I like to read the postings, but am not a regular contributor. It was time to redress some of the negativeness. Amanda was the brains behind the posting, I just did the typing.

It read:

There was nobody more disappointed with the result and performance last Sunday than me and mine. Lets be right about it at 0–36 down against the best club side in the world what are we going to do? Saints played a style of rugby alien to the rest of the competition and I along with many others in the WRE applauded them back after they crossed for another spectacular try.

For us it's a 4 game season now with our destiny in our own hands. Remember Brad after the cup defeat at Widnes on that freezing day in April? "Nobody will care about this defeat if we stay in SL".

We have 4 games to go and when we survive, who will care about the Saints defeat?

After the Rhinos victory, who remembered the debacle of the Wire 6–64 defeat?

Remember where we were this time last year and for those with longer memories…remember the support at Widnes 2 seasons ago in that 7–6 victory?

As a team we are miles better than the one that got relegated.

Look at the table after week 23, we are 2 points away from 7th. Look at the teams around us. They are all established SL outfits. The competition in our year out got tougher and with a few months lead in to it, we have done absolutely brilliant to be where we are.

The ref at Huddersfield robbed us of our star man for 2 games, lets hope Danny leads us to 2 victories so that we can go to Wakey and enjoy the day.

Let Terry do his job and let us unite as one to do our bit. It starts at Odsal on Friday.

We are the best and most loyal supporters in SL. Lets show the rest what we are all about'.

When you send a posting like that you are of course inviting a response. I thought I would either get shot down in flames or that some kind soul out there would support the points I was trying to make. Thank God for Big Steve, who responded with:

'This is awesome. I was there for all of those games and I totally agree with you, let's not slate the players, lets get behind them!!!!

We've got to take the good with the bad!!'

Whoever you are Big Steve, thank you.

If we were feeling demoralised then so must everyone else associated with the club. What about everyone associated with other clubs? They must have all been having the same thoughts about relegation as us. Huddersfield Giants were 2 weeks away from a Challenge Cup final. They could also be a month away from relegation. How were their supporters feeling at that time? Elation because they were going to Twickenham or deflation because their team could be going down?

Young people these days seem to take everything in their stride. 'A' level results day arrived and Jess was rewarded with a place at York St John University for her efforts. She was the first person from either side of the family to be going to University and as parents I think this ranked up there as been one of our proudest moments.

As we awaited a phone call from school, Amanda was pacing up and down in the kitchen with dish cloth in hand and wiping down everything that didn't move. When the call came, Jess said, "I've sailed it". Amanda thought she had said that she had failed it, which all added to the excitement.

Cal Simpson also got her results and would be heading off to Northumbria.

Both sets of parents were over the moon but the enormity of having a family member leave home hadn't really dawned on any of us. Both Jess and Cal were due to move out on the weekend of the round 28 clash against Wakefield.

Odsal, or the Grattan, Stadium is one of my least favourite grounds. I once saw Hunslet get 70 odd put on them by Bradford Northern. "And the try scorer for Northern was Ellery Hanley", was the cry that day.

It is a stadium that generates little atmosphere because of its vastness. The weather during the day leading up to the evening kick off must have changed people's minds about going. There are places to be in the world if you are going to get wet through and Odsal isn't one of them.

Leading up to the game, I said to Amanda that my dad was bound to mention the cup final replay of 1954 between Warrington and Halifax, when there was 102,569 spectators in the ground. His dad, my granddad, was in the crowd that day. I think it was one of those occasions when half of the population of the western world was there.

That conversation never took place because fearing a soaking, my dad wisely stayed at home.

It was also the final of Big Brother, whatever that meant. I hope nobody prioritized that in front of watching the Tigers.

As you enter the Odsal bowl you realize the potential of the place and just how far you actually are away from the pitch.

Amanda said, "It's like looking at Playmobile people or been at a concert. There should be a big screen"

Bradford Bulls are the masters of pre match entertainment and this occasion was no different. They had a group on that performed The Jams, 'A town called Malice' and The House-martins, 'Happy hour' amongst others. They were as good if not better than the 'Beautiful couch' that we had seen performing at the KC in Hull a few years ago. Having live music on gets you into the mood and when they play songs you particularly like, it is always a bonus.

The sound system is spot on and it is a surprise that Odsal isn't used to stage concerts.

There was also a parade of military vehicles before the game. The passengers in some of the vehicles were war veterans complete with their medals. They received the biggest ovation of the season so far. It was hair standing on the back of the neck stuff.

The Bulls mascots are also top drawer. Bullman and Bullboy rank as good as any mascots out there. I think one of the Bulls used to be a Rhino, if you can work that out.

There is a Bulls supporter who parades up and down near the front of where the away supporters congregate. He would also make a good mascot. He has all the moves and gestures and knows how to wind up the visitors. All he needs is a costume. If you have ever stood behind the sticks at the front of the away end, you will know exactly who I mean. Entertaining? Not at all. He gets right under your skin. The stewards seem oblivious to the fact that he could actually instigate trouble if the wrong crowd was in town.

This was one big night in our fight for survival. At the same time over at Belle Vue, Wakefield, the Wildcats were entertaining our friends from Headingley. If the Rhinos lost again, it would be their 6th defeat on the trot and their worst run since

1958. If ever we needed a Rhinos victory then there it was. John Kear's Wakefield team were playing with a renewed confidence after back to back wins and were well capable of making it 3 on the bounce. Over at the JJB, Wigan were entertaining the Giants.

All 3 games kicked off at the same time. Whatever happened at Odsal, we couldn't afford a Wildcats victory.

The Bulls have nicknames for their players and as the teams are read out, they play a short blast of music. This is great entertainment and all adds up to a value for money package. Paul Deacon is known as the 'baby face assassin' and former Tiger, Andy Lynch is known as the 'Rock', for whatever reason

There seems to have been a promise of massive investment to redevelop the ground for years. Loads of money has been spent and there is always a warm welcome, but at the end of the day, the pitch is miles away from where you are and you are open to the elements.

Earlier in the season I had received a text from Russ Hanwell who was at the match at Odsal. Fog had descended making viewing a near impossibility. His text asked, "How are the Bulls getting on?"

A massive Stuart Fielden image still hangs as a reminder to the home faithful of their departed legend.

We had a confidence about going to Odsal and returning with the spoils. They were the current world champions but we had Danny Brough returning after suspension and he would be our saviour.

Janet and David arrived just before kick off via Spain and from Manchester Airport. Knowing what her dad is like Cal had brought along his big winter coat. We all expected Fleeceman to arrive bedecked in his 'J.C's' (with white socks), shorts and vest. When they arrived they couldn't wait to show us a photograph that they had taken of David Beckham and his Real Madrid team mates who were in the airport in Spain at the same time that they were. I once had a photograph taken with Becks at Madame Tussauds in London. Nobody believed it was the real one, but on this occasion there was no doubting it, Becks was there.

Sophie and niece Naomi were on their holidays in Spain with Amanda's mum and dad. They remembered to text asking for score updates.

Bulls fan and best man Russ with his wife Diane always get into the ground about 2 seconds before kick off. How could you do that at Odsal with all the pre match entertainment? Russ is a traditionalist and goes for the rugby. They stood with us throughout the first half and similar to when the Bulls came to the Jungle in round 16, they said that they would sacrifice a victory if it meant that we avoided relegation. We competed well in the first half, but disappointedly trailed 4–18 at half time.

The Bulls employ a man in a go kart contraption to zoom around everytime they score. Unfortunately for us, he did a lot of zooming that night.

Despite the players looking like Playmobile characters we still managed to see every forward pass and offside. There was a friendly exchange of "Boo's" between the 2 sets of supporters. The Bulls booed because they thought that we were offside at every tackle or that every tackle was an illegal one. We just booed because it brightened up proceedings and there wasn't much to cheer about.

Amanda even spotted that Jason Payne looked really upset as he trooped off the pitch near the end after receiving a red card for a high shot on Stanley Gene. There are times when 'bionic' eye sight comes in handy. Some people already have the power.

Regular scores were coming in from Wakefield and Wigan. We were on the end of another heavy defeat and once again the commitment and passion were being questioned. We lost 10–48.

In the last 4 games we had scored just 24 points and conceded 172.

We needed Leeds to beat Wakefield. They did, just. It ended up 12–14 and across at the JJB, Wigan beat the Giants 14–10.

Our league position wasn't affected. We were no worse off and with 3 games to go, our destiny was still in our own hands. There was now a weeks break for the Challenge Cup final. We had Harlequins at home followed by a trip to Salford and finally Wakefield away in round 28.

3 games left and in a month's time we would either be gearing up for Super League X11 or gearing up for National League 1.

There was a surreal moment at Odsal that put our plight into perspective. WPC Sharon Beshenivsky had been killed whilst on duty in Bradford. At half time there was a ceremony because the Bulls had put a bench in Sharon's memory in their reception area as a lasting tribute. It was a great gesture that was warmly received by everyone at Odsal. WPC Beshenivsky's husband was there. How must he have felt? And there was us thinking about another drubbing and relegation.

The bottom of the table at the end of week 25 and with just 3 games to go, read:

	P	W	D	L	Diff	PTS
Harlequins	25	9	1	15	− 275	19
Wigan	25	10	0	15	− 114	18* deducted 2 points
Huddersfield	25	9	0	16	− 146	18
TIGERS	25	8	1	16	− 386	17
Wakefield	25	8	0	17	− 124	16
Catalans	25	8	0	17	− 223	16

Wigan looked safe now with the gamble of bringing in Brian Noble and Stuart Fielden paying off. How much is it a gamble bringing in one of the greatest club coaches in the world and one of the worlds best players? They had to complete their programme without Kris Radlinski who was forced into retirement for a second time. He may not have set the world alight with his performances but I bet his presence at training and in the dressing room was a major influence in the Wigan revival.

There was a big 'hoo-hah' at the cricket when England were awarded a test match against Pakistan after the visitors forfeited the game. It was the first time in history that a test match had been decided by that outcome. The events from the Oval were in the news for days and were blown up out of all proportion. The Pakistani captain was accused of not bringing his team back out to field after they were accused of tampering with the ball. It was by far the most exciting thing to happen at the cricket all year. It still amazes me how the sport is given so much national coverage when most county championship games are played out in front of a few hundred people. The Twenty20 competition brought in new supporters and I have to admit to having been to a couple of Yorkshires Twenty20 games. That is top quality entertainment which demonstrates how the game should be played.

If teams can score 200 runs in 20 overs when the fielders are scattered all over the field, then why can't they score more when 90 overs are bowled in a day and all the fielders are around the bat?

It is hardly fair to criticize cricket lovers. The games are played during the week as well as on a weekend and where else can you enjoy hours of your favourite sport sat in the sunshine, eating and drinking? If you support any cricket team full time you have to put miles in to get to the away fixtures and if they are playing county championship matches it must cost you a fortune paying for hotel rooms.

"Do we deserve to go down?"

"Do we deserve to go down?" asked Amanda. "Well", I said, "the league table doesn't lie". "Not the team, I mean the supporters", she replied.

The best thing about rugby league finals is the camaraderie amongst the supporters who generally represent every club side, professional or amateur, in the country. Castleford were well represented. It was documented that Super League supporters were out in force, but there was a notable lack of supporters representing National League clubs.

We stayed at home, but the Simpson family went to Twickenham, with David even managing to leave his fleece at home. Rumour as it that he even had a browse around the shops in Wandsworth Arndale centre to try to find one, but all to no avail. It appears that Southerners and fleeces just don't go together in the middle of summer, which is no great surprise.

Young Josh Gibbo bought a bomb shaped foam dart in Harrods that whistled when it was thrown.

Playing with it on the Saturday morning of the final in the hotel car park, it landed on a canopy. "Mi bombs on roof", said Josh, leaving Uncle David to go to reception to report that his nephew's 'bomb' needed retrieving. The male receptionist brought out a pair of step ladders no higher than Josh to get onto the roof. No chance. Eventually he climbed through a window and got a long stick to knock it back onto the car park. Priceless. Surprisingly with David's previous and in these troubled times, the anti-terrorist squad were not called out. Josh always has to have a ball of some kind in his hands. A 200 mile trip south wasn't going to change that.

Other Tigers fans in the cup final crowd were the 'smelly egg family' last seen at Hull. I wouldn't have liked to have been sat near them when they opened their picnic hamper. There presence could be the explanation for all of the empty seats that day.

The Giants supporters must have had a great day at Twickenham despite their 12–42 defeat against a buoyant St Helens side. As a neutral watching the game on T.V the result was never in doubt. The coverage of the whole event on terrestrial television is a world away from the product rugby league supporters are now used to on Sky. It does however reach the people who don't have Sky. Despite the admirable efforts of the well respected studio pundits, Brian Noble and Ian Millward, the commentators tended to spoil what has always been regarded as the games best opportunity to widen its appeal.

The Saints were always going to win. The result put our 4–72 defeat into perspective. To concede 42 points in a showpiece final is on paper a bit of an annihilation. The Giants competed for the first 50 minutes, but came across a side that was just too good for them. The magnificent Sean Long collected his third Lance Todd trophy as man of the match. If only he could replicate this club form for his country.

For whatever reason, there was no member of the Royal family to present the cup this year and it was left to Martin Offiah to do the honours. My mam would have been cursing the fact that 'Chariots' couldn't even be bothered to put a tie on for the occasion. Offiah apparently stood in for former England football manager Sir Bobby Robson, who was too ill to attend.

Sir Bobby seems a decent chap but why couldn't the RFL line up a rugby league legend to hand over its greatest prize?

I just hoped that the Saints kept their form, desire and ability to hammer teams for just 1 more week at least. Next up for them were Wakefield Wildcats in round 26 of the Super League competition.

The Tigers confirmed the signing of Liam Higgins from Hull for the 2007 season. The question was, which competition would he be playing in?

Bulldog spirit

It goes without saying that the Harlequins game at home was one of the biggest games in the Tigers history. The importance of recording a victory in our final home game could not be underestimated. This was the one. Win at all costs.

I wonder if in years to come there will be any bigger games than this?

On the marketing front the Tigers offered free tickets for juniors in an attempt to boost the attendance for what is traditionally one of the lowest crowds of the season. That was a wise move and one that saw pop, crisps, sweets and burger sales go through the roof. Sky also recognized the importance of the game by switching it to a Saturday evening for live coverage.

The club and several of its sponsors acted quickly to put on free transport for the following away match at Salford. There was a typical 'owt for nowt' scramble for places on the coaches. Everyone wanted to be there.

The players and staff also paid for coaches to allow supporters to travel to the game for free. That gesture demonstrated the regard the squad had for its fans.

'Never before has the light at the end of the tunnel been as bright as it is today at the start of a brand new Super League season. The club is steadily moving forward on all fronts and we are now hopefully putting in place the foundations for the future both on and off the field'.

These were the words written in 'The Wright stuff' by CEO

Richard Wright in the match day programme for our round 1 encounter at the Jungle against Hull FC. That was over 6 months earlier and 25 games ago. Who would have thought that we were now just 2 wins away from retaining our Super League status, but more worryingly we were also 3 defeats away from a return to where we had come from.

In the pre match hype to the Quins game, CEO Richard Wright said, "We started back in October 2005 with 3 simple objectives. Super League in 2007, a new stadium in 2008 and a Grand Final in 2009. We thought back then and still do that the first objective would be the most difficult. The new stadium will give us for the first time the resources to compete at the highest level, to spend the maximum under the salary cap rules. The off field team is coming together really well and the future for the Club has never been as bright. We have to make sure that all the hard work done in the last two years is not for nothing which is why we need the fans on Saturday to come down and rock the Jungle to its foundations"

The journey was nearing its end. The lives of thousands of rugby league supporters were in turmoil wondering if their team would survive the threat of relegation. Our destiny became clearer before the Quins game, when Wakefield battled all the way at Knowsley Road before eventually going down 12–34. That was a top against bottom clash and although the scoreline made the game sound 1 sided, it was anything but. We had the opportunity to extend our lead on Wakefield to 3 points with 2 games to go.

The news that Danny Ward was staying for 2007 and beyond was just what we wanted to hear going into the Quins game. Wardy goes about his business in a quiet unassuming manner and will have benefited in 2006 from playing alongside the departing Nutley.

In history there have been some remarkable personal achievements in the face of adversity. I cannot think of any greater achievement than Rothwell based, Jane Tomlinson's epic bike ride across America. Despite suffering from terminal cancer, Jane completed a remarkable 4,200 mile bike ride lasting 9 weeks. One of her partners on the ride said, "Jane turned the impossible into the improbable, into reality. 6 years ago, Jane was given 6 months to live. She has dedicated herself to her family and raising around £1.25m for some very worthwhile causes.

"For gods sake it's only half past 5, go back to sleep", said Amanda as I was itching to get up and get down to the Jungle for the Quins encounter. Getting up at that time meant it was a long day with plenty of clock watching. As soon as we got into the ground I could sense an air of expectation. Wakefield's defeat put the ball in our court. If we won then they would have to go to Odsal and beat the Bradford Bulls.

We were in the worst form of the season after suffering 4 defeats on the trot and another defeat against the Londoners would have probably meant having to go to Wakefield on the last day for a winner takes all, loser gets relegated encounter.

I have to admit to having some sympathy with the plight Wakefield were in. They were not a bad side and if John Kear had been appointed a few games earlier then who knows where they would have been? The computer that works out the fixtures wasn't kind. Leeds, Saints and Bulls as 3 of the last 4 games meant that they were always going to be playing catch up. That was their concern. Our concern was securing 2 points in our last home game and seeing what happened after that.

It was the last home game for loyal servant Deon Bird who had being the true professional throughout his time at the Jungle. Deon seems to have been at the Jungle forever. He hadn't even clocked up 50 appearances for the Tigers, but put his body on the line every time he walks onto the pitch. Ben Roarty was also returning home to Australia along with our skipper Danny Nutley.

Brad was back at last. The 38 year old Davis was named on the bench. Another comeback and probably Brads last game at the Jungle. His selection was no surprise. He is a big game player and this was a big game.

The Quins away support numbered about a coach full. They were still fighting for their Super League lives, the match was played on a Saturday tea time and they had about 50 supporters.

We had the opportunity to raise the roof and get behind the team without a whimper from the away support.

We went 10–0 up in no time through tries from Luke 'Dishy' Dyer and Ryan McGoldrick. Dishy had been out injured for weeks and his return was a real tonic for the run in. In fact the full squad baring Flash and Roarty were now fit. This left coach Matterson with a very rare selection dilemma.

The 17 men fought their hearts out and despite going behind 10–12, we managed to sneak back in front on half time after a Peter Lupton try from a Brough kick through.

16–12 at half time and game on. 40 minutes to play and no indicator which way the result was likely to go. The first score in the second half was vital. When Willie Manu powered on the a pass 20 yards out, he wasn't going to be stopped. I jumped so high that I came down and had a 'head rush'. I thought that I was going to pass out. The relief could be felt around the ground. Brough converted making it 22–12. There was then one of the best tries of the season to cap a magnificent display. I was screaming at Danny Sculthorpe to kick the ball on the last tackle before he got held up on the half way line. What did I know? Scully slipped a back handed pass out to Brad Davis and despite the pass been about a yard forward Brad burst onto the ball with speed. His 38 year old legs weren't going to carry him all the way, so he chipped a measured kick into our corner for Adam Fletcher to race onto and score to clinch the victory.

There was still time for man of the match Sculthorpe to drop a goal to make it 27–12. The victory was hard fought, but we had the points in the bag.

Scully's dog Molly who was the mascot for the day must have been proud of her owner and her owners mates for putting us 3 points clear of the relegation spot with just 2 games to go.

At the start of this book I mentioned the emotional night on the car park back in October 2005 when we celebrated our promotion. This was the last home game and we celebrated as if we were already safe.

As is the custom at any club, the departing players spoke after the game and the squad did a lap of honour to receive the plaudits of a truly loyal bunch of supporters. We knew what that victory meant to the team and the team knew what it meant to us. I even threw my prized baseball cap towards Danny Nutley as he walked around the pitch at the end. Unfortunately, it got caught in the wind and never reached its intended destination.

Halifax were in Super League not too very long ago. Their name like that of Hunslets and Featherstones is known around the world. Their plight is a lesson for all of the clubs currently occupying a place in the elite competition. To stave off the threat of going into liquidation, the club was forced to auction off items of memorabilia-including the 2004 National League 1 qualifying final winners salver, to make up a financial shortfall that threatened their very existence. The club were set to go into liquidation after failing to raise £35,000 of the £90,000 needed to cover an overspend on players' wages. As always seems to happen, there was an 11th hour intervention and the club were rescued. A massive personal loan from a former Chairman bailed Halifax out on this occasion. One day a professional club will fold and it will be sad to see a domino effect with others following suit. The game is about more than the 12 clubs in Super League and it pleased me when the Leeds Rhinos sponsored the struggling Hunslet Hawks final game of the season. That type of gesture needs applauding.

The Super League season lasted longer than Naseem Hamed's prison sentence. The Prince was released from jail in a hail of publicity that saw him driven off in a flash car. This created a public outcry with people wanting to know why celebrities were always released from custody early. They actually get out at the same time as everyone else, but the press are not there to maximize the publicity and stir up the emotions.

The bottom of the table at the end of week 26 and with just 2 games to go, read:

	P	W	D	L	Diff	PTS
Wigan	26	11	0	15	− 92	20* deducted 2 points
Huddersfield	26	10	0	16	− 140	20
Harlequins	26	9	1	16	− 290	19
TIGERS	26	9	1	16	− 371	19
Wakefield	26	8	0	18	− 146	16
Catalans	26	8	0	18	− 237	16

Our South sea islanders, Manu, Fa'aoso and Viane had enjoyed their first season at the Jungle. Every time one of the trio scored a try, they celebrated with an 'M' sign to the crowd. This was in recognition of being one of the 'mongrel mob'. It caught on and the crowd started to do it back when one of them crossed the whitewash. I thought that I had it down to a tee until I say a picture of our crew all doing it. "You don't do Manu same as me", I said, to which the girls collapsed in a heap with laughter. I was apparently making the shape of matchbox rugby goalposts from my younger days and it wasn't called the Manu, but the Mongrel sign. I much prefer my style although the pointing down of both the fore and middle fingers to make an 'M' shape looks better and is much more comfortable to do than my way.

The end of season was nigh and it was time for the playing squad to stock up with gear to take back home for their friends and family. Luke Dyer had played well since returning back from a lengthy spell on the sidelines. His dad must have also thought that his son was doing okay. Why else would Dishy Senior purchase a replica Tigers shirt and have 'Dyer' printed on the back?

Salford City blues

The survivors on that remote island in the Pacific were still stranded as the Super League season drew to its most exciting conclusion. They had been there for a couple of series and to be honest most looked pretty well on it. The girls looked to have enough make up to last for a while longer and the good looking dudes still maintained a degree of designer stubble. No-one had lost any weight and there seemed to be an endless array of new clothes to wear. Still, 'Lost' must be good because I am still watching it and there are loads of twists in the story line to string a few more series out.

Over at Mount Pleasant, Batley, Craig Lingard had had a productive season. Like us, Batley were the pre season favourites for relegation, but finished a creditable 6th in National League 1. Craig extended his record as the clubs all time try scorer. The previous record older Glen Tomlinson has a stand named after him. I asked Craig if they were going to name one after him. "No", he replied, "but I have got a pie stall named after me". I am sure that is still something to be proud of.

On the Wednesday before the Salford game, Amanda said. "It's all about Friday". Any negativeness in our house was cancelled out with, "Those negative thoughts don't need to sprout"

We were heading to the Willows with Michael Shenton becoming the latest player to put pen to paper in extending his contract at the club.

Michael said: "I'm very happy to have agreed a new deal with the club and commit myself for an additional year. I have enjoyed my time at the Tigers and it has been great to play on a regular basis in Super League this year. The club has some ambitious plans for the future and wanting to be part of those plans was a big factor in my signing this new contract."

As well as the renewed confidence after the victory over the Quins, this was a real positive going into the game where victory would see our Super League survival confirmed. If only things were that simple.

We were now only 160 minutes away from the end of the season

Wakefield had to go to Odsal and win, if they didn't win, then that would be it. In normal circumstances, our chances of getting something at Salford were certainly greater than Wakefield's chances of going to Odsal and getting anything. What were normal circumstances?

The problem was that this season had been a season when the form book had been ripped up more than once and there was no such thing as normal circumstance. After the week 15 defeat at Warrington, The Salford coach, Karl Harrison said that he thought another 2 wins would see us safe. Since then we had won 4 games and drawn another. Not the 4 points we needed for safety, but 9 points and we still weren't safe.

The Tigers traveling army headed over the Pennines in a fleet of 20 coaches that were paid for by several of the club sponsors. The mood in the car park before setting off was one of optimism, with most expecting that we would lose at Salford, but that Bradford would stand up on the day to relegate the Wildcats.

This was one of the tensest occasions any follower of any sport was likely to be involved with. For starters, our game was delayed by 15 minutes due to congestion at the turnstiles.

Credit to the authorities for allowing extra time for the Tigers support to get in. It was just a pity that Salford had only 3 turn-stiles open when they knew that at least 20 coaches were heading their way.

Salford have plans for a new stadium to replace the Willows which is another from the traditional mould of northern rugby league ground.

The Salford fans sing, "I feel the Salford reds are rising" to the tune of 'bad moon rising' which featured in the film 'An American werewolf in London'. That is the only film I have ever been back to the cinema to watch again. It is a classic horror movie with special effects way before its time.

Credit to the Salford fans for their unique song.

I wish I knew the second line of 'Salford reds are rising'. It's a bit like

"You're everywhere and nowhere baby, that's where you're at" from Jeff Beck's classic party song 'Hi ho silver lining'. Just what is the next line?

We kicked off 15 minutes later than the Bulls v Wildcats game. By the time their game finished we would still have 15 minutes to play. If they had lost then we would have had 15 minutes to conga our way around the pitch.

Alas, the conga was put on hold for another week. My mate Russ was at Odsal and agreed to text regular updates of the score. It was an occasion when score updates were flying around, making it difficult to know who was telling the truth and who was not. Half time came at Odsal. The Wildcats were in front. 15 minutes later, half time came at Salford and we were in front 14–8. We played well throughout that first period. Salford were heading for the play-offs and were as mean in defence as the best. Luke Robinson looked a threat every time he touched the ball. Despite conceding a soft try on half time, we looked good value for our lead. If it stayed the same, then we would be safe and Wakefield would be going down.

On our coach going over, everyone was singing. This continued inside the ground. The supporters couldn't have done anymore to lift the team. There was an air of tension and you could cut the atmosphere with a knife. We were making every tackle and every hit up.

40 minutes from safety. By the time the second half kicked off at Salford, Wakefield had nudged further in front at Odsal. John Kear had instilled a confidence in his charges and credit to them. Nobody goes to Odsal for an easy game. Wakefield looked like pulling off an unlikely victory and we just had to hang on. Half way through the second half a Danny Brough penalty made it 16–14 to the Tigers. We knew then that Wakefield had won. If we wanted to avoid a last day scenario of having to go to Wakefield to win to stay up, then we had to hang on. On the night we couldn't hang on. We conceded a try and a goal but were still well in it at 16–20. The genius of Robinson and the powerful Reds forwards got on top towards the end. The introduction of Brad Davis didn't work on this occasion. Our players couldn't have given any more and despite some outstanding individual performances, we went down 16–26. A last minute try and goal made the score line look more convincing than it actually was. Terry Matterson and his team were cheered and applauded for ages afterwards.

We sang a defiant, "we are staying up, said we are staying up". The Salford fans sang, "going down, going down, going down", as our dejected troops left the scene of what was a tremendous battle. According to Amanda, that was "mean and horrible". "They felt bad enough and they shunt 'ave to go through that 'an all"

We got back on our coaches and the convoy of dejected

disciples traveled back home across the Pennines in deadly silence.

We now had to avoid defeat at Belle Vue to stay up. Matterson commented that, "the players are shattered because of the effort they put in but they will be all right against Wakefield. At the start of the year people thought we would be down by now but it's gone down to the wire and we are confident. It's going to be the local derby to end all local derbies."

I imagined all of the Wildcats supporters from HMP Leeds at Odsal waiting for our result to come through. I had seen 2 of them, Mick Kelly and Geoff Wake that very day and I thought that both of them had an air of confidence. What had they to lose?

Those 2 games also had an impact on the lives of everyone concerned with Huddersfield and Wigan. They both had 2 games left to play, but they were now safe from the drop. Who would have thought that after 26 completed rounds that Wigan were still in danger of going down. Brian Noble had turned them around and they will no doubt be a force in the domestic game in the not too distant future. It took 26 rounds, but they eventually got there. Noble had worked his magic and whatever they paid for Fielden was money well spent.

If they were to be a force in years to come, it would have to be without Wayne Godwin who signed a contract with Hull FC for 2007. Tigers fan, Wagga looked unlikely to be a Tiger ever again.

The 2 extremities of emotions were unbelievable. A week earlier we thought that our win had secured survival. Now we really were teetering on the brink and relegation was on the cards. I couldn't imagine this ever happening after we had beaten half of the sides in top 6 and secured 19 league points. We were relegated in 2004 with only 12. We had taken league points from everyone besides the top 2, St Helens and Hull and our friends from Wakefield.

Our signings for 2007 had reassured us that everyone was confident of being in Super League for years to come. I felt that we were maybe 3 or 4 players away from a side that would challenge for a place in the top 6 in 2007.

It was all back in the melting pot now. An hour into the journey back home, I asked Fleeceman what he thought would happen. I could see that any belief that we would survive had drained from him that night in Salford.

We dissected events over several packets of cheese and onion crisps when we got back in the house just before midnight. They were Seabrook's crinkly cut ones and if you are going to dissect your performance over a bag of crisps, then they are the sort to do it with. Niece Naomi said, "Terry had tactics, but they dint stick to 'em. Don't blame Terry". Naomi was just 2 days away from becoming a teenager and her observations were very profound.

Mattersons credentials as a Super League coach rested on 1 game. His reputation hinged on 80 minutes of rugby.

Wakefield were playing well and with a winning mentality.

People's jobs were on the line and 80 minutes of rugby league would impact on the lives of players, officials, management and supporters. After a year in the wilderness we knew that Super League was where we belonged. The squad of 2006 had 1 hour and 20 minutes to put that theory into practice.

It was 0110 hours on the morning following that defeat at Salford. I felt like hibernating for a week, too ashamed and demoralized to come out of the house. How had we got to this point? Amanda and the girls said that they didn't want to go through any more heartache and that Wakefield wasn't a place where they wanted to be if we were going to get relegated. Wakefield had sent us down on the last day in 2004 at the Jungle. That was bad enough. We deserved to go down that year. This season we didn't deserve to be relegated, but I am bound to say that as a supporter. Everything about Castleford Tigers said that Super League was where we belonged. In 7 days time we were facing another year in the National League.

This post appeared on the Tigers website on the day after the Salford defeat:

I have watched Cas since 1953. I am bitterly disappointed the way this season has gone. I don't blame TM, he has done a good job with the time he had to build a side, he has bought wisely in mid season with the likes of Brough and Lupton- the truth of the matter is that in today's structure you cannot build a team overnight to sustain a years intensity in the Super League. That is why Catalans have 3 years to do it in. I am afraid we are doomed to National League again, as only a fool would back Castleford to win at Wakefield, we have only won 2 games away all season at Harlequins and Wigan.

I think this is it folks, I hope I am proved wrong.

Amanda asked about players like Danny Brough and Danny Ward, would they stay or would they go? Would Danny Sculthorpe head back to Wigan for good? What about Shaun Timmins and Awen Gutenbeil? Would they be hanging on the end of a telephone in the southern hemisphere waiting to be told to find another club because the club they were heading for was no longer in the competition? What about Claws? Would Sophie have a future dancing with the Tigers cheerleaders?

There is no other word than heartbreaking to describe that evening at the Willows. To see people close to you in tears at a sporting occasion demonstrated to me how this club had affected our lives. I knew that I would be in a bad mood for days, but at least we could console each other and at the end of the day, nobody had died. Nobody had died, but a part of us probably knew that life was about to change.

The Rhinos were on the end of an 18–54 reversal at St Helens. In normal circumstances I would have been dancing from the rooftops at a result like that. Putting our situation into context, I didn't care what happened to the Rhinos and I didn't feel like dancing.

The best thing about that game was when the Saints giant prop forward, Paul Anderson landed a conversion from the touchline. Great entertainment with a hint of taking the Michael. Barrie McDermott did the same for Widnes and I wondered then whether we would be celebrating at Belle Vue after a Danny Nutley conversion.

The bottom of the table at the end of week 27 and with just 1 game to go, read:

	P	W	D	L	Diff	PTS
Huddersfield	27	11	0	16	− 132	22
Harlequins	27	10	1	16	− 289	21
Wigan	27	11	0	16	− 93	20[*] deducted 2 points
TIGERS	27	9	1	17	− 381	19
Wakefield	27	9	0	18	− 138	18
Catalans	27	8	0	19	− 245	16

As expected. Les Catalans did finish bottom. They had done themselves proud and 16 points in their first season was a remarkable achievement.

When Astley came around on the Saturday morning after the Salford game, he was really critical of the teams performance. "They let you down", he proclaimed. Despite my best efforts to convince him that we never for one minute felt let down, he was adamant that Salford were an average side and after leading at half time we should have put them away. Salford are a good side and after consistent performances throughout the season, they fully deserved their place in the top 6. We gave everything and came away with nothing. We now faced having to give everything again and a little bit more. It was time to clear out the car boot and brush down the banner. The banner that got us back into Super League was set for a swansong appearance.

The winner takes it all

The week leading up to the 'judgement day' was also the week when our Jessica was packing up to leave home for university. It should have been a week of celebration with a hint of sadness. We were proud that she was going out into the big wide world, but obviously sad that she would not be living under our roof for much longer. Some might say that getting rid of one of your children is worth celebrating in any circumstance.

Everyone I bumped into wanted to talk about the Wakefield game, with the majority saying that we didn't deserve to be relegated. Nice words I suppose and words I might have clung onto a bit more if they had come from people who knew something about the game. A colleague who supports Hull KR was having his own jitters about their loss of form as the National League play offs begun to determine who would take ours or Trinity's place in Super League. I told him that "You will come straight back down if you take that team up". Afterwards I thought that it was a very churlish thing to say. Good luck to whoever gets promoted. There was no point in being sour at Hull KR.

The Tigers Supporters Club had arranged a meeting to update its members about developments with our new stadium. The mood that night was somber and even though the audience was reminded that we were there to discuss issues around a new ground, the questions everyone wanted to ask were about what would happen if we went down and who would be leaving the club?

The vultures from other clubs would obviously be hovering over Belle Vue ready for easy pickings in the shape of Tigers or Wildcats.

There was also an opportunity to get on the TV and with a speaking part to boot. It is not every day that you get the chance to rub shoulders with Angela Powers from Sky Sports and I wasn't going to miss my chance. Angela was at the Jungle to interview some fans about the prospects for the Wakefield game. I have never been one to avoid the media. My first role was to lean against a barrier and look out onto the pitch, pondering what could happen at Wakefield. I stood there for what felt like an hour and a half with the cameraman moving around taking different shots. Total air time when it was shown on Sky was about a split second.

Next it was time to talk and prompted by Angela's questions, I answered as honestly as I could. Total air time when it was shown on Sky was once again about a split second.

The piece was actually very moving whether you had an allegiance to either club or in fact neither club. Crowded House singing 'Don't dream it's over', was on in the background. That song contains a classic line:

'you'll never see the end of the road while you're traveling with me'.

Our Supporters club secretary, Graham Smith was also interviewed. He was in full flow until the longest train in the world decided to go past behind the Railway End. Graham had just about regained his composure when his mobile phone rang. It is not everyone that has the Flintstones soundtrack for their ring tone, so it made everybody laugh.

There was a scramble for tickets to go to Wakefield. It was a sell out, which must have really infuriated as well as pleased the administrators at Belle Vue. They had struggled all season to get supporters into the ground. Barry Gibbo wanted to go to the game, but he wasn't allowed after seeing us hammered in the 2 most recent matches he had attended. There was no room for sentiment and no room for unlucky charms. Barry was resigned to watching at home.

It was Saturday 16th September 2006. This was no ordinary Saturday. It was the day of the biggest game in Castleford Tigers long history.

Blurry eyed, I glanced at my alarm clock. It read 3:53. Too early to get up I thought, although I was wide awake and had the game well and truly on my mind. Our Jess must have decided that it was better not to go to bed at all. She came in from her usual Friday night out with her mates just before 4 0' clock on the Saturday morning. For her that night/morning out wasn't as usual as normal. That would be the last time her friends would be out together before they all departed to go to university.

I will never understand how anyone can go out at 1930 hours and still be out until 0400. What do they talk about all night? And why don't they feel the cold?

A full crew was out in force at Wakefield. Carolyn Simpson was the only absentee. Cal was a day ahead of Jess in moving to university. Talk about experiencing a range of emotions in one day. Fleeceman and Janet packed their daughter off to university and then headed to Wakefield for the game.

This 1 fixture was billed as a £1 million pound game. Not because the winners would collect a cheque for £1 million, but because that was how much the defeated club were likely to lose by being relegated. It meant more than that though. This game meant everything. A second relegation in 3 seasons could be our death knell. On 3 successive seasons we had faced last day encounters that would shape the clubs future. The club couldn't carry on with this trend. It was time to lay down some foundations for the long term future and stability. As supporters, we were getting used to it, but matches like this should come with a health warning. I knew one fan that couldn't go to Belle Vue because of a heart condition. When a game of rugby affects you like that, it is more than a game.

A trip to Wakey is like a trip to Cas, Ponte, Swilly, Fev or Miggy, in that Amanda dislikes shortening of any name. That is why she is still Amanda and not Mandy or Mindy. Jessica is now Jess and Sophie is now Soph, proving that there are exceptions to every rule.

Regardless of where you stand at Belle Vue, there are always pockets of Wakefield fans stood around you. We got into the ground about an hour before the kick-off and the atmosphere was already building. Unlike our last visit at Easter, there were no crème eggs, but the atmosphere was white hot. Cas fans had the away end and some had even booked a room in Wakefields equivalent to a façade of a Benidorm hotel. The Tigers flag flew with pride just like it would have done if it were being flown from any hotel in any resort.

We were in position and set for an evening of unprecedented tension and high drama. It was worth getting in early to see some boys dancing with the Wildcats dance squad. I am not sure there is any future in that, and those lads were either really brave, or doing it for a bet.

When the players came out for their usual warm up, they received an unbelievable reception. We intended to unfurl our battered and torn 'It's not the size' banner, but a rather hostile family of Trinity supporters put pay to that. Amanda got her revenge by depositing about $1/2$ a ton of confetti on their unsuspecting heads. Any doubts about the Tigers being short of support due to ticketing restrictions proved to be unfounded. We were there in force and out sung our hosts from start to finish.

Everything was on the line as Danny Brough launched his usual kick to start the game. We got the ball back and began to press from the start. It was imperative that we got off to a good start.

We did and despite an early penalty goal for Wakefield, we were soon in charge after tries from Willie Manu and Adam Fletcher. Brough landed 1 conversion and a drop goal to give us a commanding 11–2 lead in what seemed like no time at all. All we needed now was the final whistle.

The final whistle was way off and as usual we leaked points prior to half-time. In fact we leaked 12 points and went in trailing 11–14. Wakefield's first try came as a result of an incredible stroke of fortune, but you take all of the good luck you have on such occasions.

I think we would have settled for that scoreline before the game. It was now down to the motivation abilities of 2 men; coaches Kear and Matterson.

The season and the future of both clubs boiled down to 40 minutes of play. This was no ordinary game. Destiny was calling.

At half-time, academy player, Alex Shenton out sprinted a Wakefield counterpart in a length of the field foot race. Unfortunately, Mr. Purrfect was a distant second against Daddy Cool. Purrfect had 'keeping his head on' difficulties which definitely hampered his performance.

Not long into the second half, Danny Nutley crashed over under the posts and we were back in front. Brough converted making it 17–14. We were in the ascendancy and looking safe.

It was time to turn the screw. One more try and that would be it. An attempted Brough '40–20' drifted about a foot over the touchline and instead of getting the ball back in an attacking position, we were defending our line within a minute of scoring. Individual errors went on to cost the Tigers and Wakefield went back in front. It was a lead that they would not lose again. Was it the pressure on the night or the superior form that Wakefield finally delivered in the last quarter? By the hour mark, we looked like a spent force. We were out on our feet and only a miracle would save us know. Enter our 38 year old miracle worker Brad Davis.

Not even Brad could turn this one around. We conceded 2 more tries to eventually lose by 29–17.

We lost a game of rugby, not by a big score, but nonetheless we lost that game. Wakefield won it and deserved to win it on the night. Even the most biased of opinions couldn't say that we were unlucky. John Kear had led his charges to 4 wins out of 6 to mastermind their recovery.

This was our 32nd game since Boxing Day 2005. We had been to 31 of those games. Others will have been to all 32, but what can you do when your plane breaks down?

I must have been to hundreds of games since I first ventured into the world of rugby league supporting over 30 years ago. This result had more riding on it than any other game I had ever been to and probably more than any game anyone in that crowd of 11,000 had ever been to.

How did we react at the final whistle after our team gave everything for the cause only to come up short? We stood there and applauded them from the pitch. We had lost a game of rugby and as a result we were relegated for a second time in 3 years. We would have loved to have received our team for one last ovation, but unfortunately we were robbed of the opportunity by hundreds of mindless people who decided to invade the pitch, not to celebrate their victory, but to taunt and abuse the massed colony of Tigers faithful.

Our reaction to the taunts was to ignore them and I wondered how many of the mindless people would be at Belle Vue next season.

Nobody died that night at Belle Vue, but it hurt. It was time for tears and time to dissect why our season had ended in a worst case scenario. Only 2 weeks earlier we believed that we had secured our place in Super League for 2007 after beating Harlequins at the Jungle. Look at us now? Back in the National League with the prospect of losing the majority of a side that was put together at short notice less than a year earlier.

We were relegated in 2004 and lost a coach and a team.

We were promoted in 2005 and had to find a new coach and build a new team.

We were now relegated in 2006 and it wouldn't be long before the first player to leave would be out of the exit door.

An early indicator of what lie ahead came when we went straight to the Jungle to 'welcome' back our troops for one last time.

When the team coach pulled up, you could see the astonishment in the players faces that hundreds of supporters were still willing to cheer them on despite us being relegated a few hours earlier.

Castleford fans are loyal and before the first foot hit the car park at the Jungle everyone began to applaud and continued to applaud until the last man stepped off.

To be relegated with 19 points will never happen again.

Out of the 32 games played, we had only won 11 and 2 of those were pre season friendlies. Where else in the world would a team that had lost 20 and drawn 1 game out of 32 be received as heroes?

There was no consoling the players and no consoling the supporters. It was surreal. They were hurt and we were hurt. It was just that they hurt in a different way to all of us. We will be back in 2007, still hurting and having to wait a year before this seasons disaster is behind us.

The players hurt is tempered by the likely offers of contracts and employment at other clubs. Who can blame them? Playing rugby league is their job of work. They have short careers and have to pay the mortgage like the rest of us.

Amanda gave Hendo her scarf. He is a legend. He still had it around his neck a couple of hours later. How must Hendo have felt? He led us in our promotion season and had just been relegated by a team containing his brother. Our banner was laid to rest. It got us back into Super League and secured 2 vital points at Wigan. The rest as they say is history. A squad hastily put together and lacking in a quality play maker cost us in the long run. Handforth and Kain who had the 6 and 7 shirts only started 11 games between them. That tally wasn't enough for this level.

We now had the prospect of seeing our best players leaving the club. Danny Sculthorpe had thrown his shirt into the crowd. He would probably return to Wigan. The 'Mongrel mob' were too good for the National League and were mercenaries in a foreign country anyway. Home grown talent in the shape of Shenton and Huby had long careers in front of them. If they wanted successful careers than they would need to look further a field. A colleague who supports Wakefield mentioned that they wouldn't mind signing that 'Shelton'.

Loyalty is difficult to demand. We had averaged 7,096 supporters in 2006

Would our support remain loyal after a second relegation? What else could we be? Were we prepared to sack it all and not watch rugby league again? Or are we likely to sack the Tigers and consider supporting Wakefield, Leeds, Featherstone or even Hunslet?

Nobody died that night at Belle Vue, but it hurt and that hurt wouldn't go away for a long while. When we drove back into Kippax, life was going on as normal. We were 3 miles from the Jungle and hundreds of households in this hamlet outside Castleford wouldn't have even known that the Tigers were playing that night let alone playing for their future.

It mattered to the supporters but not many more people outside of that bracket.

I received a couple of text messages. Russ, the Bradford Bull said, *'Gutted 4 u all'*

A colleague from Bristol said, *'Hard luck. Watched some of it- Bristol went down, came back the next year and this year are of the top of the table. Who knows?* We had even made an impression in the south west and with a supporter of the other code.

We suffered another day of hurt the day after relegation when our eldest daughter Jess moved to York. When your family of 4 becomes a family of 3, it really hurts. Seeing one of your children becoming dependant in the big wide world pulls on your heartstrings.

For me, there was no difference from the day we took Jess to school for the first time. At 18 years of age, her fellow students all looked timid and anxious as they began a new life. Jess went with her Tigers bedspread and pillow case and the first thing she put up in her room was her 'Wheldon Road' sign. She will no doubt be spreading the name of Castleford Tigers around the halls of York St John University.

Sophie is doing her GCSE's this year. She hasn't chosen a career path yet, but psychology was mentioned the other day. "What's that about?" I asked. "It's in your 'ead or summat", she replied. I would be surprised if she becomes a psychologist.

For the record, the table at the end of the season read:

	P	W	D	L	Diff	PTS
St Helens	28	24	0	4	+509	48
Hull FC	28	20	0	8	+142	40
Rhinos	28	19	0	9	+326	38
Bulls	28	16	2	10	+234	34* deducted 2 points
City Reds	28	13	0	15	+61	26
Wolves	28	13	0	15	+22	26
Harlequins	28	11	1	16	−267	23
Warriors	28	12	0	16	−71	22* deducted 2 points
Giants	28	11	0	17	−144	22
Wildcats	28	10	0	18	−126	20
TIGERS	28	9	1	18	−393	19
Catalans	28	8	0	20	−293	16 **

** Exempt from relegation

The Saints coach Daniel Anderson had been right all along. The top of the table had been of little interest to the majority of the rugby league public throughout 2006. Their achievements this season hadn't received the accolades that they clearly deserved.

Our flirtation with Super League in 2006 had been a real rollercoaster and we had all experienced the highs and lows of supporting the greatest club in the world. We suffered record defeats at home and on our travels. We also took some notable scalps, against Leeds and Warrington at the Jungle. No-one will ever forget that Friday night at the JJB and Fleeceman has finally got over the indigestion. He tried it once and may now have the opportunity of sampling a delight from the Craig Lingard pie stand at Mount Pleasant, Batley.

We had seen some wonderful players. I asked Amanda who she had enjoyed watching in 2006. She replied, "I don't watch the opposition"

Saints Paul Wellans and Jamie Lyon stood out for me, but there was no better performer all year than our own skipper Danny Nutley. A real gent and fully deserving of a place in the Super League dream team.

The Tigers and their thousands of fans were now entering another era. It would be a chapter of a book that no-one could begin to write until the dust settled down and until it finally sunk in that we had been relegated.

The pain and agony of relegation was made worse after the club made representations to the Rugby Football League that Castleford should not be relegated. Rumours were flying around that the Catalans had gone bust, that Harlequins had gone bust and that the RFL were giving in to the sway of public opinion that dictated that we deserved to stay in Super League because we were a decent club from the heartland of the game and with a massive following that deserved top flight rugby league. After a couple of days, a statement from the club hit everyone like an express train:

'After discussions with the RFL, following the Club's relegation at the weekend, the Tigers have accepted that there will be no reprieve on the basis of Super League expanding to 13 or 14 teams and have agreed to the RFL's request to accept the current process.

The Tigers would like to thank the many Super League clubs that have offered to support the Club's request for a review of the current rules of promotion and relegation. In addition, the Club thanks those clubs that have given their commitment to allow the Tigers to continue to progress the development of the Club's leading junior players. The Club is appreciative of the wide-reaching and genuine support received and would like to believe that such support is a reflection of the respect for the Tigers from within the Game and the concerns surrounding the current promotion and relegation rules

Everyone acknowledged that the challenge facing the promoted club is incredibly tough. The Club believes that this season it has proved this challenge to be too tough. No other sport lays down such an insurmountable challenge.

The dice are impossibly stacked. The Tigers had, and continue to maintain, a solid financial base. The Club averaged well over 5,000 per game in the National League and attracted the 7th highest average in Super League in 2006. Even with this degree of stability (shaken to its core by a season in National League), the commercial platform of our fan base, an excellent coach and the likes of Nutley, Manu, McGoldrick and Sculthorpe the Club failed. 19 points, but failure. In short, the Club believes that the games promotion and relegation rules are flawed, a view clearly held by the Game at large as evidenced by the introduction of the franchise system in 2009.

In conclusion, the Tigers would like to thank, in particular, those Super League clubs that were prepared to accept reduced revenue distributions for the greater good of the game and also thanks the wider rugby league community for their overwhelming support in fighting for a change in the rules. The Tigers thanks its coach and its playing squad for the marvelous efforts of 2006. Most of all, the Tigers thanks the fans; our Super League journey has been temporarily suspended. We will be back'.

That was that then. Loyal servant 'Viva' Brad Davis left the club to join the coaching staff at Bath rugby union. Where that deal came from nobody knew. Brad had been Mr. Castleford and his contribution would never be forgotten. It was time to move on now. Brad had gone.

Over at Elland Road, Leeds United parted company with their manager Kevin Blackwell after only 8 league games. How the mighty had fallen and more heartache for the troubled club and its supporters.

The mighty also fell across the city of Leeds when the Rhinos were beaten, 17–18, in the elimination play-off against the Wolves. A drop goal from Lee Briers clinched an enthralling encounter and despite finishing 12 points ahead of the Wolves in the table, this contest proved once again that anything can happen in a one off encounter. Leeds ended the season with an empty trophy cabinet. I would have usually taken great delight in this, but I couldn't have cared less. Amanda was delighted.

"It's made my weekend. I've just seen some crying Rhino women"

A challenge cup semi final and a 3rd place finish and Leeds supporters cried. Get real.

'You'll never see the end of the road while you're traveling with me', was never more apt for this group of weary Tigers supporters. We were heading back to the National League and heading back to Cumbria. Whitehaven prolonged our hurt for a few more weeks, before relegation was 'officially' confirmed. If Haven had won the National League Grand Final then we would have stayed up because their ground was deemed unfit for Super League. They didn't win.

At least we wouldn't have to endure the trip south to London or face the disappointment of another cancelled trip across the channel.

The rumour mill was in full swing regarding the likely destination for the majority of the 2006 squad. How many teams would be strengthened with the addition of ex Tigers?

At least we were entering our next chapter with stability at the top. Terry Matterson confirmed that he was staying on as Head Coach and vowed to lead us back to the promised land.

Terry said: "Relegation was a real blow and it took some coming to terms with. It certainly gave me a lot to think about, but I came over here to do a job, which was to see the Tigers succeed in Super League and although relegation was a setback my aims are the same and I am totally committed to the task in hand.

The National League looks a tough competition and obviously we will lose quite a number of our current players, but I am confident that we will put a squad together that will get us back into the top flight. That is my immediate task and everyone at the club is fully focused on making it happen."

Time will tell Terry. 2006 was an adventure. What will 2007 bring?